AF605891

# Borges Between Singularity and Sovereignty

SUNY SERIES
LITERATURE...IN THEORY

# Borges Between Singularity and Sovereignty

Kate Jenckes

SUNY
**PRESS**

Cover art: Close-up photograph of an Alberto Burri painting.
Published by State University of New York Press, Albany

Printed in the United States of America



EU GPSR Authorised Representative:
Logos Europe, 9 rue Nicolas Poussin, 17000, La Rochelle, France
contact@logoseurope.eu

For information, contact State University of New York Press, Albany, NY
www.sunypress.edu

Library of Congress Cataloging-in-Publication Data
Name: Jenckes, Kate, author.
Title: Borges between singularity and sovereignty / Kate Jenckes, author.
Description: Albany : State University of New York Press, [2026] | Series: SUNY series, Literature . . . in Theory | Includes bibliographical references and index.
Identifiers: ISBN 9798855805406 (hardcover : alk. paper) | ISBN 9798855807011 (epub) | ISBN 9798855805420 (PDF)
Further information is available at the Library of Congress.

# Contents

# Acknowledgments

Thanks to the many teachers, friends, and students who taught me how to read Borges, who in turn taught me how to read.

An earlier version of chapter 1 was published as “Jorge Luis Borges: Probing the Limits of World War,” in *Latin American Literature in Transition, 1930–1980*, edited by Amanda Holmes and Par Kumaraswami, Cambridge University Press, 2023, pp. 32–45, © Cambridge University Press. Reproduced with permission. An earlier version of chapter 2 was published as “Walls, Towers, Books: Borges, Kafka, and the Limits of the Proper,” *The Yearbook of Comparative Literature* 63 (2017): 2–21. Reproduced with permission.

# Abbreviations

| | |
|---|---|
| CF | *Collected Fictions* |
| *L* | *Labyrinths* |
| *I* | *Inquisiciones* |
| OC | *Obras completas* |
| SNF | *Selected Non-Fictions* |

# Introduction

## Reading After Borges

> How does one account for the performance of another's writing if not by producing a performance of one's own?
>
> — Carol Jacobs, *In the Language of Walter Benjamin*

> The formula of the human being as a living being having language — *zoon logon echon* — can be clarified by the modification: he is a *zoon logon euchomenon* — a living being appealing for language, longing for it. He is a *zoon philologon.* His longing for language is a longing that exceeds every given language. His experience of the given one cannot do without the experience of its giving and its refusal; his exploration of the finite one cannot do without the opening of an infinitely finite one.
>
> — Werner Hamacher, *Minima Philologica*

While I was writing my dissertation on Borges in the late 1990s, I was met with a lot of groans. Friends and teachers suggested that Borges's work was obsolete, that everything that could be said about his work had already been said, and — most damning to me — that a focus on his work placed me either on the wrong side of the political spectrum, owing to Borges's initial approval of the Argentine military dictatorship, or was fundamentally apolitical, insufficiently attentive to the concrete realities of Latin America or late capitalism more generally. Otherwise kind and supportive mentors suggested that opting to write a dissertation on Borges was reactionary in the strictest sense of the word, akin to the gesture staged at the end of "Tlön, Uqbar, Orbis Tertius" in which a fictionalized Borges turns away from the catastrophic worlding that is Tlön to continue working on an indecisive translation. I addressed some of these concerns in the dissertation that developed into my first book, *Reading Borges After Benjamin: Allegory, Afterlife, and the Writing of History*, in which I paired some of Borges's earliest writings with another figure who dedicated his life to indecisive translations of a sort, albeit with a more evident political purchase, Walter Benjamin. Although I was aware that I had barely scratched the surface of Borges's work, I had other projects to pursue, and I did not intend to continue working on him. It even took me some time to start incorporating his work into my classes, but with time I came to teach an annual Borges class at the undergraduate level. It was the experience of reading Borges's fictions for this class and discussing them with my students that led me to think about writing on him again. His temporary support for the military dictatorship is inexcusable, but it is not, for me, insurmountable, in part due to his unqualified renunciation of that support, but also due to what I perceive as a persistent critique of sovereignty throughout his work in a variety of historical periods, geographical areas, and registers. Although this critique has certainly been touched on by some critics, while others have continued to explore other aspects of his writings, I do not in any way think that his work has been exhausted. Indeed, a key component of his writing seems to suggest that such a thing would be impossible.

This perception was reinforced when I came across the following description by the Chilean philosopher Willy Thayer, buried in the footnotes of his book *Technologies of Critique*:

> If a passage, a work, a signature — things that we approach only as singularity and constellation — is *the becoming of their readings* (Borges), of their quotations and rewritings (and never, then, an identity in progress as a voyage of conquest), there is no way to do justice to the signatures that we cite, except by using them, in each case, with the knowledge that each version (including the hypothetical "original") experiences suffering inasmuch as it is regarded as "proper," [and by] destroying any supposed identity or ipseity *until that which was never written appears, as though its ink had miraculous properties* (Benjamin), like a *book of sand* (Borges). (Thayer 181–82)

Borges appears here, together with Benjamin, as a central figure for thinking about reading understood as the inexhaustible and infinitely finite encounter with the singularity of a body of work. Invoking Derrida's reflections on the structure of the signature and Benjamin's on translation, Thayer understands reading as a fundamentally temporal action, an engagement with an afterlife that exceeds and alters the putative original, itself emergent and ephemeral and always already marked by difference. He describes the relationship between the reading subject and the textual object as a constellation, which brings things together but allows for distance and difference. Furthermore, he links such an approach to the possibility of "doing justice" — to the work, but also more generally, relating to a sense of justice that he contrasts with a form of conquest that inflicts suffering, resulting from the imposition of a unified and homogeneous structure of properness or self-identity.

Erin Graff Zivin presents a similar account of reading in her recent book, *Anarchaeologies: Reading as Misreading*, where she considers the practice of reading as an experimental engagement with knowledge that disrupts its grounds (*arche*) and the pretension to representational coherence (*logos*). She observes that such a grounded and cohesive structure of knowledge — what she calls *archaeology* — forms a critical component of sovereignty, understood as both control over meaning and knowledge, and political and institutional power. She cites Derrida's account of sovereignty from *Rogues*: "A pure sovereignty is indivisible or it is not . . . this indivisibility excludes it in principle from being shared, from time and from language. From time, from the temporalization that it infinitely contracts, and thus, paradoxically, from history. In a certain way, then, sovereignty is ahistorical; it is the contract contracted with a history that retracts in the instantaneous event of the deciding exception, and even that is without any temporal or historical thickness" (qtd. in *Anarchaeologies* 149).[1] For Derrida, sovereignty is based on a fiction of indivisibility, instantaneity, and immediacy. It cannot be divided, because an exclusive claim to division is its constitutive quality. As Carl Schmitt famously put it, "sovereign is he who decides on the exception" (qtd. in *Anarchaeologies* 113). Such a deciding exception withdraws from history, seeking to dominate time and language.

Graff Zivin proposes that reading engages time and language in such a way that disrupts the purported contraction of immediacy and indivisibility of sovereignty. She stresses that in contrast to the ideal of a comprehensive grasp of meaning often associated with it, reading always involves an element of misreading, or exposure to the unknown and unknowable. She illustrates this idea with an anecdote in which Ricardo Piglia describes having once seen Borges, who suffered from a degenerative eye disease, with a book up against his face, trying to discern the residual glimmers of words on a page. Piglia extrapolates this memory into a theory about reading. He writes that any reader, in the last instance, "reads badly, distorts, perceives confusedly. He who has the clearest vision is not always he who reads most clearly" (qtd. in *Anarchaeologies* 5). Piglia's essay is titled "The Last Reader" (*El último lector*), and Graff Zivin stresses that the sense of ultimacy that Piglia's anecdote illustrates is not final in a historical sense, but is structurally constitutive of reading, understood as a non-totalizing engagement with the objects of perception and comprehension. She finds this exemplified by Borges's writings, which repeatedly stage the irrepressible divisibility in any relation, including that between reading and writing, text and reader, origin and derivation, precursor and successor, literature and philosophy, politics and ethics, and the singular and the collective. She suggests that we are always "reading after the last reader," that is, we are always reading "after" Borges, in the sense of following the practice of misreading exemplified throughout his writing, which was fundamentally an-archeological, which is to say, disruptive of the grounds of sovereignty in all its forms (*Anarchaeologies* 4, 95).

Samuel Weber is also dedicated to exploring the relationship between sovereignty, reading, and singularity in the wake of deconstruction. Writing about how to approach the work of Derrida in the wake of his death, Weber emphasizes the need to resist any sense of a work's totality. Quoting Derrida's remark that "there is but one state of mind from which you can 'set out' — you start from the situation in which you find yourself," he stresses the singularity of every situation, which he describes as being "de-termined — closed and opened — by its relation to what lies outside itself, spatially but also temporally" ("Once and for All" 106).[2] Singularity, understood as something that does not fit in, that is odd or left over, names for Weber a uniqueness that is not a self-contained identity or undivided individuality — a word that he writes as *in-dividuality* to emphasize the association between individuality and coherence. Singularity is determined by the limits that demarcate it from what it is not, but to which it is inevitably related, including the ongoing nature of time. Never fully present to itself, singularity emerges as an event that is only ever legible in and through the divisive structure of repetition, which is exemplified by the temporalized nature of perception, including memory, and different representational practices, including writing.[3] Weber observes that the singular "does not thereby come into its own so much as make room, by withdrawing, for other singularities to come. This is why the singular is always associated with the secret . . . The singular can thus be considered to be the secret of the individual" (Weber, "Once and for All" 110).

Taking this description together with Thayer's and Graff Zivin's accounts of Borges as an extreme reader who disrupts the structure of sovereignty, I want to propose that Borges's works perform an engagement — often staged as a process of reading, and one that is both de-termined (in Weber's sense) and iterative — with the singular secret of the in-dividual in all its forms. Like Thayer, Graff Zivin, and Weber, I approach the question of sovereignty and its limits in relation to the legacy of twentieth-century philosophy, especially deconstruction.[4]

Borges's writings repeatedly explore claims to sovereignty by individuals, collectives, political bodies and apparatuses, cultural institutions, religions, philosophies, and all manner of combinations therein, and stress the irrepressible divisibility and finitude that afflict them from within. He is especially attentive to what Carl Schmitt calls political theology, that is, the intimate relationship between politics and theology that endures even after the ostensible secularization of the political. The struggle between human finitude and the ideal of the divine that is illustrated by the Biblical fable of the Tower of Babel is central to many of Borges's writings, even when not explicitly named as such.[5] The fable tells how the tool of human language (purportedly unified) is used to build a tower that would touch the heavens, that is, reach the level and totalizing perspective of God. God — the personification of both the ideal of pure sovereignty and its impossibility — interrupts this project, smashing the tower and scattering the once-unified people and language into foreign multitudes. Taking a cue from Franz Kafka, who fictionalizes the hope of a triumphant reprise of this endeavor, Borges recounts repeated efforts to surmount the divisions of time, language, and history, and reach the heights of sovereign knowledge and control.[6]

His depictions of such efforts span centuries and continents, from Ancient China and Rome to twentieth-century Europe and Latin America, and include a variety of protagonists, from exultant philosopher-kings and faceless bureaucracies to solitary archivists puttering at the global periphery. They also include a range of registers, from forms of control both political (cities, countries, continents, the world) and personal (perception, memory, finitude), to structural systems of thought such as theology and philosophy.

One of the more striking articulations of the political register appears when Borges makes the surprising observation, apropos the siege of Paris that led to its liberation from the Nazis, that "for Europeans and Americans, one order and only one is possible (*hay un orden — un solo orden — posible*): it used to be called Rome, and now it is Western Culture" ("Anotación" OC 2.112; SNF 211).[7] This statement describes a structural similarity between the Nazi ideal of sovereignty and that of democratic imperialism, both ancient and modern, with the name of Rome serving as a metonym for the interlacing of secular politics and theology. In another essay, Borges makes an even more pointed observation about the structural similarities between fascism and democracy: "Defenders of democracy, who believe themselves to be quite different from Goebbels, urge their readers, in the same language as the enemy, to listen to the beating of a heart that answers the call (*mandatos*) of blood and the land" ("Dos libros" OC 2.108; SNF 208). It is not just an abstract ideal of totality that brings these two vastly different ideologies together, but also the claim of a direct connection between the particular and the general: the beating of an individual heart that responds to the mandates of belonging enshrined in the form of nationalism. Furthermore, Borges associates the nature of such belonging, described here on the basis of a vitalist and consanguineal connection to a delimited territory, to that most common figure of belonging, familiarity, and delimitation of the proper, the *house*. He describes those who structure their lives seeking "a place . . . in some Order" with the taxonomic term "*homo domesticus*" (prologue to Franz Kafka, *The Vulture*, SNF 503).

The predominance of a political-ideological drive to totality in which the individual is incorporated into the body of the whole corresponds to central tenets of the Western philosophical tradition. Borges ironically cites Coleridge's division of this tradition into two basic camps, one that privileges the general, synecdochically captained by Plato (although he seems to really mean Neoplatonists, primarily Plotinus[8]), and the other that privileges the particular, associated with Aristotle. In his caricatured description of the former, Borges affirms that the Platonist "knows that the universe is in some way a cosmos, an order," an order that is established through ideas that are taken to be realities, and language, understood as forming a "map of the universe" ("From Allegories to Novels," OC 2.130; SNF 339). At the opposite extreme from this position is the caricature of a nominalist Aristotelian who considers the Platonist's claim of a totalizing order to be "an error or fiction" resulting from our limited understanding, and the ideas and language with which it is established to be arbitrarily applied generalizations. Borges mischievously amplifies the cacophony of this seemingly erudite squabble as though to distract us from the observation that the distinction endures through to the modern period in the form of two basic ways to approach reality, as "abstract concepts" or "individuals" — or perhaps as a way of performing the historical multiplicity of the particularity of generalization and the generalization of the particular. For his point is precisely that despite this long-standing and iterative distinction, generalization is never completely free of particularity, and there is an element of generalization in the figure of the individual. Abstraction, even when it is employed to make a map of the cosmos, is always marked by limits, including the fundamental ones of time, language, and history. Conversely, the individual is an abstraction when it is regarded as in-dividual or not divided — that is, sovereignly proper, immune to time and language. Borges points out that, paradoxically, the preference for the individual has become universal, which can be understood, among other things, in relation to the shift from loftier efforts to devise maps of the universe to the more practical production of terrestrial forms of order through the fraternal and domestic bonds of nationalism.[9]

Borges's depictions of the construction of sovereign order frequently bring together the individual and the general, and the political-institutional and the philosophical or semantic. Individual, mortal agents of sovereignty lurk behind the impersonal façades of institutions or the scaffolding of the divine — a trait that is likely inherited from Kafka. For instance, in "The Lottery in Babylon," the all-powerful leadership that goes by the name The Company determines the most intimate aspects of Babylon's inhabitants and can only be hoped to be reached (which is never guaranteed) through random sites, including, suggestively, a latrine called Qaphqa. In "The Library of Babel," anonymous authorities issue orders to curtail any questioning of universal (dis)order. In "Tlön, Uqbar, Orbis Tertius," the philosophical project of building a world — initially supposed to be an innocent pastime, like Minecraft — is increasingly totalitarian, with a structure of authorship and authority that is as impersonal as it is absolute, and which is ultimately compared to both imperialism and fascism.

The impersonality of sovereignty is often depicted in relationship to texts that must be read or deciphered by their inhabitants. However, this reliance on writing, transmission, and interpretation also tends to mark the limits of the claims to sovereignty. Weber's discussion of Kafka's "Building the Great Wall of China" — a story that Borges translated into Spanish and declared the most memorable of Kafka's fictions[10] — is instructive for understanding this aspect of Borges's work. In Kafka's story, a dying emperor sends a message to his people, but the messenger cannot get out of the palace grounds. The emperor sends his message as if it will reach his subjects; the subjects receive decrees as if they are absolute. And yet, there is no guarantee that the sovereign missive ever arrives.

Furthermore, the direction of the missive takes a detour mid-text when the story addresses the reader: "But you sit at your window and envision it as in a dream when evening comes" (Kafka 120). Weber stresses the importance of the word *but* (*aber*) in this interjection, which he reads as introducing the possibility of a difference with respect to the relation to sovereignty that is described within the story (Weber, *Singularity* 398). Even without the conjunction the address to the reader — described in very Borgesian terms as sitting at dusk between a window and a dream — shifts the narrative enough for us to introduce an element of doubt into the structure of sovereignty represented in the narrative. To the extent that we expect the emperor's message to arrive, we will never receive it, like the subjects in the story. But, invited by the story to occupy a crepuscular gap in this fictive empire, we may discern that the missives of sovereignty *never can* fully arrive, just as its frontiers are never complete. Weber suggests that this passage indicates the limits of sovereignty "without urging its readers to transcend them vertically, by rising (phallically) above them. It is sufficient to take to heart the way the text exposes and solicits certain expectations, which include first and foremost that of a vertical transcendence from signifying to signified, from text to meaning, from singularity to universality" (Weber, *Singularity* 398).

Borges's texts similarly expose and solicit expectations regarding sovereignty in both semantic and political registers. Like Kafka's parable of the messenger, they depict different ways that the missives of sovereignty may not always reach their mark. In other words, they are conditioned by what Derrida calls destinerrance, which suggests that the intended destination of a form of communication is always subject to elements of errancy and transformation (*The Post Card* 489).

Borges's essay "The Wall and the Books" can be taken as an example. The text, which shares much in common with Kafka's "Building the Great Wall of China," describes an ancient Chinese emperor's efforts to subject time and space, or history and territory, to his command. However, starting from the first word, *leí* (I read), the essay performs the ways in which the afterlife of those commands is transformed as they are contemplated by a reader (and writer) who is not only not subject to that command but is actively attentive to what they do not include (OC 2.13; SNF 34). The essay concludes with a powerful, albeit slightly cryptic theory of aesthetic action that involves a relation to something akin to messages that never fully arrive. This can be understood as suggesting that for Borges the register of aesthetics or the literary names the possibility of acknowledging the destinerrance intrinsic to all transmission, including something as intimate and singular as perception, and as general and unifying as sovereign "orders" (both *el* and *la orden*, that is, order and command).

Other examples of the destinerrancy of order include "On Exactitude in Science," in which an enormous map functions as a long-distance missive that aims to communicate the contours of the imperial territory to the imperial sovereign, its giant surface eventually left to the destruction of the elements and the adaptation of beggars and animals who nestle in its tatters. In both "The Lottery of Babylon" and "The Library of Babel," order is imparted in writing, subject to misinterpretation and variation, and subsequently recounted by the narrators in epistolary form — letters that might transmit absolute authority, like the Pauline epistles, but that are also subject to destinerrance.[11] The risk that a text not transmit an intact sovereign meaning is a common feature in Borges's fictions. As readers, we are repeatedly invited to observe how a sovereign order does not arrive at its destination, and, as in Kafka's story, we are occasionally addressed directly, asked to consider whether *we* are subject to the structures of sovereignty illustrated by the stories, and to what extent we expect to receive a sovereign meaning from the text: "You who read me — are you certain you understand my language?" (OC 1.505; CF 118).

Like Weber's description of Kafka's story, Borges portrays the limits and divisions of sovereignty without providing a "vertical" edifice or solid ground from which to develop an alternative approach. Borges's writings resolutely resist any clear moralistic structure or redemptive endings. This quality led Paul de Man to describe his fictions as tending to feature a "presence of villainy at their very heart" ("A Modern Master," n.p.). Alberto Moreiras suggests that the term *villainy* in this sense can be understood as resistance to closed structures of interpretation, and he notes that this element has proved confounding to many of Borges's readers (Moreiras, *Tercer espacio* 295).[12]

Borges criticism has long been divided along celebratory and denunciatory lines, with the former emphasizing ludic and self-referential elements of his work and the latter accusing him of elitist universalism.[13] Starting in the 1990s, readers started to stress the relationship of his works to his regional and historical context. However, there were two main approaches to this relation: the first tending to view his works as political allegories grounded in referentiality and intention, and the second attending to the "villainy" or resistance to closure as a critical component of his engagement with history and politics. Moreiras gives the example of Josefina Ludmer, who, in her reading of "The Traitor and the Hero," denounces the betrayals described by the story — both political and historiographical — rather than seeing them as literary devices designed to question the political-theological dimension that informs the ideals of collectivity and inheritance invoked in the story (Moreiras, *Tercer espacio* 304). He suggests that our role as critics should not be to reject or repair the manifestations of villainy and uncertainty that we find in Borges's texts, but rather to understand them as radical interrogations of the structures they seem to threaten.

Any schematization of the vast and varied archive of Borges criticism risks oversimplification, but the distinctions that I have just described provide backdrop to my own contribution here. Although my approach is primarily influenced by the call to attend to the points of villainous deconstruction of authority as articulated by de Man and Moreiras, I recognize that my critical debt is more heterogeneous than that and includes, in a sense, all those who have read Borges before me. I cannot hope to acknowledge the varied aspects of this debt, since to do so would replace *reading* with an archival recitation that would, in turn, require its own reading. Instead, I have striven to practice a readerly engagement with criticism, privileging and building on critical texts that contribute to my understanding of the tension between singularity and sovereignty that runs throughout Borges's work. Throughout the book I endeavor to be a villainous heir and anarchaeological reader of his work, privileging uncertainty and contingency over any sense of mastery. I do this because I consider it to be the best way, in Thayer's words, to address the singularity and constellative relationality that lie within them, to read that which may never have been written, or written only with miraculous ink, and thereby, perhaps, to approach the possibility of "doing justice" to his work.

***

The book begins with a consideration of the figure of sovereignty in one of its more overt forms: the fantasy of world domination and its implementation in the form of war. Chapter 1 opens with Emmanuel Levinas's association between the structure of totality and the threat of war. It then moves to several of Borges's fictions that address this association, including "The Maker," "Tlön, Uqbar, Orbis Tertius," "*Deutsches Requiem*," and "The Garden of Forking Paths." Each of these fictions depicts a totalizing perspective or structure and the indication of the limits of such a structure.

Chapter 2 delves into the relationship between Borges and Kafka, starting out with the claim in Kafka's story "On Building the Chinese Wall" that the Great Wall of China represents a perfection of the Biblical Tower of Babel. Just as Derrida suggests that the scattering of the legendary symbol of human sovereignty was not only a result of divine vengeance but was also already latent in the materials of its construction, both Kafka and Borges stage the structures of sovereignty while also calling attention to the differential excess that underlies them. The chapter focuses on Borges's essay "The Wall and the Books," which is structured as an allegory of the sovereign control of time and space based on the emperor Shih Huang Ti, who ordered the construction of the Great Wall of China and the destruction of all books written before his reign. The essay performatively unworks the structure of sovereignty represented by the imperial commands and ends with a kind of postface about the nature of aesthetics and its facticity (*el hecho estético*), which can be understood as a kind of excessive materiality that underlies sovereign orders, whether constructive or destructive. The chapter concludes with a consideration of the limits of sovereignty of an author's name or work in relation to the essay "Kafka and His Precursors."

Chapter 3 examines political-theological apparatuses of sovereignty relating to the motif of the world as text. It begins with a consideration of a pair of essays, written nearly two decades apart, which introduce the figure of the world as text, and the extent to which human writers can approximate the fantasy of divine writing, defined by its absolute calculation, which involves the subjection or elimination of the "incalculable alliance" of possibility ("Vindicación" OC 1.223; SNF 85). It then turns to "The Library of Babel" and "The Lottery in Babylon," which feature structures of sovereignty built around the political-theological premise of such an elimination. Although subjugation is nearly complete in these two dystopian tales, the narratives touch on the intrinsic limits of the political-theological structures that govern them, introducing elements of errancy and incalculability to the doctrinal texts in which they are embedded.

The following chapters consider the legacy of political-theological ideals of sovereignty in more individual and local settings. Chapter 4 looks at how a sense of political and metaphysical order is built into the human-sized figure of the house, which represents the grounds and limits of individual and collective life. In "The South," the rural property purchased by the protagonist, Juan Dahlmann, serves as an idealized ground for a homogeneous and nationalistic sense of identity that excludes internal difference and the temporality of life itself. In "Man on the Threshold," the space of a house in British-occupied India functions as a space of anti-colonial judgment, which mirrors that of the occupying colonialists. Both stories stress the thresholds of these structures of national, imperial, and anti-colonial identity, which are less secure than they initially seem. Language and literature are shown to form part of these structures, but also to indicate their fictive, and therefore contingent nature, opening up possibilities for individual and collective life beyond the controlled space of the proper.

Chapter 5 considers the metaphysical ideal of sovereignty in "Funes the Memorious." As in "The South," there is a strong association in this story between self, family, and nation, in which internal defense mechanisms battle perceived threats of loss and disunity. Whereas "The South" is oriented toward the structure of endings, "Funes the Memorious" can be seen as a multifaceted origin story, relating to the absence or finitude of fathers, the legacy of the tradition of metaphysics, and ultimately the nature of representation itself. Both origins and ends are related to time and its disavowal, a topic that is explored in relation to Ireneo Funes's namesakes, Irenaeus and Friedrich Nietzsche.

Chapter 6 gives another turn to the relationship between the totalizing ideals of subjectivity and its prosthetic extensions, including the structures of house and writing, in "The Aleph." Similar to the stories analyzed in the preceding chapters, "The Aleph" situates archival efforts to protect against time, change, and disunity in relation to the figure of the house and the structures of property and profit more generally, including in idealized forms of memory and language. The doubled protagonists engage with such structures in initially similar, but ultimately different ways, performing what may be regarded as a common desire for security, possession, and profit, and diverging around the recognition of their impossibility. The plot is constructed primarily around a personal antagonism between the two protagonists that concerns literary and sexual prowess, set in a family house atop the fantastical Aleph, but it also invokes the nature of sovereignty in a variety of registers, from early modern questions of political sovereignty to the nature of technological and territorial modernization.

The final chapter considers Borges's fascination with Zeno's paradox of Achilles and the tortoise. It begins with the idea that his lifelong fascination may lie in the fact that Zeno appears to have designed his paradoxes as heuristic devices to prove the impossibility of change, in support of the Parmenidean principles of unity and immutability and as refutation of Heraclitus's belief that the world is characterized by constant change. As paradoxes, however, their rhetorical strategy founders on the dizzying nature of infinity that they invoke. After tracing the enduring challenge of Zeno's paradox as it is picked up throughout the Western philosophical tradition, Borges offers one of his most acerbic critiques of that tradition, understood as a series of different efforts to suture the effects of infinity. He concludes his essays on Zeno's paradoxes with what appears to be an uncompromising belief in Schopenhauer as the only philosopher to have come close to a different approach. However, careful reading suggests that Borges undermines Schopenhauerian idealism for believing too much in its capacity for understanding the world, and gestures rather to an aesthetic mode that, inasmuch as it acknowledges the limits and contingencies of its inscriptions, does not seek to disavow the infinitely finite nature of existence. The chapter concludes with a look at how Borges invokes Zeno's paradox in "The Nothingness of Personality," where he uses it to describe how the effort to affirm a stable sense of self can never be won, and in "Death and the Compass," where it is used to challenge the structure of enmity that girds the pursuit of sovereignty.

# Chapter 1

## World (as) War

### "The Maker," "Tlön, Uqbar, Orbis Tertius," "Deutsches Requiem," "The Garden of Forking Paths"

One of the most salient features of Borges's work is its attention to the structure of totality and its effects. Borges wrote his best-known fictions during the Second World War, and many of them explicitly address the structures of war and authoritarianism, as well as other apparatuses of power. As I note in the introduction, he considers these manifestations as iterations of a common structure, which he describes as the drive to "a single order" (OC 2.112; SNF 211). He associates this single order with an imperial logic that he metonymically describes as "Rome," which he sees repeated not only in the totalitarian tendencies of the Axis powers, but also in the presumption of a unified ("Western," democratic) culture associated with the Allies.

Borges's attention to the relationship between epistemological totality and war in a single and unifying sense of order resembles Emmanuel Levinas's association between epistemological totality and what he calls "the permanent possibility of war" (Levinas 21). Levinas, who lost family members in the Holocaust and who spent most of the Second World War as a prisoner of war, stresses that violence is constituted not only by "injuring and annihilating persons," but also by how we think of the world: "The visage of being that shows itself in war is fixed in the concept of totality, which dominates Western philosophy" (21). He affirms that in Western philosophical thought, "Being reveals itself as war . . . war does not only affect it as the most patent fact, but as the very patency, or the truth, of the real, by an objective order from which there is no escape" (Levinas 21). The bellicose register of the effects of knowledge presumes what Levinas calls an *adequation* between thought and its object, whereby the thinking mind achieves correspondence with the structure of totality, and in which there is no subjectivity or possibility of relation outside of this totality. In a mode of being determined by war, he says, "individuals are reduced to being bearers of forces that command them unbeknown to themselves. The meaning of individuals (invisible outside of this totality) is derived from the totality. The unicity of each present is incessantly sacrificed to a future appealed to bring forth its objective meaning" (Levinas 21–22). In other words, there is no singularity, only an in-dividuated wartime that can persist even when there is not active fighting.

Levinas insists, however, on a differential excess that has the infinite potential to undermine the structures of totality that would determine our experience of the world. As opposed to an autonomous individuality that both grounds and reflects the whole, he describes a singularity that, in its infinite difference and non-presence, is always encountering itself, others, and the world as fundamentally unknowable. Whereas in a bellicose register, thought is presumed adequate to comprehend the whole, such differential infinity defies comprehension and representation. It is "pre-eminently non-adequation" (27). Levinas relates this to what he calls the eschatology of messianic peace, which he understands as an insistence on a future not determined by totality (22). Although he calls this a form of peace, he considers that any thought — "the act of thought — thought as an act" — that challenges the sovereignty of totality engages in an "essential violence": "What, in action, breaks forth as essential violence is the surplus of being over the thought that claims to contain it" (27). The violence of the act of thinking exceeds and disrupts the intentionality and consciousness of the putatively autonomous subject: "The incarnation of consciousness is therefore comprehensible only if, over and beyond adequation, the overflowing of the idea by its ideatum, that is, the idea of infinity, moves consciousness" (27).

Alberto Moreiras evokes Levinas's reading of the disruption of the adequation between war and understanding in relation to Borges's "The Maker." The story describes a warrior for whom nothing exists outside the "immediate indifference" of war, until one day he becomes blind, and the immediacy of the world (as war) retreats — "it began drawing away from him" (OC 1.169; CF 292). After his initial despair, he begins to sense that, in Moreiras's words, the "withdrawal of world" also offers a "return of the world (*Tercer espacio* 427). Confronting the "blurred things that lay about him" with a different perspective, the warrior descends to the "vertigo" of his "interminable" memory (Borges, OC 1.169; CF 292). In the vertiginous world of "this night of his mortal eyes," he senses a rumble (*rumor*) of meters and myths, "*Odysseys* and *Iliads*" that would go on resonating "in the cupped hands of human memory" (OC 1.170; CF 293). We are led to understand that this blind warrior who moves from the "indifferent immediacy of war" to a tenuous engagement with the interminable returns of experience and relation is, in fact, Homer. Moreiras describes the story as a reflection on poetic practice as "an uncomfortable mode of inhabiting the world only accessible through the withdrawal of a vision of the world, or rather an approach to vision . . . as dark depth" (*Tercer espacio* 427). He links this to Levinas's understanding of essential violence: "If essential violence is the excess of being over the thought that attempts to contain it, literature is an opening to the facticity of that excess" (428).

The story in this sense can be read as a fable of the shift from a totalizing and atemporal model of understanding the world as a form of war to an opening to the excess of being or life not contained by such a model. Although he warns that what goes by the name of literature can also contribute to the war games of totality, Moreiras gives the name of literature to the possibility of such an opening. He suggests that Borges's description of Homer's awakening to the "night of his mortal eyes" (OC 1. 170; CF 293) inscribes poetic or aesthetic action — at its putative origin, namely Homer's epics — as a potential engagement with the limits of structures of totality. As with this short fiction, Borges eschews any heroic stance related to such an engagement.[1] Nor does he place it on center stage, but rather tucks it into the folds of the numerous warlike structures of totality that surround and inhabit their protagonists.

In the rest of this chapter, I will examine several stories in which Borges invokes the violence that wracked the mid-twentieth century in relation to the structural and conceptual dimensions of totality. "Tlön, Uqbar, Orbis Tertius" is exemplary in this regard, describing the creation of a world — a single order — through knowledge, which comes to resemble and merge into real-world structures of totality, including Nazism and Stalinism. "*Deutsches Requiem*" zeroes in on the former of these two structures, Nazism, which it describes as the agent of one of the most violent totalizing structures of our time, which is, paradoxically, so totalizing that it requires its own self-sacrifice. The story demonstrates how literature can be used to justify such a structure of totality, but also how it can touch on a differential singularity that fundamentally resists it. "The Garden of Forking Paths" addresses the logic of "world" war from the perspective of an Axis spy who hardens his resolve to uphold that logic, although it also demonstrates how the logic of war relies on missives of sovereignty that, even when they purportedly arrive at their intended destination, move through a dense and divergent materiality that complicates and divides the structure of enmity that they aim to transmit. In each of these stories, Borges insists on the "non-adequation" of the bellicose imposition of structures of totality, stressing points of excess and fissure that represent the condition of possibility for encounter with the infinitely finite singularity of existence.

## *Appearance of Order*

"Tlön, Uqbar, Orbis Tertius" stages the construction of the bellicose adequation between knowledge and world. The story, published in the critical year of 1940, describes the discovery of an international and transhistorical project to create a virtual world. Efraín Kristal points out that it was the first story that Borges wrote after the war broke out and followed the publication of a newspaper article about national socialism in which he states, "The unbelievable, indisputable truth is that the directors of the Third Reich are procuring a universal empire and the conquest of the world" (from "1941," quoted in "Jorge Luis Borges's Fictions and the Two World Wars" 39). "Tlön, Uqbar, Orbis Tertius" is a peculiarly structured story that recounts an effort by a secret society to create an ideal and idealist world whose totalizing impulse threatens to take over other kinds of fictitiousness and facticity. Although not directly about war, this world-making is compared in the story to real-life totalitarian projects. The story ends with the threat of world conquest looming, but incomplete.

The world-making project reportedly began with thinkers from the margins of the Enlightenment such as George Berkeley and George Dalgarno (OC 1.471; CF 78), who enthusiastically and idiosyncratically embraced the epochal opportunity to topple centuries of doctrine of divinely ordained sovereignty and replace them with a variety of absolute subjectivism. Dalgarno explicitly connected his ideal of a universal language to the tale of Babel, describing it as an effort to "to remedy the difficulties and absurdities which all languages are clogged with ever since the Confusion, or rather since the Fall" (Ars Signorum, qtd. in Schulte-Albert 54).

Indeed, one of Tlön's primary functions can be seen as that of a "universal translation machine" (Moreiras, *Tercer espacio* 68). Moreiras stresses that the affirmation that "There are no nouns in the conjectural *Ursprache* of Tlön" (OC 1.465; CF 73) posits language as an originary form of substantification (*Tercer espacio* 72). He suggests that "Tlön's (conjectural) 'primitive language'" (OC 1.474; CF 81) does not have nouns because it fundamentally substantivizes — turns into nouns — all that it says, with no Babelic errancy. The ultimate object that it constates is the world of Tlön, which soon enough becomes the world *as* Tlön. Resonating with Levinas's description of total knowledge as war, Moreiras describes this as a brutal form of totalization: "A language absolutely constructed . . . is the most totalizing and brutal act of substantivization that the human mind can imagine or accomplish" (*Tercer espacio* 72).

In apparent opposition to substantive objectivity, subjective perception is considered to constitute the very basis of reality, as articulated by George Berkeley's premise that perception determines being (*esse est percipi*). Indeed, the project of Tlön can be understood as an unfettered exercise in Berkeleian idealism. The epistemological and cultural disciplines of Tlön privilege subjective experience and immediacy over systematization and mediation: for instance, tactile geometry, creative arithmetic, poetry whose only object is itself, philosophy that seeks to amaze rather than seek truth. All disciplines are said to be subordinate to psychology, since "the people of that planet conceive the universe as a series of mental processes" ("Tlön" OC 1.466; CF 73). Like nouns, epistemological systems are rejected as reductive: "a system is naught but the subordination of all the aspects of the universe to one of those aspects" ("Tlön" OC 1.467; CF 74). However, just as the putative rejection of nouns in Tlön dissimulates the radical project of objectification, the rejection of systematic knowledge dissimulates the fact that the sovereignty of subjective experience constitutes the heart of a *system* to which all other aspects of the universe are subordinate. "We must always remember that on Tlön, the subject of knowledge is one and eternal" ("Tlön" OC 1.469; CF 76).

The transition from the speculation of the eighteenth century to a very different sort in the nineteenth century, as represented by the ideas of George Berkeley in the hands of Ezra Buckley, a US American prostitute- and slave-owning millionaire, combines the sense of perception as intuition through sensation with the *legal* sense of perception as the collection of revenue from properties.[2] The name Buckley is a near homophone of Berkeley in British and Irish English, evoking the stereotype of US Americans reducing everything to bucks (dollars), and stressing that the United States is not separate from "world" conflicts (despite its stance of neutrality at the time of the story's writing). Making explicit the connection between knowledge and conquest, Buckley suggests that the exercise of constitutive perception started by the creation of Uqbar, an idealist country, had already been accomplished by US expansionism, and he proposes enlarging the project to create an entire world. As the golden age of primitive accumulation drew to an end, Buckley invested the spoils from that era, the riches his expansionist and oppressive "perception" had yielded him — "his gold-veined mountains, his navigable rivers, his prairies thundering with bulls and buffalos, his Negroes, his brothels, and his dollars" — into the "methodical" production of this world, coinciding, not coincidentally, with the dawn of the industrial revolution (OC 1.472; CF 79).

This methodical production is repeated within the fictional world of Tlön, with the "methodical production" of *hrönir*, duplicated objects constituted by perception ("Tlön" OC 1.470; CF 77).[3] This production represents an alienation of the means not only of production but also of perception through a Kafkaesque ideological apparatus that claims to produce nothing less than freedom. The directed production of *hrönir* was first experimented with prisoners in a state prison who were shown images of objects and instructed to "find" them through an archaeological dig. It was promised that their success would buy their release. These prisoners were perhaps too jaded to trust that the retrieval of objects suggested by their jailers would lead to real freedom. The experiment was repeated with schoolchildren, some of whom were more impressionable, and "unearthed — or produced" a number of objects, including a gold mask, as a kind of prototype of the extraction and molding of value from raw materials (such as Buckley's *montañas auríferas*) into face-adorned tokens that represent (or mask) the kind of equivalence that is supposedly impossible in Tlön.[4] The malleability and freedom associated with such a mode of productive perception is extended to time, as well, which is soon mined and shaped to produce new understandings of history, the past as well as the future: "making it possible not only to interrogate but even to modify the past, which is now no less plastic, no less malleable than the future" (OC 1.470; CF 77–78). These examples show how in Tlön the Berkeleian precept *esse est percipi* is not a neutral form of sense perception, but an ideology of perception that complements and reinforces the world system ("a single order") in its different manifestations as it develops from colonial expansion to extractivism and productionism, and which includes within it the reproduction of its own means, including an institutionally sanctioned form of freedom based on sacrifice and exchange.

Such mined objects (surely Borges enjoyed puns across different languages) as the *hrönir* make the jump from Tlön to the "real" world in the form of small metal objects, including a minute cone that the narrator was able to hold in the palm of his hand. He describes it thus: "I recall that its weight was unbearable, and that even after someone took it from me, the sensation of terrible heaviness endured. I also recall the neat circle it engraved in my flesh," ("Tlön" OC 1.473; CF 80). This cone, which is an example of the tactile geometry of Tlön as well as the geometrical foundations of idealism,[5] demonstrates how the objects of perception take on a power of their own and impress, and sometimes oppress, us in turn. The narrator describes how the impression on his hand from the minute cone provokes an "impression" of disgust and fear.

Like the cones, Tlön itself is an object produced by perception, which acquires a force that impresses itself on those that perceive it, to the point of taking over their capacity for perception. In this, it resembles other constructs that appear to impose order, including some of the main ideological and imperial forces transforming the world in the fateful year cited as the present of the story, 1940: "Ten years ago, any symmetry, any system with an appearance of order — dialectical materialism, anti-Semitism, Nazism — could spellbind and hypnotize mankind. How could the world not fall under the sway of Tlön, how could it not yield to the vast and minutely detailed evidence of an ordered planet?" ("Tlön" OC 1.473; CF 81). In this pivotal sentence, which, like the intradiegetic cones, thrusts the fiction of Tlön into "our" world, Tlön is presented as surpassing other totalizing forms — forms of war, in Levinas's terms — because it is *evidence* of planetary order, as opposed to its mere *appearance*, although at these rarified extremes of Berkeleian idealism, perhaps there is no difference, since what we perceive as appearing determines being. The modifier *cualquier* (any, whatever) establishes a commonality between orders that *appear* to be different, namely dialectical materialism and Nazism, a commonality that the Hitler-Stalin pact fatefully established as the prelude to world war. In fact, the slightly anomalous term in the series, anti-Semitism (which is, unlike the other terms, not a political ideology per se), can be seen as a symbolic link that draws these different forms of symmetry together. Anti-Semitism can be understood in relation to a mechanism whereby the anxieties of disorder and uncertainty — Babel, confusion — are externalized and projected onto a scapegoat, which can then be sacrificed as a symbolic suturing of order.

The intrusion of the ideal order of Tlön into the "real" world begins with the appearance of objects such as the cone, but it is a barrage of media that ultimately threatens to make reality succumb to Tlön: "Handbooks, anthologies, surveys, 'literal translations,' authorized and pirated reprints [*reimpresiones autorizadas y reimpresiones piráticas*] of Mankind's Greatest Masterpiece filled the world and still do [*abarrotaron y siguen abarrotando la tierra*]. Almost immediately, reality 'caved in' at more than one point" ("Tlön" OC 1.473; CF 81). The word *abarrotar* suggests that this mediatic influx effects both an imprisonment (*barrotes* are bars), and a filling, packing, or pressing, which is reinforced by the use of the word *reimpresiones*. The phrase "almost immediately," however, indicates that this phenomenon (both impressive and oppressive) is compromised by a differential mediation that allows for the inscription of other differences, other impressions.[6]

Such difference is highlighted by the narrator's practice of translation at the end of the story: "At that, French and English and mere Spanish will disappear from the earth. The world will be Tlön. That makes very little difference to me; through my quiet days in this hotel in Adrogué, I go on revising (though I never intend to publish) an indecisive translation in the style of Quevedo of Sir Thomas Browne's *Urne Buriall*" (OC 1.474; CF 81). Moreiras reads this passage as an indication that, both with the intradiegetic translation of Browne and with the writing of the story, "Tlön, Uqbar, Orbis Tertius," "Borges" (the narrator's name also functioning as a translation) translates the universal translating machine of Tlön, reintroducing the differential excess that the idealist project seeks to master and objectify (*Tercer espacio* 73–74).[7] Thomas Browne's philosophical archaeology opens with the idea that many things exist in the earth that we do not see: "a large part of the earth is still in the Urne unto us" (Browne, n.p.). Not only does this undermine Berkeleian idealism, since it suggests that much exists beyond our range of perception, it also describes a world that is far from *abarrotado*, filled in, and although Browne's treatise is framed within a Christian scheme of revelation, the text can be described as darkly materialist, burrowing through mounds of cultural, historical, and physical debris. Both this text and the narrator's revision of his indecisive translation of it stress difference — temporal, material, linguistic, historical, and other shadows lurking in the crevices of an autonomous "subject of knowledge" ("Tlön" OC 1.469; CF 76). The narrator's stipulation that he does not intend to send the translation to press (*imprenta*) seems to reinforce the resistance to the molding and packing (*impresionar, abarrotar*) of the world into Tlön.[8]

## *Irrevocable Determination, Varied Futures*

The figure of totality in "Tlön, Uqbar, Orbis Tertius" is somewhat abstract, given its fantastical quality, and transhistorical, stretching from Enlightenment-era primitive accumulation to twentieth-century totalitarianism. "*Deutsches Requiem*" and "The Garden of Forking Paths" are — while still being quite Borgesian — more concrete and historically located, bringing the figure of totality to bear on the two world wars. The stories demonstrate how the fight for sovereignty exemplified by war is supported by epistemological and technological forms that are used to subject the singular and differential nature of time, existence, and the possibility of relation. These forms include long-standing representational apparatuses such as historiography, philosophy, philology, and aesthetics, as well as technological innovations including new forms of telecommunication, warfare, and transportation. Although these two war stories seem to demonstrate the imminence of a global sovereignty at once epistemological and political, they also probe the limits of the drive to totality, stressing points of fissure and excess — non-adequation, in Levinas's sense — that constitute the condition of possibility in which the singularity of existence is not subjected to a single order.

As we saw in the introduction, in an essay on the nature of fascism in the 1940s, "A Comment on August 23, 1944," Borges puzzles over the unexpected enthusiasm of Argentine supporters of Hitler at the news of Paris' liberation. He conjectures that their celebration indicates a belief that the Allied victory perpetuated, rather than opposed, the ideal of totality imposed by the Nazis. He writes, "for Europeans and Americans, one order and only one is possible: it used to be called Rome, and now it is called Western Culture" (OC 2.112; SNF 211). This totalizing sense of order forms the basis of an understanding of reality from which a differential understanding of singularity is excluded. Although this ideal of order is not new, its scale and pervasiveness have expanded during the twentieth century to include the entire world. The Nazi supporters who celebrated the liberation of Paris, Borges surmises, perceived a transition from a continental, imperial horizon to a global one.

"*Deutsches Requiem*" is a fictional exploration of the ideas presented in "A Comment on August 23, 1944." Although it is narrated by a Nazi and concerns the rise and fall of Nazism, it should be viewed not only as a cautionary tale about German fascism but also, especially in light of "A Comment on August 23, 1944," as indicating a conceptual structure that exceeds any single manifestation. The story narrates the perspective of a Nazi man of letters, Otto Dietrich zur Linde, who becomes subdirector of a concentration camp. It is structured as an account of his participation in the rise and fall of national socialism on the night before his execution.

Dietrich's declaration begins with a seemingly innocuous account of his family history, with an emphasis on ancestors who played a role — often merely by dying — in the establishment of modern Germany, leading up to his own anticipated execution. He mentions that it is natural, given the circumstances, for him to be thinking of his ancestors, "since I am come so near their shadow — since, somehow, I am they" (OC 1.617; CF 229). This reflection introduces an ahistorical ideal that forms the basis of his ideological commitment to Nazism. He insists that the Nazi worldview constitutes the ineluctable future of the world: "Those who heed my words shall understand the history of Germany and the future history of the world. I know that cases such as mine, exceptional and shocking now, will very soon be very unremarkable [*triviales*]. Tomorrow I shall die, but I am a symbol of the generations to come" (OC 1.617; CF 229). Dietrich describes himself as a symbolic link to a world history that extends into the past and future without significant change: He is at once both past and future generations (I am they, *soy ellos*). He proposes that his individuality may seem exceptional, but in reality, he represents a timeless norm, a permanent state of exception.

The "trivial" (translated by Hurley as "unremarkable") nature of his individual case does not mean a lack of significance, nor does it *only* mean — since this is a central idea in the story — that particularity is superseded by the universal. The etymological sense of the word *trivial* conjures both the sense of crossroads (*tri-via*) and the medieval trivium of grammar, rhetoric, and logic, that is, the verbal mechanics for conveying truth. Together with Dietrich's surname, *zur Linde*, which evokes the Spanish word *linde* or limit, this adjective can be seen as suggesting that his individual life is situated at the crossroads or on the limit between a present particularity and the universal, which encompasses both past and future. He thereby constitutes a symbolic manifestation of that universal, which his pre-execution declaration explains and justifies through language and logic.

The way that Dietrich describes himself and his words as a direct link to Germany's role in a new world history resembles the description that appears in the second footnote of the story. This footnote supplements his explanation of the philosophical influences that led him to national socialism, including the work of Friedrich Nietzsche and Oswald Spengler. The footnote elaborates his views on the latter's *The Decline of the West* in particular: "Other nations live naively, in and for themselves, like minerals or meteors; Germany is the universal mirror that receives all others — the conscience of the world [*das Weltbewusstsein*]. Goethe is the prototype of that ecumenical mind" (OC 1.618; CF 230). In this simplified and slightly exaggerated account of Spengler's book (a reckoning or *Abrechnung* calculated to cancel any "debt" to his contemporary), Dietrich describes Germany as an ideal space that transforms the perception of material particularities — including other nations, which, like inert, opaque objects, exist only in and for themselves — into world consciousness. Goethe is hailed as having produced a foundational version of this transformative reflection through his literature, which produces an "ecumenical mind," an understanding that grasps (*comprensión*) or domesticates (ecumenical derives from the Greek root *oikos*) the globe. From a Nazi perspective, Goethe's conception of *Weltliteratur*, like Dietrich's declaration, constitutes a prototype of a global consciousness to which national socialism will add the finishing touches.

The understanding of language as capable of constituting and transmitting a totalizing perspective of the world finds several points of contrast in the story. The first appears in the first footnote, purportedly added by the editor of Dietrich's declaration, which points out that in his description of his ancestors, he neglected to mention Johannes Forkel, a Hebrew philologist and theologian who applied Hegel's dialectic to Christology and translated some Biblical apocrypha (OC 1.617; CF 229). It is unclear why Dietrich omitted this ancestor, or why the editor considers it a "significant omission," although the implication is that a Hebraist is anathema to a Nazi, even if he is not Jewish himself (which is left as an open question).[9] But it is also interesting to consider how Forkel's projects engage with the way in which meaning is not neatly and reliably transferred through signifiers. Christology concerns the nature of the incarnation of God in the figure of Christ, which differs significantly from the transformative antagonism intrinsic to the Hegelian dialectic. In contrast to introducing strife and negativity into the direct transmission represented by the Christian incarnation, Forkel produces a "literal version" of the Biblical apocrypha, which suggests a direct transmission of the original. Nonetheless, many of the Biblical apocrypha are highly figurative (for instance in *Esdras* a woman turns into a city), so a literal version could be said not to arrive at the original sense, remaining in the errancy of human language rather than divine Logos. Whereas the second footnote of the story suggests how letters and literature are capable of creating and transmitting a totalizing image of the world through a hypernationalist, ethnically homogeneous perspective (that is, the "mirror" of Nazi Germany), the first footnote concerns the murkiness of representation in relation to the uncertain grounds of different "ecumenical" forms of comprehension.

Dietrich describes a great love for the works of Johannes Brahms and William Shakespeare, and although it might seem that his invocation of these privileged figures from the (broadly understood) Germanic canon would resemble that of Goethe, in fact, they too appear at odds with the linguistic production and transmission of a totalizing picture of the world. He describes how they diverted him (*me desvió*) from the totalizing pretensions of theology with "the infinite variety of their worlds. I wish anyone who is held in awe and wonder, quivering with tenderness and gratitude, transfixed by some passage in the work of these blessed men — anyone so touched — to know that I too was once transfixed like them — I the abominable" (OC 1.618; CF 230). In contrast to the figure of world as a static temporal and spatial totality, produced through the optics of Germany, Goethe, and Dietrich, here the world is described as infinitely differential. Likewise, in contrast to the totalizing consciousness said to be available to Goethe and the reader of Dietrich's declaration, the encounter with the worlds of Brahms and Shakespeare is described as leaving the recipient vulnerable and unsettled, "quivering with tenderness and gratitude." It is not possible to internalize these worlds; one passes before them, stopping (*detenerse*) to allow their greatness to disturb the ostensible unity of the self, leaving it trembling tenderly.[10] Furthermore, in contrast to the ecumenical mirror of hypernationalist Germany, produced by killing Jews and others perceived as threats to its limpidity, the works of Brahms and Shakespeare are open to anyone who chooses to pause before them, even someone as "abominable" as Dietrich.

Dietrich's description of the works of Brahms and Shakespeare resonates with the account of the Jewish poet David Jerusalem, the only victim of the concentration camp in which Dietrich serves as subdirector that is mentioned by name. Dietrich begins his description of Jerusalem's work with a reference to Albert Soergel (a poetry critic who became a Nazi), who reportedly compared Jerusalem to Whitman, but Dietrich rejects the comparison, stating that "Whitman celebrates the universe *a priori*, in a way that is general and virtually indifferent; Jerusalem takes delight in every smallest thing, with meticulous and painstaking love" (OC 1.620; SF 232). The poet who celebrates blades of grass and the air in his mouth appears "general and virtually indifferent" in comparison to Jerusalem, whose poetry by implication must be even more radically singular than Whitman's in its engagement with, as Dietrich says of Brahms and Shakespeare, the "infinite variety" of the world.

Although Dietrich clearly admires Jerusalem, he says he is compelled to destroy him, not only because he is a Nazi and Jerusalem a Jew (a fact that is merely implied), but because Jerusalem awakens in him a "compassion"

(OC 1.619; SF 231). Such com-passion can be understood as care for another, which might open onto care for *other* others, and even the "infinite variety" of the world, which runs counter to his philosophical justification of national socialism. Whereas the aesthetic works of Jerusalem, Brahms, and Shakespeare appeal to an infinite and endlessly emerging multiplicity, Nazism is for Dietrich conceptually bound to a totalizing order, the figure of the One.

At the beginning of the story, it appears that totality, both temporal and spatial, can be symbolically represented, by both Dietrich ("I am a symbol of the generations to come") and Germany ("the universal mirror that receives all others") (OC 1.617–18; CF 229–30). He also describes a deep affinity for Schopenhauer, who, according to his understanding, regards the individual as a microscopic version of the whole. In this theory, each individual predetermines his own destiny, which he describes as a "secret order" and an "individual teleology," through which everything a person does — all action and accident, even every failure, every chance encounter — contributes to a self-determined end, to the point that "every death [is] a suicide" (OC 1.619; CF 231).

This understanding of self-sovereignty underlies Dietrich's description of his execution of Jerusalem. He explains that despite his admiration for him, he was impelled to "destroy" him, which was really a form of destroying his own "piety" and even himself: Jerusalem had become "a symbol of a detested region of my soul. I suffered with him, I died with him, I somehow have been lost with him; that was why I was implacable" (OC 1.621; CF 232). Dietrich leads Jerusalem to death by inciting him to kill himself (*darse muerte*), as a way of destroying himself, perversely suggesting that both Jewish victim and Nazi executioner share the same secret order and teleology. Dietrich induces this double suicide not only out of anti-Semitism, but also, and primarily, based on the opposition between his commitment to a total order and the radical particularity invoked by Jerusalem's poetry. The method that Dietrich uses to drive Jerusalem insane is to push particularity to a hellish extreme:

> I had realized many years before I met David Jerusalem that everything in the world can be the seed of a possible hell; a face, a word, a compass, an advertisement for cigarettes — anything can drive a person insane if that person cannot manage to put it out of his mind. Wouldn't a man be mad if he constantly had before his mind's eye the map of Hungary? I decided to apply this principle to the disciplinary regimen of our house and . . . (OC 1.620; CF 232)[11]

Here the text breaks off, and a footnote explains that "the excision of a number of lines has been unavoidable," ironically obscuring the particulars in this description of death by particularity. Dietrich's method of inducing insanity and death seems to harness what he sees as Jerusalem's proclivity toward particularity to impose a sense of truly arriving at a particular object. However, this method reveals an important distinction between two different kinds of particularity. The weaponized understanding of particularity is atemporal and self-identical, essentially universalizing the particular, making of the part its own whole, which can be sacrificed to another whole, as the Jews are to Nazi Germany. The kind of particularity that Dietrich observes in Jerusalem's poetry, as well as in the works of Shakespeare and Brahms, on the other hand, concerns a difference that necessarily exists in time, and in a movement that one can only pause before in momentary contact (*detenerse*). It is a radical particularity (or what I am calling in this book *singularity*) in that it cannot be fully absorbed into a whole, sacrificially. It does not give itself (*darse*) because there is no unified self to give.

The sacrificial structure of a universalized part to a whole dominates the end of the story, where, as in "Tlön," the ideal of a totalizing order threatens to take over the world. Although initially such adherence to the structure of totality was represented by "in-dividual" particulars — namely Dietrich and Germany — these particulars that symbolized or reflected a totalizing world consciousness are, in Dietrich's account, ultimately absorbed into the whole.

In the end, the order of the One prevails over Nazism and Dietrich himself. Echoing Borges's conjecture in "A Comment on August 23, 1944," Dietrich describes an odd sense of satisfaction when he realizes that the structure of totality requires the sacrifice of all particulars, even its most fanatical supporters: "There are many things that must be destroyed in order to build the new order; now we know that Germany was one of them" (OC 1.622; CF 234). Although his compatriots may resist, he says he is personally pleased with this destiny, which he describes as an "orbicular and perfect gift," a sacrificial entry to a totalizing world order. The final paragraph of the story displays this sacrifice in a split image, as it were. Dietrich looks at himself in the mirror and observes the difference between his physical body and the ideal of totality, which his individuality serves merely to reflect. His parting glance in the mirror "to know who I am" confirms his earlier assertion that his existence (*soy*, I am) links past, present, and future in a single static order. Although the story concludes with Dietrich's simultaneously self-assured and self-annihilating confidence in the triumph of the One, the description of the relationship to singularity and difference in the works of Jerusalem, Brahms, and Shakespeare suggests a different possible ending, one that Borges's story — as indeed his work in general, far as it is from Goethe's ecumenical mirror — can be seen as trying to elicit.

In "The Garden of Forking Paths," there is a similar struggle between a differential experience of time and singularity, on the one hand, and the imposition of a single and atemporal form of order, on the other — in this case less the umbilical One of empire, than the divided One of enmity. Like "*Deutsches Requiem*," the story is structured as a declaration of a man about to be executed, who affirms his victory despite his impending death. Nonetheless "The Garden of Forking Paths" emphasizes the struggle between order and excess more than the other. It is for this reason that I have chosen to reverse the chronological order of the stories, since in "*Deutsches Requiem*," written later about a subsequent war, the intensification of the dominant order makes it hard to discern any excess or remainder beyond the ghostly reverberations of Brahms, Shakespeare, and Jerusalem.

Perhaps more than any of Borges's other stories, "The Garden of Forking Paths" illustrates and interrogates Levinas's precept that "Being reveals itself as war to philosophical thought" (Levinas 21). Although the story is set during the First World War, it is less about a totalizing world order than the previous two stories, and more about knowledge, including the knowledge *of* others and its transmission *to* others. These questions about knowledge are conditioned by the setting of war, in which the structure of enmity reigns supreme, although it is clear that they are not limited to that setting.

The story begins with a frame narrative, which references a small detail in a history book about the war. Historiography is a mode of knowledge that, at least traditionally, seeks to unify space and time. The book in question is Liddell Hart's *History of the First World War*, the Spanish title of which, *Historia de la Guerra Europea*, retrospectively confines the war to a continent — to which it was not in fact contained — and affirms its conclusion (although, given the story's publication date of 1941, readers would be aware that global conflict is not safely contained in the past). The specific reference concerns a short delay in a British offensive in the infamous Battle of the Somme, one of the bloodiest conflicts in recorded history. Hart characterizes this as "a delay that entailed no great consequences" (OC 1.506; CF 119), stressing the historian's authority to determine, with certainty, what is meaningful about history.[12]

The frame narrator introduces the primary narrative as one that permits a different perspective on the delay, questioning the certainty of historiographical closure. This declaration is made by "Dr. Yu Tsun, former professor of English at the *Hochschule* at Tsingtao" (OC 1.506; CF 119), who, like Dietrich in "*Deutsches Requiem*," declares victory in the face of execution: "I have most abhorrently triumphed: I have communicated to Berlin the secret name of the city to be attacked" (OC 1.514; CF 127). His abominable victory consists of a successful act of communication in which distance is bridged and a message delivered, acts that result in death and destruction. Nonetheless, the story also stages a delay and an interference in that communication, thereby performing an opening in the sutures of history exemplified by the opening reference to Hart's historiography, and stressing how delays and gaps affect understanding, communication, and relations with others in ways that are not reducible "as war to philosophical thought," as Levinas puts it (21). The story portrays the bellicose subordination of singularity and difference to totality, but it also stresses points of incompletion and differential excess.

The narrator, Yu Tsun, is a Chinese-born professor of English (from a town near British-occupied Hong Kong, who taught in a German school in German-occupied Tsingtao), who is acting as a spy for Germany. He is pursued by Richard Madden, an Irish agent working for Britain. Both characters are colonized subjects fighting for (and against) their colonizers, and both are described as reluctant and even cowardly participants in this war that is not of their own making. However, despite their reluctance, they both seem determined to overcome their perceived cowardice through their missions for the imperial powers, as though the divided totality of this "European war" were the only possible reality.

As the Battle of the Somme rages on a few hundred miles away in France, Yu Tsun, positioned in England, endeavors to send a message to his boss in Germany, who will then authorize an aerial attack on an artillery field in the middle of that ferocious battle. The story is therefore organized around the structure of telecommunication, which can be understood as collapsing distance into a common (in the sense of single or shared) space of understanding.[13] Yu Tsun spends the entire story trying to bridge difference and distance to deliver his message and thereby prove his worth as equal to both his colonizer and its enemy. The medium of his message is the name of a man he murders, Stephen Albert, which the boss deciphers as the name of the targeted artillery field, which he promptly orders to be destroyed. Both the medium and the result of his message are destructive, and they constitute a response to the destructive instruments of the enemy. Such is communication in wartime.

In addition to its staggering number of casualties, the Battle of the Somme has the dubious distinction of being among the first battles in which both trench and aerial warfare were extensively employed. In trench warfare, armed conflict is simultaneously face-to-face and mediated by the distance and depth of the trenches; in aerial combat the distance between combatants is increasingly widened, and telecommunication plays a more important role. Indeed, Yu Tsun's "sick and hateful" boss, who sits in his office in Berlin waiting for missives (*noticias*) about his subordinates in the field, exemplifies the kind of remote-control warfare that was initiated during this period (OC 1.507; CF 120). However, although the story can be seen as tracing the arc of this transformation, based on the success of telecommunication and subsequent aerial bombing at the end, it also stresses some of the ways that distance and proximity resist and disrupt any simple division into enmity or unification into a static commonality.

The story begins in a doubly disrupted fashion, in medias res due to some missing pages of the transcript of Yu Tsun's declaration, and starting with the words, ". . . and I hung up the receiver" (OC 1.506; CF 119). The introduction of the motif of telecommunication thereby exhibits an important difference from its conclusion. The opening telephone call does not constitute a successful act of communication in the sense of establishing a common space of understanding, since it is intercepted by the enemy and subsequently cut off or suspended. The rest of the story consists of Yu Tsun's circuitous efforts to contravene this interception with his own fatal form of communication.

From the intercepted telephone call, Yu Tsun rushes to take a train to the country village to find Albert, the medium of his message. Trains do not collapse distance, like telephones, but they traverse it in such a way that standardizes the experience of space and time. Thanks to the train schedule, Yu Tsun knows how far he must go to find his victim and he knows how long he has until Madden can follow him. He describes a sensation of "cowardly cheerfulness" as the train carries him away from his pursuer and toward his victim, entrusting what might in a previous form of war have relied entirely on face-to-face encounter and the will to kill to the mediation of modern technology (OC 1.508; CF 121).

Once on board the train, Yu Tsun reflects on the relationship between time and his deadly objective:

> I foresee that mankind will resign itself more and more fully every day to more and more horrendous undertakings; soon there will be nothing but warriors and brigands. I give them this piece of advice: He who is to perform a horrendous act should imagine to himself [*debe imponerse*] that it is already done, should impose upon himself a future as irrevocable as the past. That is what I did, while my eyes — the eyes of a man already dead — registered the flow of that day perhaps to be my last, and the spreading of the night [*la fluencia de aquel día que era tal vez el último, y la difusión de la noche*]. (OC 1.508; CF 121–22)

Yu Tsun's description transforms time into a linear train-track of intention, in which the future is considered to be as "irrevocable" as the past. Irrevocable here suggests resolution and immutability, but also, with the root of *vox* resonating with the motif of communication, already spoken and received. In other words, the increasing commonality of atrocity constitutes a form of already-achieved communication in which distances and differences, as well as the "flow" and "spreading" of time, are contained and controlled. Such a description, furthermore, recalls "*Deutsches Requiem*" in that it links the individual to the general, in which the past and present are fixed in an atemporal state, and in which one's own mortal perspective ("the eyes of a man already dead") reveals a general state of death ("the spreading of the night").

When he gets off the train, Yu Tsun walks along a bifurcating path in semi-darkness, where he loses his sense of certainty and preestablished completion. He reflects that there is in fact much that escapes wartime action and the generalized structure of enmity: "I was struck by the thought that a man can be the enemy of other men, the enemy of other men's other moments, yet not be the enemy of a country — of fireflies, words, gardens, watercourses, zephyrs" (OC 1.509; CF 122–23). As he moves closer to committing his atrocious act, he perceives forms of singularity that flicker like fireflies in the currents of the night, beyond the militant limits of intention and the schema of enmity in which he is caught up.

With these thoughts he arrives at a tall iron gate, and through its bars he makes out or deciphers ("*descifré*") a line of poplar trees and a pavilion (OC 1.509). The word *decipher* reinforces the motif of communication around which the story is built, and reappears at the end of the story, when the boss in Berlin deciphers Yu Tsun's long-distance message ("The Leader solved the riddle [*ha descifrado el enigma*]," OC 1.514; CF 128). That definitive and deadly deciphering evokes a play on the root of the word *cipher*, which comes from the Arabic word for zero or void (*sifr*). The successful delivery of a (wartime) missive in this sense can be seen as a double negative that negates the zero by turning it into a positive integer, of which the standard is the One. However, after describing the success of his telecommunicative act, Yu Tsun reflects forlornly that, despite successfully deciphering his sinister message, his German boss "does not know (no one can know) my endless contrition, and my weariness [*mi innumerable contrición y cansancio*]" (OC 1.514; CF 128). The word *innumerable* (innumerable or endless) stands out, since sadness and fatigue are uncountable nouns, and suggests that even though Yu Tsun has carried out his obligation to the order to which he has sworn allegiance, there is something exceeds that order, something that is not reducible to a single totality. It also contrasts notably with the end of "*Deutsches Requiem*," in which Dietrich discards the finite singularity of his body in favor of his commitment to a single totalizing order. The contrast between the boss's deciphering of Yu Tsun's message and his description of "endless contrition," indicates that although Yu Tsun has in fact carried out his obligation to the order to which he has sworn allegiance, something exceeds that order, something that is not reducible to the One, or the competition of Ones that is enmity.[14]

Returning to Yu Tsun's arrival at Albert's enclosure, it is this tension between totality and difference, or the "innumerable" excess of the One, that he "deciphers" through the bars of the gate and throughout his visit with Stephen Albert. The description of Yu Tsun's approach and first encounter with Albert emphasizes the ways in which his host is not reducible to a target (name, missive, or cipher). As he draws near, he notices the sound of music that is described as similar to language (syllabic), but which seems to prefigure a different form of communication, involving a play of distance and proximity distinct from the organization of distance crucial to the structure of enmity: "A keen and vaguely syllabic song, blurred by leaves and distance, came and went on the gentle gusts of breeze" (OC 1.509–10; CF 122). This description resembles the flow and diffusion of day and night that follows Yu Tsun's avowal of determined action (OC 1.508; CF 121). Furthermore his experience of hearing the music is compared to a firefly-like dance of light in the dark — "the sputtering [*chisporroteo*] of the music" (OC 1.510; CF 123) — which is visually echoed by Albert's approach, discernible at first only as the flickering light of a lantern, which the trunks of the trees "cross-hatched and sometimes blotted out altogether [ . . . ], a paper lantern the shape of a drum and the color of the moon" (OC 1.510; CF 123). The sparks and glimmer of both the music and the lantern's approach suggest a fragile uncertainty that does not reveal the approaching other in any solar fashion: "I could not see his face because the light blinded me" (OC 1.510; CF 123). Furthermore, the description of the music as a *chisporroteo* (sputtering or crackling, from *chispa*, spark) can be seen to evoke the paper lantern's combustibility, characterizing the moment of encounter as fundamentally ephemeral. Moreover, the word *chisporroteo* also suggests the effect of electrical overload that occurs when electrical flow is not sufficiently isolated or insulated. The sound and sight of sparks thereby do not only prefigure the perception and communication of the two characters, but also indicate an involuntary effect of their proximity, which overloads their individual systems, or "corrects" what may never really be individual or isolated in the first place. This latter sense is suggested by the first words that Albert utters as he welcomes Yu Tsun — even while mistaking him for someone else — as a "remedy [*corrección*]" to his solitude (OC 1.510; CF 123).[15]

As Yu Tsun enters Albert's house, from a winding path that reminds him of his childhood, he notices the source of the music he had heard from the gate: a gramophone turning (*giraba*) next to a bronze phoenix (OC 1.510; CF 123). The sight of the source of the music, which turns out to be Chinese, set amidst ancient books and porcelain from Yu Tsun's home country, seems at first glance to contrast with the description of the flickering of sound and light that accompanied his approach to Albert's house, representing rather a return to a cultural identity firmly rooted in the past.[16] The figure of the gramophone is key here. In addition to transmitting sound across distance, like the telephone, the gramophone also preserves its sounds across time. Nonetheless, as the sight of the gramophone suggests, such preservation does not permit a real return or arrival at an origin, but only a turning, and as its contiguity with the figurine of the phoenix suggests, the sounds that it carries are not preserved intact as they move through the turns and returns of space and time, but are exposed to ashes, the other side of the *chisporroteo*.

Sitting down before a window, the window that will eventually reveal Yu Tsun's enemy pursuer, and a round clock that will mark the time before that enemy appears, Yu Tsun resolves to put wartime (and war space) on hold — "My irrevocable determination could wait" (OC 1.510; CF 123, translation modified) — in order to learn more about his ancestor Ts'ui Pên, a Chinese ruler and scholar who secluded himself for thirteen years to produce a book and a labyrinth, whom Albert, who turns out to be an avid Sinologist, has studied. In a sense, Yu Tsun can be seen as seeking to shift the command of enmity, the atrocious imperative to kill the other, to the authority of his cultural and familial past; to recuperate a truer affiliation, through bloodline, than the one for which he feels compelled to shed blood. He wants to recover the light of his "illustrious ancestor" (OC 1.510; CF 123), which might redeem or reorient his murky present, a messianic desire peculiarly linked to the eponymous figure of the garden, which Yu Tsun invokes as the "re-creation" of an Edenic space of belonging (OC 1.514; CF 127).

Before his encounter with Albert, Yu Tsun knew only that Ts'ui Pên had secluded himself for thirteen years to produce a book and a labyrinth. He says of this labyrinth, "I pictured it perfect and inviolate on the secret summit of a mountain" (OC 1.509; CF 122). He repeats "I pictured it [*lo imaginé*]" three times, extending the image to encompass a sovereignly governed cosmos: "I pictured it as infinite — a labyrinth not of octagonal pavilions and paths that turn back upon themselves, but of rivers and provinces and kingdoms." As he struggles to find an image suitable to hold his enigmatic inheritance, his awareness of enmity and pursuit falls away and he experiences the world as a labyrinth: "The vague and living countryside, the moon, the remains of the day did their work in me . . . The evening was near, yet infinite. The road dropped and forked as it cut through the now formless meadows" (OC 1.509; CF 122). This description corresponds to Paul North's distinction between a maze, which can be visually comprehended, and a labyrinth, in which planning, intention, and calculation are rendered useless, and one is compelled to meander through it with no sense of a clear end, structure, or subjective autonomy (North, *Distraction* 102).[17]

Yu Tsun shares with Albert his frustration that the writings left by Ts'ui Pên appear incomprehensible, an unsuitable vessel for the continuity of the bloodline: "we who are descended from Ts'ui Pen execrate that monk. It was senseless to publish those manuscripts. The book is a contradictory jumble of irresolute drafts [*un acervo indeciso de borradores contradictorios*]" OC 1.511; CF 124). The word *acervo* signifies a heap or pile of things and also, oddly, cultural heritage, or the effort to shape the jumble of history into tradition.[18] Ts'ui Pên's book, however, appears to be a jumble that refuses to be shaped into a useful vehicle for the present. It does not provide a mandate that might replace or at least provide ballast to the "irrevocable decision" that drives Yu Tsun's present (OC 1.510; CF 123). It is indecisive, contradictory, and incomplete, appearing to consist of drafts that do not cohere into a single, authoritative work. It is therefore appropriate that the key to its interpretation is found in a fragmentary letter, which articulates a different mode of inheritance: "I leave to several futures [*a los varios porvenires*] (not to all) my garden of forking paths" (OC 1.512; CF 125). This fragmentary letter traverses space and time but describes the very structure of both message and legacy as constitutively fragmented, plural, and not self-identical. This structure of communication and inheritance reflects the differential nature of both space and time, which, as Albert explains, Ts'ui Pên understood not as uniform and absolute a prioris, but rather as a vertiginous web of differences that conditions thought, representation, and relation as shifting sands of possibility (OC 1.513–14; CF 127). In this labyrinthine experience of space and time, relation is determined not by the One, whether as bloodline, political allegiance, or elective affinity, but as a fundamentally differential multiplicity in which communication is possible but never guaranteed, and inevitably incomplete and unresolved, like Ts'ui Pên's fragmentary missives.

This incompletion is generative and even constitutive of life, understood not as an individual subject subsumed by a totalizing order, affiliated with a proprietary bloodline or subjected by a predetermined objective, but as an experience of finitude that exceeds and unsettles human autonomy. At various points in which the structure of enmity is recalled during his conversation with Albert, Yu Tsun describes feeling a powerful "pullulation": "I felt all about me and within my obscure body an invisible, intangible pullulation" (OC 1.513; CF 126); "I felt again that pullulation I have mentioned. I sensed that the dew-drenched garden that surrounded the house was saturated, infinitely, with invisible persons. Those persons were Albert and myself" (OC 1.514; CF 127). Jolted by the return to an awareness of the global antagonism in which he is a player, Yu Tsun perceives the vertiginous web of differences that underlies all relations, both synchronic (exemplified here by the face-to-face with Albert) and diachronic (exemplified by the texts bequeathed by Ts'ui Pên). The word *pullulation* suggests a kind of larval swarm that infests both his sense of self and his relation to the other with a plural, burgeoning, but also fundamentally fragile and ephemeral form of possibility, akin to the *chisporroteo* that marked Yu Tsun's approach to this site of encounter. Yu Tsun disavows this multiplicity and pulls the trigger, sending his message via detonation, ostensibly reaffirming the triumph of a single order and simultaneously closing himself into an irrevocable end.

Like "Tlön, Uqbar, Orbis Tertius" and "*Deutsches Requiem*," "The Garden of Forking Paths" appears to conclude with a form of totality in which "Being reveals itself as war, . . . an objective order from which there is no escape" (Levinas 21). Nevertheless, points of excess and non-adequation to this order are mentioned throughout all three stories, suggesting that the ideal of "one order" has not been definitively achieved (Borges, OC 2.112; SNF 211). In "The Garden of Forking Paths," the closing mention of Yu Tsun's "endless" contrition indicates the irrepressible multiplicity of the future, and the possibility of new drafts and rewritings — such as these stories — that explore the limits of totalizing structures.

# Chapter 2

# Walls, Towers, Books: Borges with Kafka

## "The Wall and the Books," "Kafka and His Precursors," "On Exactitude in Science"

Paul North observes that there is a tendency to read the works of both Borges and Kafka as fables of complete subordination or complete emancipation, appealingly describing the latter as "a total garden of totally forking paths" (*The Yield* 221). North condemns such a "Kafka reaction" in relation to Kafka's works, but he suggests that in Borges's case the representation of total emancipation, which he understands as constituting a form of total constraint, is probably justified. North describes this polarization in relation to Deleuze and Guattari's reading in *Kafka: A Minor Literature*, which is largely responsible for the emancipatory interpretation of Kafka's works. Ironically, North's approach to Borges appears to be influenced by Deleuze's interpretation of Borges in *The Fold*, in which the latter's work is indeed read as totally folding or forking (*The Yield* 62–63). Deleuze's reading of Borges can be seen as one pole of a similar "Borges reaction," in which readers have tended to read Borges's fictions as either bleak illustrations of entrapment or celebratory postulations of unrestrained infinity.[1]

With appreciation to North for his thought-provoking description, I want to propose that, as he argues about Kafka, Borges also eludes both extremes, and this becomes especially apparent when looking at his reactions to Kafka's works. In his writings that evoke Kafka, whether directly or indirectly, and indeed throughout his work, Borges emphasizes the internal contradictions of limits in ways that confound structures of sovereignty and exceed any simple opposition between subordination and emancipation.

Borges's most explicit ideas on Kafka's work appear in the two prologues that he wrote to accompany translations of Kafka's stories. The first prologue, which accompanied a Spanish translation of Kafka's *The Metamorphosis*, was published in 1938; the second appeared in a 1979 compilation of Kafka's stories, titled *The Vulture,* after Kafka's story of that name.[2] In these prologues, Borges stresses that Kafka's fiction tends to be structured around two main ideas — subordination and the infinite — which at first glance seem to work seamlessly together: "In the most memorable of all [of Kafka's stories, "Building the Great Wall of China,]" the infinite is multiple: in order to stop the course of infinitely distant armies, an emperor, infinitely remote in time and space, orders infinite generations to infinitely raise an infinite wall around his infinite empire [*que dé la vuelta de su imperio infinito*]" (OC 4.106). However, this does not mean that Borges is a dupe of the "Kafka reaction." He links the structure of hierarchy to the figure of, and search for, a home (*domus*), which he describes as "a place . . . in some Order" (Borges, "Franz Kafka, The Vulture" SNF 503).[3] He also describes a recurrent motif of postponement or deferral, which suggests the fundamental elusiveness of both order and a proper place within it. The word that he uses, "postergación," comes from the Latin *post tergum*, referring to something behind the back, which implies that the search for a home or the proper place in an order is not only infinitely deferred (carried off), but it is also carried off toward the back and so inherently dorsal, to use David Wills's suggestive term.[4] Such a relation of the figure of order to its underside or outside can be seen in the above description of the infinite circumscription of the empire, which in addition to inferring a paradoxically infinite making finite of the empire, also evokes a turning or turning over ("*que dé la vuelta*") of the infinite effort to dominate. Rather than seeing Kafka's work as merely staging infinite scenes of subjection, Borges stresses the ways that such infinite scenes turn toward and against each other to reveal the murky limits that lurk beneath constructions of the proper.

## *Limited and Lacunary*

Kafka's "most memorable" story, "Building the Great Wall of China"— which Borges translated into Spanish in 1938 — recounts the piecemeal and ultimately unfinished act of building the Great Wall of China. It describes how armies of workers start from different directions, and build toward each other, and when they complete one section, rather than lengthening it, they are sent to another part of the empire to construct another section. The narrator observes, "In this way, of course, numerous large gaps came about, and these were only gradually and slowly filled in, many only after the construction of the Wall had already been announced as completed. Indeed, it is said that there are gaps that have not been filled in at all; according to some people these are much larger than the completed sections . . ." (Kafka 113). The narrator explains that the reason for such a piecemeal method is to counteract the Sisyphean task of construction, which would likely discourage the workers: "the hopelessness of such work, which, however industriously performed, would not achieve its goal even at the end of a long life, would have driven them to despair" (115). Rather than become depleted by the extensive task of circumscribing the empire, they are celebrated for accomplishing short-term goals and reinvigorated to accomplish more:

> while they were still ecstatic from the festival when the sections of the thousand-yard wall were joined, they were sent far, far away. On the journey they saw, here and there, finished sections of the Wall looming up . . . they heard the cheers of new armies

> of workers streaming in from the provinces . . . at sacred sites they heard songs of pious pilgrims begging for the completion of the Wall . . . [The] desire to labor once again at this national mission became uncontrollable . . . every fellow countryman was a brother for whom they were building a protective wall and who was thankful all his life, thankful with everything he had and was: unity! unity! breast on breast, a round dance of the people, blood no longer confined in the meager circulatory system of the body but rolling on sweetly and yet returning to its source through the infinity of China. (115)

Although the primary objective of this extraordinary wall was ostensibly to keep out the nomadic "peoples of the north" (113), a more immediate motivation was to foment a sense of shared identity among the far-flung regions of the Chinese empire. Since simply imposing a sense of unity on vastly divergent regions was as daunting as constructing a wall around China, the leaders appealed to the supplements of labor and patriotic ceremony.

The ideal of infinite collective unity recalls, once again, the fable of the Tower of Babel, which concerns an effort to construct the unity of a people, only to be foiled by God's hand. The narrator of Kafka's story remarks that "deeds were accomplished" during the building of the Chinese wall that "fall just short of the building of the Tower of Babel" (115). He tells how, early on in the construction of the wall, a scholar claimed that the wall would in fact "create, for the first time in human history, a solid foundation for a new Tower of Babel" (116). Although the narrator discards this claim, contending only that elements of the wall's construction came close to the building of the Tower of Babel, the production of patriotic fervor can, in fact, be understood as providing a kind of foundation for a unified and unlimited ideal of sovereignty.

In his discussion of this story in *Singularity: Politics and Poetics*, Samuel Weber stresses the narrator's response to the comparison between the wall and the Tower of Babel. The narrator observes that the wall does not form a circle, which might be understood to serve as the basis for a new tower. He surmises that the idea that the wall serves as a foundation for an improvement on the Tower of Babel "can only be meant in some intellectual way. But what then was the point of the wall, which was something factual [*etwas Tatsächliches*], the result of the labor and the lives of hundreds of thousands of workers?" (Kafka 116; Weber, *Singularity* 394). Weber interprets the "intellectual" way in which the wall is understood to provide a foundation for a new tower that would successfully unify a people, and even, possibly, all of humanity, as an imaginary screen designed to deflect and distract from anxieties relating to finitude and vulnerability — for instance, "the meager circulatory system of the body" (Kafka 115; Weber 392). He writes, "The desire to escape such anxieties can be provisionally relieved through a process that allows an imaginary identification with a collective — a country, state, ideology — that is considered to be as 'infinite' as the 'infinity of China'" (Weber 392). Such an intellectual, imaginary, or ideal response "turns the body from a mortal into an immortal mode of being," turning singularity — fundamentally limited, contingent, and temporal — into individuality, which Weber stresses implies an ab-solute (that is, not subject to dissolution or change) form of in-dividuation or indivisibility. In the narrator's response to the idea that the wall constitutes a foundation for a Babelic structure of unification, he protests that the wall also involves something "factual" or material, which he links to "the result of the labor and the lives of hundreds of thousands of workers" (Kafka 116). This "something factual" that constitutes the other side of the idealized, infinite One involves the multiple lives and labor of the people who helped to construct the wall, lives and actions that were singular, limited, and temporal. Furthermore, the finite conditions of the lives that dwelled in the wall's shadows are reflected in its piecemeal and incomplete construction. Weber writes, "The wall, which is limited and lacunary, reflecting the finitude of the conditions under which it is built, is meant by the dominant social and political powers presiding over its construction to supplement the limitations of the singular living beings laboring on it. But . . . it inevitably also embodies those limitations" (Weber, *Singularity* 395).

Weber interprets the "limited and lacunary" construction of the wall as analogous to language. He compares the piecemeal and deferred method of construction to the nature of writing and reading, which similarly rely on an "intellectual" process of supplementation to convey or arrive at a unified and conventional sense of meaning. He stresses the etymological sense of the word convention, from *con-venire*, as implying a drawing together of multiple possibilities into a single inclination (Weber, *Singularity* 402). He compares convention to the psychoanalytic structure of repression, in which the act of convergence excludes and denies a multiplicity of tendencies or possibilities that are brought together into a single idea or figure, but not completely: They "still exert a centrifugal pull away from the 'point' in which they have converged," and, indeed, they can have concrete effects, much like the "return of the repressed" (402). In the case of "Building the Great Wall of China," the gaps and limits of the wall, as well as the lives and labor of those who built it, are elements that underlie the ideal meaning spelled out in its bricks, unsettling the effort on the part of the leaders to affirm the convention of identity, the "unity" and "infinity of China" (Kafka 115). This is another aspect to the narrator's description of the wall as "something factual": Its facticity, which, like language, is "limited and lacunary," serves as a material resistance to prescribed conventions of meaning, which recalls "a signifying potential" that exceeds and underlies them (Weber, *Singularity* 395). In this way, Kafka's story effectively underscores the unattainability of the "towering aim" of the wall and so many other structures and systems of sovereignty throughout history, in the spirit of the Tower of Babel, to assert in-dividual and ab-solute unity and infinity over and against singularity, finitude, and difference. In his essay on the Tower of Babel, Derrida points out that incompletion, fragmentation, and difference do not only constitute the tower's final consequences but are also present in its very construction, that is, the ultimate scatter is present even in the careful laying of bricks, and polylingualism is present in a single language or name ("Des Tours de Babel" 104). Kafka and Borges stress this differential excess and its potential for disruption, even as they also explore, and often exaggerate or distort, the structures and systems that seek to master or deny it.

Derrida's description of difference and incompletion in the construction of the Tower of Babel, as "the inadequation of one tongue to another, of one place in the encyclopedia to another, of language to itself and to meaning, and so forth," is oddly evocative of Borges's work ("Des Tours de Babel" 104). Indeed, like Kafka, Borges's writings abound with Babel-like structures that purportedly constitute and defend "a place . . . in some Order" but within whose limits lurk a constitutive inadequation that unsettles their claims to completion and sovereign containment (Borges, "Franz Kafka, The Vulture," SNF 503). Borges repeatedly pushes at these sites, as though to make them less subtle, less "behind the back" (*post tergum*), more of a challenge to the ostensibly infinite hierarchies that continue to structure our world. Although this gesture is not always linked to Kafka or to Babel, the specter of Kafka's evocation of Babel in "Building the Great Wall of China" can be discerned in a number of his works concerning the structures of sovereignty and their ruins or excess. In what follows, I examine two of Borges's texts that are exemplary in this regard: "On Exactitude in Science" ("Del rigor en la ciencia") (1946) and "The Wall and the Books" ("La Muralla y los libros") (1950). I consider the latter essay at some length, in part because it appears to constitute a kind of response to Kafka's Great Wall story and, in part, because it is one of Borges's more interesting and under-recognized efforts to address the relationship between political structures of order and (aesthetic) representation. I then turn to "Kafka and His Precursors" ("Kafka y sus precursores") (1951), which also concerns the relationship between literature, the structuration of the proper, and its inevitable *postergación*.

## *Systems of Shadows*

Although not directly linked to Kafka or Babel, Borges's "On Exactitude in Science" provides a condensed depiction of the Babelic aspiration to unity and subordination through knowledge as well as its intrinsic inadequation. This well-known vignette describes the development of an imperial map "whose size was that of the Empire, and which coincided point for point with it" (OC 2.241; CF 325). Like the Tower of Babel, the imperial map is a prosthesis of sovereignty, although the two fables are spread on inverse axes. The tower is constructed vertically, to raise humans up to the absolute perspective of God, whereas the map is constructed horizontally, as an affirmation of the effects of absolute perspective, or what Alberto Moreiras describes (apropos the invocation of Babel in Borges's "Tlön, Uqbar, Orbis Tertius") as the immanentization of transcendence, in which God is no longer needed (*Tercer espacio* 69).

The drive to approximate divine perspective is only implied by the fable of Babel. What is explicit is the builders' desire to "make a name" for themselves, to rise from telluric dispersion to the celestial plane of the proper. The map of the empire, of course, is part of a process of imperial appropriation that endeavors to convert material extension into territory. Such a creation of the proper as property happens not merely by virtue of a proper noun or name, although each of its "points" does indeed correspond to the process of Adamic (re)naming. But builders of empires can be seen as aspiring to be God, rather than merely Adam. The word *empire*, which comes from the Latin *im-pero* ("to command or order"), replaces the structure of the name with that of the command. The imperial map does not only render the territory legible, it also makes it intelligible. The map does not merely "coincide" with territorial points, it mandates them into existence as imperial possession. Empire exemplifies the incorporation of a place into an Order, to paraphrase Borges's description of Kafka.

Borges's vignette stages the emplacement of imperial subjection as well as the natural history of its dispersion and disintegration. After the structure of imperial command is exchanged for more plastic practices of administration, the map shreds and tears from the "inclemencies" of time, weather, and neglect. In the end, animals and beggars — creaturely figures possessing neither the ability to name nor to command, thereby indicating an intrinsic inadequation in the economy of the human — wander among the tattered remains of the map.

Four years after publishing "On Exactitude in Science" and twelve years after translating Kafka's "Building the Great Wall of China," Borges wrote "The Wall and the Books," which offers a similar portrait of an imperial effort to establish the proper through architectural and linguistic structures. The text presents itself as a simple commentary on the interesting fact that the emperor Shih Huang Ti (Qin Shi Huang), who ordered the construction of the Great Wall of China, also ordered that all books written before his reign be burned. Nonetheless, the essay turns into a performative exploration of the relationship between construction and destruction, naming and unnameability, and concludes with one of Borges's most compelling reflections on the nature of the aesthetic. It is a fable about the construction of a *domus* or "place . . . in some Order" and its inevitably aporetic foundations (Borges, "Franz Kafka, The Vulture," SNF 503).

Borges begins "The Wall and the Books" with the observation that some Sinologists consider defending territory and burning books to be common sovereignly behavior, and that the only unusual thing in Shih Huang Ti's case may have been the scale on which he operated. Regarding the emperor's actions, Borges admits to feeling a simultaneous sense of satisfaction or sufficiency (adequation) on the one hand, and unease or disquietude on the other, which is not explained away by the fact that this is just how sovereigns act (OC 2.13; SNF 344). He describes the objective of the essay as the effort to understand that "emotion," which can be understood as a dynamic response to the tension between adequation and non-adequation, sovereignty and excess, exemplified by the actions of the ancient emperor.

Propelled by this emotion and resembling the piecemeal construction of the wall in Kafka's story, or as Carlos Rojas suggests, the actual forking nature of the Great Wall itself (Rojas 122), Borges's essay proceeds through a series of hypotheses, none of which is accepted as definitive. These hypotheses are performed and referred to as conjectures, punctuated by the anaphoric use of "perhaps," and, once articulated, they are immediately supplanted by additional considerations: for example, "[b]oth conjectures are dramatic, but" (OC 2.14; SNF 345). The essay does not mention Babel, but the similarities between Shih Huang Ti and the Biblical fable are striking. Shih Huang Ti came to power during the century-long unification of China. Like the Shemites, he sought to create unity on a symbolic plane and transcend his mortal condition through architectural construction and the structure of the name, endeavoring to fortify the physical limits of his empire, and assert himself as its center and foundation by renaming himself as first emperor — after a previous ruler known as "the one who names" (Huangdi). No Pascalian circle this. Shih Huang Ti sets himself up as a sun king, aiming to abolish any threat to his power, including three thousand years of Chinese history and his own mortality. He mandates not just territory but also history into a *domus*, an enclosed space of the proper, based on the wager that, as Borges puts it, "decay" ("*corrupción*") — that is, mortality, dispersion, difference — "could not enter a closed sphere" (OC 2.14; SNF 345).

In his recounting of the details of Shih Huang Ti's life and speculating on what may have motivated him, Borges performatively unworks any proper exposition of historical explanation, any closed circle or frame of meaning, through the paratactically arranged conjectures. For instance: perhaps Shih Huang Ti really imagined himself as magical, believed the mystical foundation of authority even as he engineered it; perhaps he only stumbled accidentally onto such imposing actions; perhaps they were a mere effect of indecision (should I destroy or should I create?). In one of the final conjectures of the essay, Borges speculates on the possibility of the complete inverse of what he suggested formerly: he considers the idea that Shih Huang Ti "walled his empire because he knew that it was fragile [*deleznable*], and destroyed the books because he knew they were sacred books, books that teach what the whole universe teaches or the conscience of every man" (OC 2.14; SNF 345–46). Eliot Weinberger's translation of *deleznable* as "fragile" runs the risk of sounding too much like "delicate," whereas the word can also mean contemptible, flimsy, perishable, and prone to disaggregation — that is, the very qualities the imperial constructions were designed to keep out. Where an earlier conjecture posits the idea that mortal "decay could not enter a closed sphere," this one insists that it does and suggests that Shih Huang Ti's imperial actions may have sought to preserve the impossibility of preservation — the delicate nature of finitude — at the same time that it destroyed books, which can threaten to appropriate the infinitely finite nature of the world as doctrine. The final sentence in this paragraph of conjectures suggests that the end game of Shih Huang Ti's despotic dialectic may be zero, with the symmetrical, but inverse, endeavors of construction and destruction canceling each other out. Nonetheless, nothing in this final conjecture suggests that it is any more authoritative than any of the previous ones.

After this dorsal swirl of hypotheses, Borges pauses to observe that, whatever its origins, the "unyielding wall" (*muralla tenaz*) persists to this day, as well as its "system of shadows" (OC 2.15; SNF 346). I understand this as saying that not only do the relics of ancient structures intended to unify and exclude endure, but also that they are endlessly reconstructed, as are their shadowy undersides, which have the potential to unsettle their persistence and rigidity. Such transmutability of the ostensibly solid defense structure is described in "The Story of the Warrior and the Captive Maiden," in which Borges describes how the Mongolians, whom the Great Wall was purportedly designed to keep out, ended up living in the same Chinese edifications that they had previously sought to destroy — an instance, which resembles the titular case of the warrior and the captive, of what he calls a "secret impulse" that unmoors and disrupts ostensibly rigid structures of enclosure and exclusion (OC 1.599; CF 211).

Somewhat unexpectedly, "The Wall and the Books" ends with a striking reflection on the nature of aesthetic representation, which has interesting implications regarding the relationship between politics and aesthetics. The final section is at first glance confusing, in part because the transition from the discussion of the foundations of Chinese imperial history to aesthetic considerations is abrupt and without any typographical marker such as a paragraph break, and in part because it is tempting, as it is throughout the essay, to take conjectures at face value and thereby misunderstand essayistic contemplation as authorial assertion. Structurally, the concluding section resembles the beginning of the essay. It starts with an affirmation, which is followed by an attribution, which is then followed by a parataxis that undermines the initial affirmation.[5] The opening affirmation states that what most resembles the truth is that the idea of Shih Huang Ti's dual actions "is what moves us in itself, quite apart from the conjectures it allows [*es verosímil que la idea nos toque de por sí, fuera de las conjeturas que permite*]," from which, he says, "we might infer that *all* forms have virtue in themselves [*en sí mismas*] and not in a conjectural 'content,'" which he associates with Benedetto Croce's and Walter Pater's theories on the intrinsic unity of form and content (OC 2.15; SNF 346, translation modified). Borges here considers the possibility that the conjuncture of construction and destruction exemplified by Shih Huang Ti's foundational actions embodies an idea that supersedes any mere conjecture and is perfectly contained within its own boundaries, like Shih Huang Ti's empire. Nonetheless, the use of the word *verosímil* suggests that this idea is not fully self-referential or enclosed ("*de por sí*," "*en sí mismas*"), but involves a relation to something outside of itself, something that is like it (*símil*), but not identical. Borges furthermore elaborates such an idea of a self-enclosed truth beyond conjecture *with* a conjecture ("we might infer") about the universality of such an idea, which, in the conditional mood, he reflects *might* agree with the aesthetic ideals of Croce and Pater. This string of inference and analogy appears to affirm a similarity between imperial sovereignty, such as that exemplified by Shih Huang Ti's imperial circumscription, and aesthetic form understood as structurally self-sufficient. Nonetheless, like the notion of verisimilitude, the syntactical structure performatively subverts such an idea.

Borges's reference to Croce and Pater tends to be understood as an acknowledgment of affinity with their understanding of art, although the association is highly mediated (the sequence of ideas in this section so far is roughly this: the idea that form is content is truth-like ["*verosímil*"], by which we could infer a generalization about form's intrinsic worth, which agrees with Croce's thesis, which Pater anticipated). It is perhaps due to my own disbelief in the self-sufficiency of form that I cannot help thinking of how Borges skeptically describes Croce's belief in the unity of form and content in several contemporaneous essays.[6] I am also struck by the ways in which the essay by Pater that Borges cites resonates with some of the concerns we have considered. For instance, in the same section in which Pater states that "all art constantly aspires toward the condition of music," in which form becomes (or "should become") an end in itself, he compares the "mere matter" of an artwork to the "topography of a landscape," and affirms that aesthetic form, as a mode of "handling" such matter, "should penetrate every part of" it (Pater, n.p.). Such a description recalls the map in "On Exactitude in Science," which similarly "obliterates" (Pater's word) the matter on which it rests. In a different section of the same volume, Pater stresses that art transcends time as well as matter: While "all melts under our feet" in a temporal flux that results in a "strange . . . weaving and unweaving of ourselves," aesthetic perspective enables us to rise above the tumult, sunlike, and "burn always with [a] hard, gem-like flame."[7]

The following and final sentence in "The Wall and the Books" contrasts with such an idea of aesthetics as luminous sublation of time and materiality: "Music, states of happiness, mythology, faces worn by time, certain twilights and certain places, all want to tell us something, or have told us something we shouldn't have lost, or are about to tell us something; that imminence of a revelation as yet unproduced, is, perhaps, the aesthetic fact (*esta inminencia de una revelación que no se produce es, quizá, el hecho estético*)"[8] (OC 2.15; SNF 346). The placement of the word *music* seems to set up this remarkable sentence as a supplement to the previous statement regarding Pater's notion of music as pure form. As the list progresses, however, it becomes clear that the relation between the reference to Pater and the list is paratactic rather than subordinate. If music can be understood as embodying the union of form and content, like the imperial map and its terrestrial contours, the subsequent terms on the list not only resist the very distinction of form and content (what is the form of happiness, for instance, or of the ephemeral interval of twilight?), but they also exceed any sense of unity or eternity. Furthermore, far from constituting forms of imperial production or appropriation, these things, including music, seem to provoke a kind of "weaving and unweaving" of solar sovereignty (Pater, n.p.). Borges's peculiar phrase, *el hecho estético* — which recalls the "something factual" (*etwas Tatsächliches*) from Kafka's story on the Chinese wall — implies both a facticity that exceeds any proper realm of art and a *poeisis* or making that exceeds sovereign production or appropriation. Rather than a means of transforming and transcending the weaving and unweaving of temporal existence, Borges suggests that art can *perhaps* — the final perhaps of the essay — offer a means of attending to what calls to us from the shadows of sovereign structures, the secret impetus lodged within architectures of the proper.

## *Unstable as the Dust*

Such a possibility is at stake in Borges's well-known essay "Kafka and His Precursors." Although structures of sovereignty do not form a focal point of this essay — that is, there are no imperial walls, maps, or would-be divine towers — the essay addresses the structure of the proper in a number of different registers. Most obviously, it concerns the structure of the proper name, specifically that of Kafka, initially regarded as a marker of unique greatness, and the place of such a name in the pantheon of literary tradition. It also describes structures of unity and permanence evoked by Kafka's work. The essay turns these structures on their heads, effectively performing a Kafkaesque *postergación* of such permanence, stressing the unruly element of temporal difference.

First and foremost, "Kafka and His Precursors" concerns the structure of tradition and its implications for an understanding of time.[9] Borges begins the essay with a reflection about how he once considered conducting a study of Kafka's precursors. The idea of cultural precursors presupposes the fixity and coherence normally associated with the proper name, tracing one such immutable property to another in a kind of patrilineal line of descent and discarding the intervening course of time and all else as mere substratum. Borges explains that his plan to study Kafka's precursors relied on a belief in the distinctive quality of his writings, which he illustrates with an intriguing metaphor: "I had thought, at first, that he was as unique as the phoenix of rhetorical praise" (OC 2.93; SNF 362).

This comparison appears to link Kafka's exceptional greatness with the marvelous and unusual attributes of the mythical phoenix. However, the analogy can also be seen to suggest impermanence and finitude more than monumental self-identity. In the entry on the phoenix in *The Book of Imaginary Beings*, Borges recounts various versions of this mythical bird. The first, from Herodotus, describes its distinctive nature as stemming primarily from its custom of paternal interment in the temple of the sun. This legendary ritual gave way to the more well-known pattern of cyclicality and incineration, associated with various ancient philosophers, including Tacitus and the Stoics, who, Borges notes, believed that "the universe dies in fire and is reborn in fire and that the cycle had no beginning and will have no end" (*Book of Imaginary Beings* 118). Laura Jansen cites Roland Barthes's insightful interpretation of the Tacitean phoenix, which represents the world as an "open system" in which "everything repeats and nevertheless nothing repeats" (Barthes 111, qtd. in Jansen 39). In *The Book of Imaginary Beings*, following the description of such a combustible iterability, Borges notes: "Time simplified the method of the Phoenix's generation. Herodotus speaks of an egg and Pliny of a maggot, but the poet Claudian at the end of the fourth century already celebrates an immortal bird that rises out of its own ashes, an heir to itself and a witness of the ages" (118). It would seem that Borges's invocation of the "the phoenix of rhetorical praise" at the beginning of "Kafka and His Precursors" alludes to this Roman version, which transformed the vulnerable symbol of finitude into an immortal being that can engender and inherit itself, thereby providing an omniscient perspective on history, not unlike how the giants of cultural tradition are sometimes thought to do. Nonetheless, his comparison of Kafka to the figure of the phoenix appears to be tongue in cheek since the singularity of the mythic bird is in all cases linked to repetition as well as incineration, which, furthermore, evokes the fact that Kafka instructed his executor to burn his writings after his death.[10]

The word *precursor* is comprised of the prefix *pre*, meaning before, and *cursor*, from the Latin *currere* ("to run"). The conventional understanding, as described above, presumes a legibility of stylistic singularity and greatness that effectively transcends the changing currents of history, much as the poet Claudian transformed the Tacitean-Stoical figure of radical instability and finitude into Christlike redemption. Borges observes that repeated reading of Kafka's work ("a poco de frecuentarlo") led him to reject such an understanding of tradition, and to consider Kafka's distinctiveness in relation to the divergent and roily waters of literary and philosophical history (OC 2.93; SNF 362).[11] My play on the figure of water in relation to the etymology of the word *precursor* is an admittedly ham-handed way of evoking what I see as a muted resonance with the numerous allusions to Heraclitus that pervade Borges's work, generally in relation to the figure of an endlessly changing river, in which, as he repeatedly insists, the bather is also changing (as Borges puts it in "A New Refutation of Time," "[t]ime is a river that sweeps me along [*arrebata*], but I am the river") (OC 2.158; SNF 332).

Borges does not mention Heraclitus explicitly in "Kafka and His Precursors," but he is nevertheless implied, first, because the figure of the phoenix, understood not as a myth of intransient auto-generation but, rather, of recurrent conflagration, bears a strong resemblance to Heraclitus's extant writings, which describe endless change through the figures of both fire and water (indeed, Heraclitus was an important precursor for the Stoics). Second, Borges's first example of a non-linear antecedent of Kafka's work is Zeno, who, as part of the Eleatic school and together with Parmenides, had a long-standing antagonism with Heraclitus concerning the question of difference and change. Borges states that the moving bodies in Zeno's paradoxes constitute the first Kafkaesque characters in literature (OC 2.93; SNF 362). This idea appears to be tinged with irony since, by both Zeno's logic and Heraclitus's, one could never determine the first instance of anything. It also constitutes a subtle joke since Borges is positing as a precursive instance of Kafka's work a figure that runs without running or moves without changing, not unlike the phoenix in Claudian's account. As I explore in more depth in chapter 7, Borges considers that what is at stake in the Eleatic perspective is nothing less than the fundamental question of whether "anything could happen [*suceder*] in the universe" (OC 1.257; SNF 43). The paradoxes, indeed, appear to answer in the negative: Change cannot occur because everything already is, fully, in the Parmenidean One. The refutation of change illustrated by Zeno's paradoxes would seem to exemplify a "place . . . in some Order," a state in which the *domus* of an eternal and unchanging One banishes difference, time, and possibility (SNF 503).[12] We are back with Pater's gem-like flame and, for that matter, Shih Huang Ti's closed circle, the imperial map, and the Tower of Babel. However, as we have seen with all these examples, Borges is quite insistent that things do in fact *suceden,* and not in successive fashion.

"Kafka and His Precursors" affirms this as its primary idea: "The fact [*hecho*] is that each writer *creates* his precursors. His [or its: *su*] work modifies our conception of the past, as it will modify [*ha de modificar*] the future" (OC 2.95; SNF 365). This is a far reach from Achilles running without running, in a world in which things cannot happen because they already are. With writing, something happens, and that happening is never absolute. As Borges says in "The Wall and the Books," aesthetic action or the aesthetic event ("*el hecho estético*") concerns a temporal imminence, not only never fully arriving but also not suspended in an all-encompassing present. Aesthetic creations are always susceptible to change, even though their forms may appear immobile. This is illustrated in "Pierre Menard, Author of the Quixote" by the two identical sentences from *Don Quixote* set side by side: They are the same, as anyone can see, but they are also different since they change as their context and our perspective change (OC 1.480–81; CF 94). Menard and his admiring narrator are buffoonish speculators, striving to appropriate temporal difference and call it original creation, like Claudian's self-inheriting and self-generating phoenix. When Borges states in "Kafka and His Precursors" that "each writer creates his precursors," he does not mean that writers have sovereignty over the effects of their writing. Rather, it means that the fact of writing, as an instance of the *hecho estético*, creates the conditions for there to be precursors as well as other temporal flows and relations, which are never fully produced or revealed and are constantly changing. They certainly do not conform to conventional understandings of legacy or even identity. Borges mentions, for instance, that the early Kafka is not even a stable precursor to the late Kafka. This example supports the idea that, rather than the work of the writer as sovereign subject that creates precursors and modifies the past and future, it is the fact of the work of writing ("*su labor*") that affects time, even that of the writer himself (OC 2.95; SNF 365). In this way, the *hecho estético* is also an *hecho temporal*, swept along by the swirling currents of time and contingency that condition all structures, even those most heavily fortified against change and difference — and even works, such as Kafka's, that raise the question of how fortified structures of sovereignty can be, or whether they are "essentially changeable, unstable as the dust" (Kafka 239).

The texts that I examine in this chapter correspond to Pablo Oyarzún's discerning reading of Borges's work as one that engages with the boundary between fiction and essay. He suggests that, if essays at times endeavor to "make an experience of the singular" and fiction to claim its originality based on nothing more than "the breath of language as its instigating force," Borges's work pushes the limits of both essay and fiction into a zone in which the singular emerges as a kind of "aesthetic" facticity that fleetingly traces the possibility of an event, beyond any structure of sovereignty, including that of the writing subject (Oyarzún, *Literature and Skepticism* 174–75).

To return to the question with which we began, Borges's reading of Kafka does not leave us in a "total garden of totally forking paths" (North, *The Yield* 221). Rather, it demonstrates how writing, as a mode of *postergación*, stresses the precursive space-time of difference, which disrupts any putatively totalizing structure, whether of the constrictive or emancipatory variety. It indicates the finitude that inhabits all structures of the proper, which constitutes the condition of possibility for things to occur, even though they can never be fully produced or revealed.[13] Given the numerous forms of domination that continue to exercise force in our world — including walls, towers, and discursive constructions of timeless ideals — this fact, and Borges's and Kafka's interrogations of the limits of architectures of the proper more broadly, are no less relevant today than they ever were.

# Chapter 3

## Incalculable Alliances

### "The Library of Babel," "The Lottery in Babylon," "On the Cult of Books," "A Defense of the Kabbalah," "Ramon Llull's Thinking Machine," "The Total Library"

"The Library of Babel" and "The Lottery in Babylon" are Kafkaesque fictions of political-theological constructions of order, related to what Pascal once called the "mystical foundations of authority" and supplemented by man-made structures of institutional authority.[1] The invocation of Babel (explicit in one title, and implicit in the other, since Babylon was the supposed location for the fabled tower) can be seen as alluding to the structural prostheses of sovereignty by which human beings have endeavored to achieve the perspective and power they attribute to a monotheistic god. As I have noted, the fable of Babel underscores the relationship between language and the ideal of absolute knowledge. The possession of a common human language is an infrastructural component that makes possible the project to construct a tower that would provide a Godlike perspective and name, and is also, of course, what God destroys in order to draw a limit between divine knowledge and human knowledge. It was, perhaps, a small jump to move from this association between divine power and language to the conceit of the world as a text created by divine writing, which humans endeavor to read, and possibly also write. The idea of the world as a divinely created text concerns the question of possibility: whether every singularity is already determined and can therefore be symbolically mastered, or not. This question motivates the political-theological structures depicted in both stories and is also addressed in the two essays that Borges wrote about the world-as-book conceit, "A Defense of the Kabbalah" (1932) and "On the Cult of Books" (1951). I will begin with a consideration of these two essays, which, although they are often read as impartial accounts of a recurrent quirk of intellectual history, pose important questions about the relationship between language, knowledge, and sovereignty. I will then turn to "The Library of Babel," which fictionalizes some of these questions, and subsequently to "The Lottery in Babylon," which focuses on the question of the mastery of possibility, with both stories attending to the ways in which belief structures are supplemented by institutional power and yet are always undermined by the nature of language.

## *The World as Book Motif*

In "A Defense of the Kabbalah" and "On the Cult of Books," Borges focuses on the idea, which appears in both Kabbalistic and Christian thought, that the world was the product of "deliberate writing [*redacción*] by an infinite intelligence" ("Defense" OC 1.223; SNF 85). He notes that the Kabbalistic text *Sepher Yetzirah* affirms that God created the universe by means of symbols — like any other writer, but better. God is said to have used "the cardinal numbers from one to ten and the twenty-two letters of the alphabet" to produce "everything that is and everything that will be" ("Cult" OC 2.98; SNF 360–61). The Kabbalistic text then reveals the code that he used, that is, which letters have power over which elements of creation, including wisdom, peace, Wednesdays, and ears. Borges observes that the conflation of divine creation and writing also appears within the Christian tradition, in which divine logos is understood as constituting an *abecedarium naturae*, although his examples — Francis Bacon, Thomas Browne, and Galileo — point to what might be thought of as a historical moment of translation from Christian dogma to Renaissance empiricism. This is evident from his quotes from Thomas Browne — "Thus there are two Books from whence I collect my Divinity; besides that written one of God, another of His servant Nature, that universal and publick Manuscript, that lies expans'd unto the Eyes of all" — and Galileo, who replaces the word "divinity" with "philosophy": "Philosophy is written in that very large book that is continually opened before our eyes (I mean the universe), but which is not understood unless first one studies the language and knows the characters in which it is written. The language of that book is mathematical and the characters are triangles, circles, and other geometric figures" ("Cult" OC 2.99; SNF 361).

From this anthropo-theological faith in the ability to decipher God's writing, Borges turns to two examples that appeal to the same motif but suggest a little less confidence in humans' role vis-à-vis the textual universe. The first comes from Thomas Carlyle, who ventured that "universal history was a Sacred Scripture that we decipher and write uncertainly, and in which we too are written" ("Cult" OC 2.99; SNF 361). The second is from Léon Bloy, who wrote,

> There is no human being on earth who is capable of declaring who he is. No one knows what he has come to this world to do, to what his acts, feelings, ideas correspond, or what his real *name* is, his imperishable Name in the registry of Light . . . History is an immense liturgical text, where the i's and the periods are not worth less than the versicles or whole chapters, but the importance of both is undeterminable and is profoundly hidden. ("Cult" OC 2.99; SNF 361–62)[2]

If the belief in human capacity to unlock the secrets of the universe in the *Sepher Yetzirah*, Chrsitianity, and Renaissance Humanism can be seen as resembling the Babelic endeavor to raise human perspective to that of divine absolute knowledge, the ignorance and uncertainty described by Carlyle and Bloy can be seen as acknowledging the difference between divine creation-as-writing and the human capacity for reading.

Perhaps the most important element of this difference is the domination of chance (*azar*). In "A Defense of the Kabbalah," Borges describes on the one hand "the perfected God of the theologians," for whom "the vague concept of chance holds no meaning" (OC 1.223; SNF 85). This God "sees all at once (*uno intelligendi actu*), not only all the events of this replete world but also those that would take place if even the most evanescent — or impossible — of them should change." Divine Scripture (*Escritura*) is regarded by some as embodying this "astral intelligence" and its dominion over everything, even things that might be or cannot actually be. Borges calls the idea of such an "absolute text, where the collaboration of chance is calculated at zero [,] . . . a greater wonder than those recorded in its pages," and suggests that it is no surprise that some, such as the Kabbalists, "study it to absurdity" (*interrogarlo hasta lo absurdo*) ("Defense" OC 1.224; SNF 86). His vindication of the Kabbalah is not a logical justification of the merits of this school of thought, but an appreciation of how in its zeal to grasp absolute meaning and thereby dominate contingency, it reintroduces excess and absurdity.

In this essay he also considers the relationship of secular forms of writing to chance. Somewhat counterintuitively, he describes journalism as a genre that involves a considerable amount of chance: He says that it exists solely to report on the unpredictable actions of the world, and its form reflects that unpredictability. Discounting years of modernist experimentation, including his own, he describes poetry as governed by laws that subject "meaning to euphonic needs (or superstitions)" and hence reduce its relationship to chance. The category of writing least exposed to an "incalculable alliance" (*alianza incalculable*) with chance is oddly named "intellectual," for which he cites Paul Valéry and Thomas De Quincey as examples ("Defense" OC 1.223; SNF 85, translation modified). He posits that these writers have certainly not eliminated chance, but they deny it as much as possible, "remotely" approximating the ideal of an "astral intelligence" that accounts for all possibilities, even the ephemeral or impossible ones.

Although Borges does not elaborate on this category here, it is perhaps not surprising that he begins the later essay with a quotation by Valéry's mentor, Stephane Mallarmé: "The world exists to end up in a book" ("Cult" OC 2.96; SNF 358). Borges mordantly characterizes this idea as an "aesthetic justification for evils [*los males*]," as though Mallarmé's quip were affirming writing's capacity to transcend and redeem the good and bad of existence, not to mention any incalculable collaboration of contingency, like the ideal of divine Scripture. Nevertheless, Mallarmé (and Valéry and De Quincey), are far from "the perfected God of the theologians," understood to reduce the world to a single act of understanding (*uno intelligendi actu*). One of Mallarmé's signature works is, after all, "A Throw of the Dice," a poem that performs the inevitability of chance as something that exceeds any structure designed to comprehend it. In Mallarmé's poem this is invoked in the reference to dice (an early form of representation that mimetically responds to contingency) and is intensified in a poetic form that ruptures aesthetic conventions designed, as Borges underscores, to minimize the effects of chance. The typographic spacing in this poem invokes chance as something that can emerge interlineally in writing, that is, within and beyond what the author — who is no longer master of his realm — actually writes. Although the final sentence of "On the Cult of Books" seems to draw a contrast between the swagger of Mallarmé and the humility and uncertainty expressed by Carlyle and Bloy, all three of them can be seen as affirming reading and writing as an engagement with the incalculability that conditions our existence.

## *Weaving Through Hexagons and Circles*

In "The Library of Babel," Borges combines the mystical-metaphysical topos of the world as text as described in "On the Cult of Books" with institutional structures intended to prop up the belief in an absolute order. Like the Kabbalists described in "A Defense of the Kabbalah," the inhabitants of the library of Babel are readers and custodians of texts, rather than writers or creators. Their tower of Babel is constructed by means of interpretation, not outright creation, although they are no less assured of reaching God's level, securing absolute meaning and confirming the foundation of authority. The political-theological logic undergirding the narrator's account of his world is not explicitly Kabbalistic, however, but a hybrid belief system based on a mix of philosophy and religion, dedicated to defending the mystical foundations of (its) authority, even amidst Babelic chaos. At least in the beginning of the story, this system is naturalized by the narrative, as part of a seemingly innocent search for meaning in an apparently meaningless universe. But little by little, it is revealed that there are institutional mechanisms in place to ensure that the library's occupants continue to believe in a single, unshakeable meaning, which is immanentized by the institutional order that insists on it. The agents of this order (a word that suggests at once followers of a religious sect, punitive measures — "strict orders" [OC 1.503; CF 116] — and an overall organization or totalizing structure of the universe) aim to eliminate any sense of contingency, and indeed, to reinforce a belief that hope itself has become obsolete. Nevertheless, almost in spite of himself, the narrator reveals and contributes to some interlinear cracks in the system.

The narrator's account begins with an Enlightened belief in reason and slowly reveals its political-theological underpinnings, suggesting not only the relationship between reason and belief, but also that between both modes of knowledge and political domination. The story begins with an ethnographic-like description of the features and dimensions of the library, which performs a kind of scientific objectivity: "The universe . . . is composed of an indefinite, perhaps infinite number of hexagonal galleries . . . From any hexagon one can see the floors above and below — one after another, endlessly" (OC 1.499; CF 112). Soon the narrator inserts his own experience and perspective on different matters in contrast to various sects ("Idealists argue . . . ," "Mystics claim . . ."), which is then formalized into a pseudo-philosophical tract of his own, replete with axioms, premises, corollaries, and a conclusive deduction that leads to "the fundamental law of the Library" (OC 1.499–500; CF 113–14).

Before I get to this fundamental law, I want to comment on the impersonal nature of the narrative and the structure of logic to which it appeals. The pseudo-scientific description of the library universe suggests an omniscient narrator, or at least one whose familiarity with this world, and commonality with its other inhabitants, leaves no room for error ("Like all the men in the Library, in my younger days I had traveled . . ." [OC 1.499; CF 112]). Many readers fail to question the reliability of the narrator, taking his objective tone at face value. One of the books that is described from this library consists only of the ceaseless repetition of the letters M C V (OC 1.500; CF 113). Although the narrator uses it as an example of apparent senselessness, the letters C V, when sounded out, are homophonic with the Spanish passive reflexive "*se ve*," which translates to "one sees" or "it is seen," a discursive kingpin of objective, scientific language. It is as though the book does nothing more than assert its categorical authority over and over. And yet hidden in this perverse "cryptography" is another assertion: When read over and over again, the sound of *veme* (see me) emerges from the contiguity of the letters V and M, calling attention to the writer and the conditions of enunciation, which undermine the unbiased and detached stating of truth. In other words, the narrative warns us that we should consider the narrator's use of an objective tone as a rhetorical strategy rather than as outright truth.

This recalls Borges's description in "The Nothingness of Personality" of the general tendency to accept logical propositions out of laziness, and to synthesize the results afterward, reducing even dubious steps to a single idea. In order to prevent the reader from falling into that trap, he vows to "cast aside all strict and logical schemas and amass a pile of examples" ("desecharé . . . toda severa urdimbre lógica y hacinaré los ejemplos," [*Inquisiciones* 94; SNF 3]). This affirmation, made somewhat in jest — and with a focus on the contingent nature of the self ("personality") that underlies any text and conditions the acts of reading and writing — can be seen as a description of many of Borges's texts, including "The Library of Babel," in which the examples the narrator amasses are loosely held together by a thinly logical framework. The translation of "schema" for *urdimbre* conveys the basic idea, but it leaves out the word's primary sense of "warp," as in the structural basis for weaving, through which the weft (*trama*, which also means "plot"; or *hilo*, a word also used for conceptual threads or trains of thought) passes.

One such logical "schema" is what is known as the logical hexagon, an extension of the square of oppositions, which functions as a model for explaining relations between categorical propositions (all books are . . . ), including predicates (all books are finite, no books are finite, and so on) and modalities (regarding possibility and contingency, for instance).[3] The narrator of "The Library of Babel" does not refer to this geometrical model of logic, but the hexagonal shape of the library's galleries can be seen as representing the basic structure through which he weaves his logical propositions, which aim to confirm, recursively, the unassailability of their foundation, even though the structure of his "methodical writing" resembles a pile or bundle of examples more than a tidy weft. His description of the idealists' affirmation that the hexagonal shape of the rooms relates to the capacity to intuit absolute space (OC 1.499–500; CF 113) corresponds to this underlying belief in logic, which is distinct from, but analogous to, mystical cosmogony, associated with the circle, representing totality without positions of contradiction.

A precursor to the logical hexagon is Ramón Llull's "thinking machine," which Borges associates with the idea of the total library. He describes Llull's "machines" in an essay from 1937 titled, precisely, "Ramón Llull's Thinking Machine." He begins with a prototype of the Ars Magna, which consists of a circle, around which are written letters and words designating the attributes of God, for instance *potestas*, *aeternitas*, *veritas*, *gloria*, each of which is linked by lines that form interlocking polygons. This immobile prototype affirms that the attributes are "systematically interrelated" (in contrast to the logical hexagon, which designates opposites) for instance, that "glory is eternal or that eternity is glorious; that power is true, glorious, good, great, eternal, powerful, . . . etc., etc." (OC 4.344; SNF 156). Borges calls attention to "the full magnitude of this etcetera," stressing that it creates an impressive number of predicates, linked together "with impeccable orthodoxy," effectively affirming not only the multiple attributes of God, but also the human and institutional (ecclesiastical) capacity to know and represent them. This static model of representation merely whetted Llull's appetite for the power of combinations. His Ars Magna was a much more complex production, consisting in several interlocking, revolving circles, each with numerous compartments, designed to produce truths and resolve problems by virtue of the association of multiple predicates. In his introduction to this essay, Borges considers that, in "mere, lucid reality," Llull's thinking machine is not "capable of thinking a single thought," that is, "measured against its objective, . . . the thinking machine does not work" (OC 4.343; SNF 155). Later, he retracts this assessment and says that on the contrary, "*elle ne fonctionne que trop*, it works all too well [*abrumadoramente*]" (OC 4.345; SNF 157). The machine may not be able to think, but it is eminently capable of affirming its capacity to postulate and produce truth, understood tautologically as the confirmation of what is postulated, to an overwhelming degree. The beauty of the device is the combination of a closed system with the mathematical sublime, imitating infinity in such a way that can astonish its beholders and affirm the Godlike capacity of its makers and operators. It can be seen as resembling the Kabbalistic *Sepher Yetzirah*, which similarly proposes a method for deciphering the universe, understood to have been created by a vast combination of letters and numbers, although Llull's machine can perhaps be seen as privileging the effort to *create* a system of legibility, rather than merely interpreting divine creation. The fact that the machine was designed in order to convert Jews and Muslims to Christianity hints at the ideological coordinates of this legibility, as well as the limits of its version of infinity. Borges proposes that although Llull's machine may seem vacuous and archaic, its basic structure is not fundamentally different from other "metaphysical and theological theories that . . . declare who we are and what manner of thing the world is" (OC 4.343; SNF 155).

In "The Library of Babel," the narrator begins his logical account of his world with a "classic dictum": "The Library is a sphere whose exact center is any hexagon and whose circumference is unattainable" (OC 1.500; CF 113). The word *dictum* means essentially that it is true because it is said to be true, a condition underlying all premises, ratio-logical and theological (at one point the narrator remarks that "no rational mind can doubt" his logical steps).[4] This particular dictum is a variation on Pascal's sphere, which, as Borges points out in his essay by that name, was for Pascal less a cartographic delineation of the shape of the universe than an expression of the impossibility of such a thing (OC 2.18; SNF 353). The combination of sphere and hexagon evokes not only Llull's graphics, but also the way that logical structures, based on categorical propositions, are embedded within a mystical master structure, thereby illustrating other observations of Pascal, including the idea that "might" is capable of producing its own "right," and that forms of authority tend to obfuscate their origins, so that they are not questioned — this is the "mystical" foundation of authority (Pascal, section V, n.p.). In the context of "The Library of Babel," this combined Pascalian legacy can be seen in the idea that logic (that is, the logical hexagon) will confirm the mystical figure of totality, represented by the sphere, whose center is everywhere, and whose limits will never be known.

The narrator structures his account linearly, like an argument, with axioms that appear to be extensions of, and in turn extend, the mystical qualities of immutability and totality. For instance, he claims that the library exists *ab aeterno* and all the books consist of twenty-five symbols (OC 1.500; CF 113). In a circular logic, these axioms both precede (narratively) and follow (chronologically) what he calls "the fundamental law of the Library," the "incontrovertible" fact that "the Library is 'total'" and "that its bookshelves contain all possible combinations of the twenty-two orthographic symbols . . . that is, all that is able to be expressed, in every language" (OC 1.501–02; CF 114–15).

## *Masters of the Babelic Universe*

The library, then, is effectively a giant thinking machine, consisting of a vast, if not infinite, number of combinations of symbols. In his 1939 essay "The

Total Library," Borges considers the intellectual genealogy of this idea, describing its recurrence throughout history in figures as different as Cicero, Pascal, and Lewis Carroll. He ends with Kurd Lasswitz's short story "The Universal Library" (which Theodor Wolff suggests can be read as a parody of Llull's thinking machine), which plays with the mathematically sublime dimensions of the idea and speculates on what a universal library might contain (SNF 214). Borges furthers this speculation in both this essay and "The Library of Babel," enumerating possibilities of what might be included in a total library, including texts and events real and imagined, lost and unwritten, and still to come, including "the detailed history of the future" and "the true story of your death" (OC 1.502; CF 115). In addition to works that can be named, there would also be commentaries upon commentaries, translations, and thousands of catalogs of the library, with no way to verify which one is accurate, which is described in "The Total Library" as "millions of meaningless cacophonies, verbal farragoes, and babblings" (SNF 216).

The librarians' belief that the space they inhabit "contained all the books" endows them with a sense of mastery grounded in a secret, mystical foundation: "All men felt themselves the masters [*señores*] of an intact and secret treasure" (OC 1.502; CF 115, translation modified). Rather than the ground of logic or reason emphasized by the narrator in the opening pages of the story, this "intact and secret treasure" corresponds to the mystical foundation of authority that the Llullian technician uses to interpret the results of the combinatory machine. Even though the librarians in the story are baffled by the materials in their jurisdiction, they feel certain that the archive in its entirety contains nothing less than the justification of the universe ("The universe was justified"), and they were its masters (*señores*). The terms *justified* and *masters* straddle the theological and the political, and both registers of mastery are considered to be both spatial and temporal, indeed encompassing all of time, even the future: "The universe was justified, the universe suddenly usurped the unlimited dimensions of hope" (OC 1.502; OC 2.502; CF 115, translation modified).[5] This usurpation of possibility is an onto-teleological coup — the narrator calls it the "most important event in all history" (OC 1.500; CF 113) — that marks the subjugation of existence to a structure of sovereignty that the librarians presume to possess, even if they do not understand its operating functions.

Like Borges's remark that Llull's thinking machine did not work and that it worked *abrumadoramente* (astonishingly), the library illustrates the fact that exponentially numerous combinations produce exponentially numerous combinations, but if you claim authority to call this order or totality, you will be able to dazzle those who want to believe. Such a claim to authority stands in an interesting relation to the eponymic allusion to Babel. Unlike the builders of the fabled tower, the librarians, dispersed as they are throughout the library, are unfamiliar with unity. They have a common language — they seem to understand one another — but this language is imbued with Babelic confusion and is therefore hardly a key to unity. They try appealing to a virtual and unifying authority despite the condition of dispersal, although things begin to unravel anyway.[6]

The librarians seek the key to the "intact and secret treasure" of mastery with increasing, and increasingly ferocious, determination. This starts with an effort to understand their own lives, as promised by the so-called Vindications, texts in which the meaning of their own existence was said to be written (OC 1.502; CF 115). In an especially Babelic description, we read how "thousands of greedy individuals abandoned their sweet native hexagons and rushed . . . upstairs, spurred by the vain desire to find their Vindication." Simply declaring themselves masters of (a secret, if inscrutable, code to) the universe is not power enough. The librarians want to master the meaning of their individual existence (in-dividual and undivided) and will risk their lives to do so. They strangle one another, toss books into the depths of the ventilation tunnels, and are themselves tossed into the same abyss, all in pursuit of the towering ideal of unity.

## *Institutional Inquisitions*

When the feeling of mastery is depleted in the face of the vastness of the library and the "meaningless cacophonies" of its numerous combinations, it is surreptitiously supplemented by an institutional imposition of power (OC 1.502; CF 115). The acts of pilgrimage and searching, which resulted in violence and despair, are ominously formalized into the function of "official searchers," known as *inquisitors* (OC 1.503; CF 116). These inquisitors replace the erstwhile search for the meaning of the universe or the self. Rather than illumination or justification, they scour the library's galleries for "disgraceful or dishonorable words," words that would presumably undermine the secret treasure-like foundation of authority. Reflecting the fall from the exuberance of the builders of Babel and their heirs, the Vindication-seekers, they too risk falling to their deaths on faulty stairways.

While the unnamed orthodoxy is evident only as the empty exercise of power, heretics and the institutional mechanisms to suppress them proliferate. We learn of a blasphemous sect that tries to create meaning from random combinations of symbols, in a parodic version of an anecdote from Cicero that Borges recounts in "The Total Library," cited as a precursor of the infinite monkey theorem (SNF 214–15). These heretics are accused of "feebly mimicking the divine disorder," and, the narrator observes, "the authorities were forced to issue strict orders" (OC 1.503; CF 116). The anonymous "authority" and the law that forces them remains troublingly unexplained, an ominous escalation of the rational passivity of "se ve."

In contradistinction to the sect that sought to create, we are told of the Purifiers, who are driven by a "hygienic, ascetic rage" to destroy millions of "useless" books (OC 1.503; CF 116, translation modified). Although described as religious fanatics, they are virtually indistinguishable from the civic authorities anonymously imposing order, suggesting an intrinsic similarity between the theological and the political: They "would invade the hexagons, show credentials that were not always false, leaf disgustedly through a volume, and condemn entire walls of books." The Purifiers claim a capacity for judgement between what is useful and useless, and flash credentials that no one else has the capacity to judge as true or false. As if to purge the groundless nature of their authority, they pursue an autoimmune action par excellence, destroying in order to preserve and "purify" the power to distinguish value from worthlessness. The narrator observes that purity or immunity is not really an option, since the library is filled with "imperfect facsimiles."

The first heterodox sect was determined to create meaning out of chaos; the second, to filter chaos out of meaning. The third, which the narrator admits is one to which he subscribes, affirms simply that there is meaning somewhere in the chaos, a master signifier that grounds and justifies all others: "the cipher and perfect compendium *of all other books*" (OC 1.503; CF 116).[7] Although the belief in this master key, which makes its solitary reader "analogous to a god," is called a superstition and a cult, it can be seen as constituting the core element of all religion, and specifically religions of the book. The narrator recuperates this belief from "vestiges" of an ancient cult and prays to "unknown gods" for the book that would transcend time and heterogeneity and justify his mortal existence amidst the bewildering heterogeneity of his world. Although he would clearly love to find this object himself, he has resigned himself to searching for a trace of it. The narrator invokes Job in his efforts to maintain faith in redemption while he slogs among the shelves and shelves of "meaningless cacophonies" (OC 1.500; CF 113). He proclaims, "Let heaven exist, though my own place be in hell" (OC 1.504; CF 117).

Interestingly, the Nazi narrator of "*Deutsches Requiem*" utters a nearly identical sentence: "If victory and injustice and happiness do not belong to Germany, let them belong to other nations. Let heaven exist, though our place be in hell" (OC 1.622; CF 234). Both articulations of this Jobian sentiment epitomize what Paul de Man calls ideological idealism (*Aesthetic Ideology* 146). De Man describes this idealism with reference to Schiller's sense of an "ideal security," born of a "link between the divine and reason," that rescues us from any mortal weakness, fear, or suffering: "We call . . . practically sublime any entity which makes us aware of our weakness as a natural creature, but which at the same time awakens an entirely different kind of resistance in us, resistance to the terror. This counterforce in no way rescues us from the physical existence of the danger . . . It is therefore not a particular and individual material security but an ideal security, which extends to all possible and imaginable situations" (de Man, quoting Schiller in *Aesthetic Ideology* 146). De Man calls this security and the drive to self-preservation that motivates it a principle of closure, which he associates with Joseph Goebbel's understanding of the relationship between aesthetics and political power (*Aesthetic Ideology* 155).

The beleaguered narrator of "The Library of Babel" is no Nazi, but the resonance can be understood as highlighting the extreme, real-world consequences of the political-theological, a totalizing structure grounded in a timeless, absolute principle whose origins and nature are posited as beyond question. In both cases, this structure, associated with a (Babelic) immanentization of heaven, is called "order." In "*Deutsches Requiem*," the narrator declares, "There are many things that must be destroyed in order to build the new order; now we know that Germany was one of them" (OC 1.622; CF 234). In "The Library of Babel," the narrator avers that his solitude is lightened by the hope that the unlimited repetition of the library's disorder constitutes "order: the Order" (OC 1.505; CF 118).

## *The Heresy of Possibility*

In contrast to the systematization of the whole, secured by the linchpin of a single book and its presumptive reader, the fourth heterodox sect embraces disorder and chance. These "infidels" (*impíos*) claim that nonsense (*el disparate*) is normal, and that "rationality (even humble, pure coherence) is an almost miraculous exception" (OC 1.504; CF 117). This description, deemed heretical within the story, evokes the mathematically slim possibility of producing sense through chance and combination, despite efforts that claim to do so, from Llull's thinking machine to the use of algorithmic probability that increasingly shapes our world today. The word *disparate* primarily means "something absurd," but — deriving from the Latin *disparo*, to separate — it also indicates excess, unevenness, incommensurability, and non-equivalence, that is, something that does not fit within a closed structure. The belief of this heterodox sect is the opposite of the story's final syllogism, in which everything in the library forms part of an order — effectively, disorder is order is Order (OC 1.505; CF 118). The narrator says of this sect, "They speak, I know, of the 'feverish Library, whose random volumes constantly threaten to transmogrify into others, so that they affirm all things, deny all things, and confound and confuse all things, like some mad and hallucinating deity.' Those words, which not only proclaim disorder but exemplify it as well, prove, as all can see, the infidels' deplorable taste and desperate ignorance" (OC 1.504; CF 117). The prosopopoeia insinuates not only a generalized state of febrile delirium, but also the absence of any divine foundation — prosopopoeia, after all, is a figure that endows a face where there is none (de Man, *The Resistance to Theory* 44). The description of chance, change, and indistinction between affirmation and negation suggests that the foundation of authority is not so much shrouded in mystery but simply missing.

The quotation marks in the above sentence and the parenthetical interjection ("I know") endow the narrator's account with firsthand certainty. They also perform a kind of formal incommensurability or rupture (a kind of *disparate*) with his account, since the quoted phrase is a version of the final sentence of Borges's "The Total Library," from 1939. This inside joke, in which Borges effectively insults himself — from one register of narration to another — for being ignorant and having bad taste, indicates an outside to the hermetic space of the Library as recounted by the narrator. Furthermore, the rupture and externality do not refer us to another inside, an "intellectual" text in which the author asserts his authority like the "perfected God of the theologians," as Borges calls it in "A Defense of the Kabbalah" (OC 1.223; SNF 85). Rather, this parodic self-quotation can be seen as an instance of how texts "constantly threaten to transmogrify into others" (OC 1.504; CF 117). Even when ostensibly fixed by the form of the printed word, every inscription or mark bears within it the potential for change and encounter with other temporalities and textualities.

The description of the fourth sect's privileging of randomness and chance over rationality and intention recalls the references in "On the Cult of Books" to Carlyle, in which mortal life is described as a fallible form of reading and writing the world with no other author to guarantee the "text" in which we live, and to Mallarmé, who despite his description of books as a putative end, undermines teleological and hierarchical structures in his writing, partly by affirming the indomitable nature of chance. Chance here should be understood not only in relation to models of probability, as in the exponentially small but nevertheless calculable possibility of composing a coherent text through random assortments of letters and symbols, but also, critically, as *possibility*, the chance that something cannot be anticipated or accounted for, whether by a superior intelligence, the logical hexagon, or nameless authorities.

## *Phantasmatic Order and the Scribbling of Survival*

In response to the heterodox belief of the infidels, the narrator spends the remainder of his tale defending his conviction that, despite the apparent senselessness of any given page, there is nothing in the library that is fully senseless. Everything has meaning and justification, even if the librarians' chances of finding it are miniscule. He affirms the *fact* of certainty and ground of authority, even though it is so mystical and mysterious that nobody can understand it and its very existence creates uncertainty among the population: "The certainty that everything has already been written annuls us, or renders us phantasmal" (OC 1.505; CF 118).[8] An absolute ground runs so counter to life that the inhabitants of the library feel depleted, and epidemics, discord, and suicide have decimated the population. The narrator fears that "the human species — the *only* species — teeters at the verge of extinction, yet that the Library — enlightened, solitary, infinite, perfectly unmoving, armed with precious volumes, pointless, incorruptible, and secret — will endure." The mention that human beings are the only species in this world reflects the auto-affection that underlies this belief in absolute being, which is an extension of a belief in a homogeneous or immunological category or genre, although it is one that, carried out to its logical extreme, requires the sacrifice of its engenderers.[9] This again resonates with the concluding idea of "*Deutsches Requiem*," in which the narrator states that "There are many things that must be destroyed in order to build the new order; now we know that Germany was one of them . . . Let others curse and others weep; I rejoice in the fact that our gift is orbicular and perfect" (OC 1.622; CF 234). The ideal of the self is so strong that it overshadows materiality, history, and even life, as summed up by the last sentence of that story, "My flesh may feel fear; I myself do not."

As already noted, the narrator of "The Library of Babel" is different from the Nazi narrator of "*Deutsches Requiem*." He marvels at the idea that the pleroma of the library will outlast human beings as a useless monument to itself, a Babelic ruin of creation, competition, and extinction towering in space. (Although the story was written several years before the first biocidal bomb was dropped, this description evokes a giant mushroom cloud, a trophy of the triumph of human sovereignty and indemnificatory autoimmunity over the conditions of planetary existence.)[10]

Meanwhile, the narrator writes as a melancholic mode of survival. He describes his own writing right after his refutation of the "impious" acceptance of disorder and chance and his insistence that everything in the library is meaningful, even if that meaning is not evident to human readers. He affirms, "There is no syllable one can speak that is not filled with tenderness and terror, that is not, in one of those languages, the mighty name of a god. To speak is to commit tautologies" (OC 1.504; CF 117). That is to say, everything a human can say has been anticipated by the library, to the point that everything is pure repetition. Even, he says, "This pointless, verbose epistle" (OC 1.504; CF 117–18). In "Plato's Pharmacy," Derrida describes two principal approaches to repetition. On the one hand, it is understood as truth or life "going out of itself to come home to itself"; on the other, as "life going out of itself beyond return . . . [an] irreducible excess" ("Plato's Pharmacy" 168–69; qtd. in Naas, *Plato and the Invention of Life* 119–20). The narrator of "The Library of Babel" argues that every letter in the library, and even the librarians' utterances, no matter how senseless or insignificant they appear, have a "terrible significance" (*terrible sentido*) already inscribed elsewhere among the countless volumes (OC 1.504; CF 117). On the surface of it, this corresponds to the returning-home model of repetition: Texts and utterances are understood to return virtually to the principle of truth represented by the library. This principle is capacious, because the meanings to which its representatives return are multiple and even contradictory. For instance, the narrator affirms that his letter already exists somewhere in the library's expanses, as well as its refutation. And yet he writes, even with the understanding that he can write nothing new, nothing original.

Perhaps it is this gesture — writing even while condemned to repeat — that breaks, ever so slightly, with the underlying principle of truth to which his wordy scribbles are supposedly bound. He writes despite his certainty that there is a home base of truth that has already said it for him, with the recognition that what he writes is unnecessary, excessive. His descriptions of his writing, starting with the modifiers "pointless" and "verbose," emphasize this excess (OC 1.504; CF 117–18). His description earlier in the story of his writing spatializes the excess: "one has only to compare these crude trembling symbols which my fallible hand scrawls [*garabatea*] on the cover of a book with the organic letters inside — neat [*puntuales*], delicate, deep black, and inimitably symmetrical" (OC 1.500; CF 113). Due to the apparent lack of blank paper in the library, he is writing on the covers of books. Inside, the printed letters are "organic" — "life going out of itself to come home to itself" — and *puntuales*, which means neat, but is also related to the geometrical point, as if to suggest that their lines are excessive, since they are always already where they need to be, as though enclosed by (or as) the orthographic period.[11] In contrast to this, the narrator's writing is described as "trembling," which implies a motion in excess of the movement of his writing. The word he uses to describe his writing, *garabatear*, means to scrawl or scribble, emphasizing the rudimentary (*rudos símbolos*) nature of his writing vis-à-vis the printed text on the inside of the books, but it also refers to a method of grappling something with a hook, as though his script were an effort to find something in the books — something not already in place or *puntual*. His writing may be tautological, a mere repetition of something already inscribed in the symmetrical pages of the library's volumes, but it is also different because it is in movement, or rather, the narrator acknowledges its movement as something that is not just a return home to a presumed organic presence.

The fact that this tremulous, searching movement is made on the books' surfaces further emphasizes its fundamental externality to self-presence. This externality is also evident in the fact that the narrator describes his narration as an epistle, a word that implies movement and distance. Since this epistle appears to be written on the covers of books in the library, hence not likely physically sent anywhere, the implication of movement and distance can be understood as an iterability intrinsic to the writing itself. Each mark is a kind of missive that has no home to return to and no guarantee of being received, a kind of sending in time to another reader of the library-world who is more like Carlyle (uncertain reader and writer) than any of those readers of the universe who believe they are uncovering a singular and immutable truth.

Although the narrator has declared that the belief in the library's totality "usurped the unlimited dimensions of hope," which is to say, an open-ended relationship to the future, the nature of his writing as an epistle to an indeterminate destination demonstrates that the "unlimited dimensions of hope" are not completely vanquished (OC 1.502; CF 115, translation modified). He imagines a reader whose only certainty is finitude ("the true story of your death"), and whose reception of the epistle is described in terms of indeterminable translatability — "You who read me — are you certain you understand my language?" (OC 1.505; CF 118). This address to a temporal and inconclusively translating "you" is the opposite of a tautological self-affirmation in which language is understood as economically confirming its own point of departure. Furthermore, just as the narrator is a Carlylean reader and writer, writing his tremulous script on the covers of the books he reads, so too might his presumptive reader also write on or over his scribbles. In other words, his narrative can be seen as a figure of reading, understood as a practice of repetition that intrinsically involves transformation that cannot be foreclosed or foreseen, no matter how bold and symmetrical the letters are. (The analogy with reading is reinforced in the final footnote, which describes an infinite book that Borges will later develop into "The Book of Sand," which can be understood as a figure for the infinite possibilities of reading, among other things). Hence although the narrator pins his hope on the disorder of his world being sublated into a totalizing Order that would usurp the very nature of possibility, the method of conveyance of this hopeless hope can be seen as subverting this objective.

## *Melancholy Method*

The narrator describes the writing of his epistle as an activity to distract him from the dismal conditions of his world: "Methodical composition distracts me from the present condition of humanity" (OC 1.505; CF 118).[12] This description is a near repetition of a line in the preface of Robert Burton's *The Anatomy of Melancholy*, in which the narrator states, "I writ of melancholy by being busy to avoid melancholy" (1.17). Burton's book is also evoked in the story's epigraph. Although the title of this seventeenth-century book sounds like a grim medical treatise, it is actually a rollicking satire that covers a number of issues, including political turmoil, religious hypocrisy, social injustice, and the nature of writing. The narrator is named Democritus Junior, which is a complex attribution that, among other things, underscores the satirical nature of the text, since Democritus is commonly known as the laughing philosopher, in a kind of sock and buskin pairing with Heraclitus, who is known as the weeping philosopher. The suffix "junior" refers to the contemporary setting, rather than a diminution, since the narrator suggests that the need for laughing or satirizing philosophers has increased manifold: "Tis not one Democritus will serve [the] turn to laugh in these days; we have now need of a *Democritus to laugh at Democritus*, one jester to flout at another, one fool to fleer at another: a great *Stentorian Democritus*, as big as that *Rhodian Colossus*" (Burton 1.53–54).

The narrator elaborates on this implied inheritance, emphasizing his lack of originality, which, he adds, is characteristic of his time:

> As Apothecaries we make new mixtures every day, pour out of one vessel into another; and as those old *Romans* robbed all the cities of the world, to set out their bad sited *Rome*, we skim off the cream of other men's wits, pick the choice flowers of their tilled gardens to set out our own sterile plots. *Castrant alios ut libros suos per se graciles alieno adipe suffarciant* (so *Jovius* inveighs): they lard their lean books with the fat of others' works. *Ineruditi fures*, &c. A fault that every Writer finds, as I do now, and yet faulty themselves, *Trium literarum homines*, all thieves; they pilfer out of old Writers to stuff up their new Comments, scrape Ennius' dunghills, and out of *Democritus'* pit, as I have done. (Burton 1.20–21)

This castrative scavenging, a performance of the impossibility of originality or autogenesis — exaggerated throughout Burton's text by the kind of intermittent quotations that are on display here — can be seen as a kind of improper repetition or reproduction, what Derrida describes as "life going out of itself beyond return . . . [an] irreducible excess" ("Plato's Pharmacy" 168–69). Melancholy names a different form of repetition, a frustrated effort to recuperate loss and repair the integrity of the living. Although Burton discusses this condition in fairly serious terms as a mode of grappling with the implications of mortality, he also plays with it, for instance in his discussion of an anecdote about Democritus in which he was found slicing up animals, looking for the source of melancholy (Burton 1.2).[13] Burton's narrator, Democritus Junior, notes the futility of such butchery, since melancholy's origins were not discovered by this gory method, but he also reenacts it literarily, excising citations from literary texts, and assembling them into a new kind of body, one that wears its melancholic incommensurability, or non-coincidence with vital self-presence, on the outside.

One of the remedies offered by this combinatory apothecary is alluded to in the epigraph of "The Library of Babel": "By this art you may contemplate the variation of the twenty-three letters . . . " The "art" in question is the discipline of algebra. Although this is just one activity available from the vast "apothecary's shop, wherein are all remedies for all infirmities of mind, purgatives, cordials, alteratives, corroboratives, lenitives, &c.," it is, of course, not a purely incidental one (Burton 2.108). The word *algebra* derives from the Arabic *al-jabr*, which means a reunion of broken parts. Burton describes algebra — which he calls the supreme form of human understanding ("*omnem humanum captum superare videtur*") — in terms that reflect this etymology, stressing how it can be used to calculate the whole from the part: "By this means you may define *ex ungue lionem*, as the diverb is, by his thumb alone the bigness of *Hercules*, or the true dimensions of the great *Colossus* . . . " (Burton 2.109). It is tempting to doubt the solemnity of this proposed remedy, partly because Burton's own style can be seen as a reveling in broken parts, resisting any direct relation between part and whole, or derivation and source. Just like the ruins of the Rhodian Colossus, the many quotations sprinkling Burton's text are parts that will never fit (back) into an anatomical whole; on the contrary, Burton's description of a new, Colossus-sized Democritus satirically doubles the figure of the original.

The suggestion to contemplate the variation of the twenty-three letters directly follows the description of calculating the whole from the part and illustrates how the "parts" that are letters end up exceeding and unsettling any sense of a whole, not just the integrity of a referent or text, but even the very universe: "the words complicated and deduced thence will not be contained within the compass of the firmament" (Burton 2.109). Burton does not make the connection between the random variation of letters and Democritus's theory of atomism explicit, but it is clearly implied, as Borges acknowledges in "The Total Library" (SNF 214). Although neither Burton nor Borges elaborates on this, it does not seem insignificant that Democritus's (and Leucippus's) theory of atomism was developed as a means of refuting Parmenides and Zeno's belief in the immutable and unified nature of the universe (Berryman n.p.). Like letters, atoms thus conceived are parts that can combine to compose a corpus (physical or textual), but not as an algebraic reunion of a presumed whole, so much as an event of contingency that is subject to change. In this, Democritus stands with — perhaps with (melancholic?) laughter rather than tears — Heraclitus's insistence on change as the only constant, also against Parmenides and Zeno (see my discussion of this tension in chapter 7). An intriguing aspect of Democritus's atomism is the theory that there is a void-like space between atoms, so that things are understood to be moving even when they do not appear to be moving, a theory that was directly oriented against Zeno's refutation of movement. Perhaps this theory of the void can be seen in "The Library of Babel" in the space of (un)translatability and (a)destination of the narrator's epistle (which, as epistle, implies a kind of movement, even though it is written on the cover of an ostensibly immovable tome; hence it is an apt figure for literature, simultaneously ponderous and ephemeral), and even in the ventilation shafts (*pozos*) that form an opening within the spatialization of possibility of the hexagonal galleries.[14]

## *Interpolations of Chance*

"The Library of Babel" begins with a naturalized anthropo-theological relation amidst and among texts, in which humans operate as custodians or readers of absolute knowledge in the world about them. This function is either sanctioned by God — human beings written, as it were, as readers — or, in Babelic competition with the divine, claimed as autonomous, with humans in charge of discovering or establishing truth and order. In both cases, it involves an ideal of absolute knowledge, opposed to the incalculability of chance. In "The Library of Babel," it is only when this relationship begins to be questioned that political-theological institutions are introduced to protect the order of things. "The Lottery in Babylon" begins with such institutions and the principle of equivalence on which they are based, a principle that is understood (to invoke Mallarmé) as abolishing chance.

As David Laraway indicates, Babylon serves as a capacious symbol in the Western cultural imaginary (Laraway 569). It was considered the "cradle" or origin of "Western" civilization, although it was also associated with decline and excess. The Tower of Babel was reported to have been built in Babylon, and Babylon can be seen as representing both the construction of the tower and its destruction. Early apparatuses of social and political institutions, such as writing, mathematics, and a written legal code, had been around for centuries, but the cultural and economic centralization of power associated with Babylon, from approximately 2000 to 330 BCE, standardized and incorporated these practices into the institutionalization of civic sovereignty and its imperial extension. An important component of these developments was Talionic law, in which transgression of the law was based on an exchange deemed equivalent (an eye for an eye), an ancient principle that endures to this day (Laraway 578).

The very notion of law based on equivalence is at the center of Borges's "The Lottery in Babylon." The lottery in the story is effectively the codification of chance, what the narrator describes as the "interpolation of chance into order" (OC 1.491; CF 104), or in other words, the instrumentalization of chance in the name of sovereignty (hence, paradoxically, its negation). The narrator provides a brief genealogical account of the development of the lottery, starting with its plebian origins as a mere game, conducted "in broad daylight" and without any other "corroboration by chance" than silver plated tokens (OC 1.489; CF 102). The early versions of the lottery failed because "they appealed not to all a man's faculties, but only to his hopefulness," with the implication that a lottery that appeals to fear as well as hope would constitute a more complete "moral force" of "Man." However, it must be said that the idea of a system that directs itself to "all a man's faculties" suggests a form of totalization from which, precisely, hope would be constitutively excluded, if by hope we understand a sentiment oriented to something not already known, a possibility that may not come to pass.

The appeal to fear through the introduction of negative consequences — including first a fine, then prison time, then all manner of corporeal punishment — upped the stakes of the lottery and caught the attention of the public, which now clamored to participate and to shame others into participating. It is interesting that "the public" is described initially as an entity that polices itself, using, effectively, peer pressure to ensure unity, although peer pressure is not completely apt.[15] An important component of this ideological policing came from the "priestly class," or in other words, a priestly governing body, which delighted in (*gozaban de*) "all the vicissitudes of terror and hope" (OC 1.489; CF 103). This collegium or corporation, performatively reveling in the ups and downs of fortune, can be thought of as the institutional base of the secret governing body that came to be known as the Company, whose existence is first explained as necessary to protect the earnings of the winners by ensuring the penalties of the losers. This Kafkaesque name evokes a covert sovereign body that bears elements of government, commercial-corporate, and theological structures (including an evocation of the Jesuits, known as the Company of Jesus, who were, incidentally, instrumental in the colonization of the Americas).

This political-theological body achieves an apparent omnipotence — involving an "ecclesiastical, metaphysical force" (OC 1.489; CF 102) — when the results of the lottery start to transcend the representational element of currency (fines and monetary prizes) and are inscribed directly on the bodies and experiences of its subjects, from the most intimate and vulnerable to the most public and institutional: "A lucky draw might bring about a man's elevation to the council of the magi or the imprisonment of his enemy (secret or known by all to be so), or might allow him to find, in the peaceful dimness of his room, the woman who would begin to disturb him, or whom he had never hoped to see again; an unlucky draw: mutilation, dishonor of many kinds, death itself" (OC

1.490; CF 103). The story begins with a description of how the narrator, along with all men in Babylon, experiences tremendous contrasts: "Like all the men of Babylon, I have been proconsul; like all, I have been a slave" (OC 1.488; CF 101). Although at first glance it seems that these states are successive, depending on different turns of chance from the all-powerful lottery, the word *all* suggests that they are not necessarily mutually exclusive states. The totalitarian regime provides the illusion of difference and vicissitudes of luck, but in a sense, the parts of this whole constitute different facets of the experience of subjectification. The condition of bearing the contradictory but complementary roles of sovereignty is manifested directly on the narrator's body, with a tattooed letter and a missing finger: an imparting of power that literally *parts* the body, cutting off his index finger, perhaps as a cautionary gesture not to try to point out or grasp the mechanisms of power, and assigns him to a specific categorization (the tattoo constituting a sinister symbol that lies somewhere between the mystical *abecedarium naturae* and the institutional imprint of power found in the branding of slaves and the tattooed numbers of concentration camp prisoners).[16]

An important moment in the Lottery's history is illustrated by an anecdote: "A slave stole a crimson ticket; the drawing determined that that ticket entitled the bearer to have his tongue burned out. The code of law provided the same sentence for stealing a lottery ticket" (OC 1.490; CF 103). A debate ensued as to why he should receive the punishment, whether due to the legal code or the lottery. Although this implies that there is a real alternative between the two, the anecdote itself suggests that there is in fact no real difference between the two justifications for the inscription of sovereignty on the slave's body, but rather a convergence or equivalence of structures of equivalence, in which this coincidence corroborates the relationship between chance and law, which is then extended to become the law of the land.

The Company's imperative is experienced through the effects of the lottery, as a mystical source of authority without explicit pronouncement or articulation: "the paths they followed, the intrigues they wove, were invariably secret" (OC 1.490; CF 104). There are rumors and assumptions about its surveillance techniques and the forms of communication between its agents (authorized or not) and central command. According to public opinion, there are routes of transmission through material portals — some stone lions, a latrine called Qaphqa — but there is no way of confirming either the truth of the communications or whether they truly reach the Company. Nevertheless, the notices are archived, providing an archontic structure to house and affirm their claims, although the alliterative description — "An alphabetical file [*archivo alfabético*] held those *dossiers* of varying veracity [*variable veracidad*]" (OC 1.490; CF 104) — can be seen as drawing attention to its fictive, poetic nature. Another alliterative word — *murmuraciones* — suggests that there are those who question the *variable veracidad* of these communications, which elicits an apparent response from the Company: "With its customary discretion, the Company did not reply directly; instead, it scrawled its brief argument in the rubble of a mask factory. This *apologia* [*pieza doctrinal*] is now numbered among the sacred Scriptures. It pointed out, doctrinally, that the Lottery is an interpolation of chance into the order of the universe, and also observed that to accept errors is to strengthen chance, not contravene it" (OC 1.490–91; CF 104). It is of course not coincidental that the name "Qaphqa" appears amid this section about communication between a sovereign power and its subjects. As discussed earlier, the parable of the messenger in Kafka's story "On Building the Chinese Wall" implies that the missives of sovereignty never fully arrive, and that the act of subjectification involves an element of fiction that sutures that non-arrival. The description in "The Lottery in Babylon" of the Company's response to doubts as to whether the portals of communication really reach the Company (including the latrine, which perhaps implies that messages *to* the sovereign are merely waste products) can be seen as an adaptation of Kafka's parable. Unlike Kafka's story, this description seems to presume the veracity of the sovereign communication and does not question whether it reaches its subjects. Nevertheless, it highlights its indirectness ("the Company did not reply directly"), which might suggest a stylistic preference of a body that shrouds itself in secrecy, but also might be understood as constitutive of the capacity for sovereign transmission. That it chose to sketch its response in the remnants of a mask factory further emphasizes its indirectness and lack of clarity, which is nonetheless compensated for by its archontic reception as sacred doctrine. The word *pieza* is significant, furthermore, given that the process of converting the Company's response from marks amidst rubble — pieces of masks, no less, that is, pieces of pieces that never formed a whole — to a coherent ideological whole is precisely the definition of doctrine.

The declaration attributed to the Company affirms that the lottery is "an interpolation of chance into the order of the universe, and . . . that to accept errors is to strengthen chance, not contravene it" (OC 1.491; CF 104). This statement echoes the idea of the usurpation of possibility in "The Library of Babel" (OC 2.502; CF 115). At its most basic, interpolation means insertion, but as its etymological resonance of the root *polare* (related to *polire*, to polish) suggests, it is an insertion intended to refurbish or restore a purportedly original meaning from gaps or errors. In historic (ecdotic) philology, it refers specifically to adding words to manuscripts or typescripts in order to resolve perceived gaps or errors.[17] Thus the pronouncement that the lottery is an interpolation of chance into the order of the world describes at once the process of inserting doctrinal certainty into the scrawls discovered among the ruins, as well as the idea that chance can be added to that presumed order, added not as chance, and certainly not by chance, but precisely as a supplement perceived as completing a structural totality. Errors are said not to fall outside such an order, but to corroborate it and the version of chance that it encompasses. The doctrinal declaration concludes with an example: Missives sent to the Company through the stone lions and the sacred latrine might arrive at their destination, or they might not — there is no guarantee, but the very possibility that they might arrive effectively represents the Company's claim to authority.

However, the narrator observes that the Company's own missives may or may not reach its audience in the form intended: "This statement . . . produced other effects perhaps unforeseen by its author" (OC 1.491; CF 104). This declaration (later qualified as officious [*oficiosa*], an adjective that implies a performance of authority that may or may not overstep its bounds) jolted the narrator's compatriots out of a complacent obedience to the *dictámenes* of chance (a word that recalls the unquestioned principles recited by the narrator of "The Library of Babel"). From their previous attitude of passive submission to the authority of chance, they begin to question the "juridical-mathematical" structure of their world, that is, the Talionic law on which their society is based, "with no official guarantee." The declaration's description of suturing chance and error into "world order," far from affirming the Company's authority, opens room for other "interpolations"; since, after all, if "order" can be corrected once, it can be corrected again. And indeed, the terms of the declaration are soon modified, from the "interpolation" of chance as a stable supplement to the order of the world, to an "intensification" (a strengthening that is also a stretching, a tensing toward inner limits) and an "infusion" (a fluid dispersion): "If the Lottery is an intensification of chance, a periodic infusion of chaos into the cosmos . . ." (OC 1.491; CF 104). This conditional statement, which purports to rephrase (interpolate) the Company's declaration, displaces chance from its instrumentalized subjection to a principle of equivalence — a juridical version of a conditional statement: if this, then that; if the moon is full, those with the mark of Beth are subordinate to those with the mark of Aleph (OC 1.488; CF 101) — to a condition of incalculability.

Chance, intensified and infused with incalculable cosmic chaos, explodes the presumption of equivalence of any conditional statement, including, exemplarily, the structure of a death sentence, the syntactical form that underlies all presumptions of sovereignty. The narrator's description of this ultimate syntax of sovereignty begins with a muffled burst of laughter: "Is it not ludicrous that chance should dictate a person's death while the circumstances of that death . . . should *not* be subject to chance?" (OC 1.491; CF 104). Chance, it turns out, is a very inefficient sovereign, since every one of its dictums is subject to an incalculable number of other dictums, infinitely deferring the first and revealing the constitutive divisibility at the heart of any mandate or order (*orden*): "No decision is final; all branch into others" (OC 1.491; CF 105). This intensification of chance, which stretches it beyond the confines of any sovereign sentence or doctrinal decree, ultimately undermines the very nature of sovereignty, which, as Derrida explains, "is posited as immortal and indivisible . . . precisely because it is mortal, and divisible" (qtd. in Graff Zivin, *Anarchaeologies* 149).

The Company, however, is not about to cede to these "labyrinthine laws" (OC 1.491; CF 104) without a fight and sets about reasserting its own authority through a kind of philosophical trick. It turns the gap at the heart of sovereign decidability into something akin to the mathematical sublime, which, for Immanuel Kant, describes the idea that the perception of quantitative excess serves to reaffirm the transcendent law of reason.[18] Kant describes the relationship between the experience of sublime excess and the transcendence of reason as a kind of harmonization or agreement; the narrator of "The Lottery of Babylon" uses the word *coincide* [*condice*] to indicate a congruency between infinite divisibility and what is called the Platonic ideal of Chance and the Celestial Archetype of the Lottery (OC 1.491–92; CF 105). That is, the intensified nature of chance, a cosmic chaos that undermines sovereignty and introduces a kind of errancy that cannot be corrected (interpolated), is reclaimed for a transcendent, political-theological structure of power. This reappropriation is indicated textually by the use of capital letters, which mark the elevation of the words (chance, lottery) to the sphere of presumed indivisible self-presence already occupied by the Company. It is not coincidental that this idea is associated with Zeno's paradox of Achilles and the Tortoise, here called not a paradox, but the "parable of the Race with the Tortoise [*parábola del Certamen con la Tortuga*]." The word *parable* suggests something not beside or against doxa (paradox), but a form of illustrated doctrine, like the Biblical parables, and also a geometrical curve, as though the labyrinthine laws of chance were being brought back to a doctrinal center. The use of the word *certamen* comes from the Latin *certo, certare*, to struggle, but, as I discuss in chapter 7, Zeno's paradoxes are intended to illustrate the ultimate overcoming of struggle and difference.

The narrator adds an observation that seems to constitute a non sequitur. He says, "Some distorted echo of our custom seems to have reached [*retumbado en*] the Tiber," and he proceeds to tell of how Aelius Lampridius, in his biography of Antonino Heliogabalus, describes the Roman emperor's use of games of chance to entertain his guests (OC 1.492; CF 105). The anecdote appears to describe a decline from an archetype of sovereignty in Babylonia, as adored by "Platonists" (presumably Neoplatonists) to the idle pastime of a profligate ruler of Rome, a distorted echo or resonance (*retumbo*) akin to falling — *tumbar* — into the turbid water of the river that bisects Rome, icon of imperial sovereignty.

The implication that the ideal form of the lottery was shattered into mere echoes due in part to geographical displacement may shed some light on the narrator's decision to leave Babylon, a departure that is alluded to throughout the story, and yet is never explained. It may also be that such disruption by transmission may already be occurring in his narration. That is, what he calls his "hurried statement [*apresurada declaración*]" (OC 1.492; CF 105), can be understood not so much as a firsthand, quasi-objective ethnographic report of the socio-political function of the lottery in Babylon, as it may seem through much of the story, but as a declaration that is characterized by its difference from the semiofficial statement [*declaración oficiosa*] of the Company, made in the process of departing Babylon, that is, already outside the unchanging eternity of any Celestial Archetype. The declaration's production on the banks of the Euphrates before an imminent naval departure resembles the reverberant fall of the idealized lottery into the Tiber River. The narrator's declaration is hurried: "I have but little time remaining; we are told that the ship is about to sail [*está por zapar*]" (OC 1.491; CF 104). *Zarpar* means departure, but also, specifically, the lifting of anchor: He is writing just before the anchor is lifted, the mystical foundations of this totalitarian society uprooted and the subjugation of this subject perhaps released.

Or is this lifting of anchor already happening in the declaration? It is perhaps not insignificant that the odd anecdote about the distant and distorted *retumbo* of the idealized lottery in Heliogabalus's brief and controversial reign concerns an installment of the Historia Augusta, a biographical account of Roman sovereignty whose veracity and authorship have long been in doubt. Although the narrator appears to attribute the fact of deformation to Heliogabalus's theatrical use of chance to entertain his guests, it can also be seen as applying to the historiographical format of this anecdote, in which an ostensibly objective representation of sovereign history is revealed to be a veritable echo chamber of error. And while this resonance is described as a kind of fall from the archetypal solidity represented by the Company's reign of Babylon, the narrator subsequently observes that Babylonian society and his own narration of it are similarly — constitutively — entangled with errors and deception. Historians have invented a method for "correcting chance," but they do so with deception; scribes secretly vow "to omit, interpolate, alter" the texts that they (re) produce, rarely passing up the opportunity to "include some error" (OC 1.492; CF 105). This description can be seen as rephrasing the Company's declaration that the lottery is an interpolation of chance into the order of the world and to accept errors serves to corroborate chance as a principle of sovereignty — *but*, rather than reaffirming the notion of an interpolated (corrected) order, it stresses how the very nature of inscription, even in the acts of affirming sovereignty or correcting errors, cannot fully rid itself of error. The official scribes of the Company's officious declarations interpolate the Company's interpolations, unsettling the difference between correction and error, history and fiction, order and chance, and highlighting the archive fever that is intrinsic to every archivization. The narrator admits that he, too, has falsified elements of his declaration, a confession that recalls the question posed by the narrator of "The Library of Babel": "You who read me — are you certain you understand my language?" (OC 1.505; CF 118). The admission that the declaration that constitutes the narrative of "The Lottery in Babylon" is not completely clear and truthful reflects the element of uncertainty and contingency intrinsic to every exercise of sovereignty, including the sovereignty of meaning.[19]

# Chapter 4

## *Homo Domesticus*

### "The South," "The Man on the Threshold"

Throughout this book, I have explored how Borges's writings probe the desire for a stable order and meaning, a desire that traverses historical periods, geo-cultural regions, and philosophical and political registers. Borges gives the name of *homo domesticus* to those figures that are driven to find a "place in some Order," a term that links the individual desire for home with a more generalized structure of order, including those associated with onto-political projects such as the nation or empire (SNF 503).[1] In this chapter I will focus on two stories that link the structure of sovereignty, both individual and political, to the figure of a house. Juan Dahlmann, the hapless protagonist of "The South," can be seen as exemplifying the drive to be *homo domesticus*, even though he never reaches the house in the South that he purchases to mark the ground and horizon of his life, as well as his sense of belonging to the imaginary of the Argentine nation. The narrative of "The Man on the Threshold" similarly moves toward the structure of a house, which can be seen as the house of judgment on the border between colonial and anti-colonial power. In both cases, the drive toward these houses is associated with a domestication or domination of life bounded by a determinable death, or a death "sentence." The stories stress the thresholds of such domestication, playing on the slippage between a *sentence* understood as a strict and anticipated limit of life and death, and the play of language (or *sentences*) more generally, which is ultimately incapable of imposing syntactical order on life and history. Both stories feature liminal figures, described in nearly identical terms, that are themselves compared to sentences that are reified and polished through time. These liminal figures can be seen as statuettes of the Roman demigod Terminus, guarding the boundaries of the domestication of time, life, and history; but they can also be seen as representing loose stones (*calculi*) of the (calculating) structures they appear to guard.

Among other things, the symmetries between these two stories, including the nearly identical descriptions of men "on the threshold," can be seen as flags alerting us to the persistence of elements across ostensibly different forms of sovereignty, including two extremes of the Argentine cultural-political landscape in the first half of the twentieth century: Creole-elite nationalism and Peronist populism. Some critics have tended to try to situate Borges ideologically as a Creole nationalist, positioned against the emergence of Peronism, but taken together, these stories can be seen as an interrogation of the domesticating urge in all its forms, and an insistence on the generative space of its multiple thresholds.[2]

## *On the Thresholds of Primal Phantasms*

As we saw earlier, Borges provocatively states that there is a thin line between democratic countries and Nazi fascism. He affirms that "Defenders of democracy, who believe themselves to be quite different from Goebbels, urge their readers, in the same language as the enemy, to listen to the beating of a heart that answers the call of blood and the land" ("Two Books" SNF 208). The protagonist of "The South," Juan Dahlmann, can be seen as exemplifying this slim distinction between democratic nationalism and fascism. He has structured his life responding to "the call of blood and the land," through seemingly innocuous patriotism related to a feeling of being "profoundly Argentine" (OC 1.562; CF 174).[3] However, such nationalist identification seems to require the disavowal of his descendance from an immigrant, who, ironically, was German.[4] He represses what he thinks of as "the discord of his two lineages [*la discordia de sus dos linajes*]" (translation modified) by ignoring his relationship to his bookish German grandfather, and grounds his sense of Argentineness in relation to his other grandfather, who was a hero of national consolidation — which was itself based on genocidal cleansing — and who died on the spatio-temporal border of the modern Argentine nation. In other words, he rejects the immigrant side and embraces the "Romantic" death of the frontiersman, claiming it as his own.[5]

This preference reflects what Elizabeth Rottenberg, glossing Derrida's seminars on the death penalty, calls a primal phantasm of mastery over finitude, which Derrida describes as an effort to "infinitize ourselves by giving ourselves death in a calculable, calculated, decidable fashion" (qtd. in Rottenberg 132–33). Dahlmann subjugates the temporality of life to a kind of ideal infinity that links his present and future, including his eventual death, to the past death of his ancestor. A librarian by profession, he extends this mastery through archival collection, acquiring various items of Creole memorabilia, including a rural property — "the shell [*casco*] of a large country house [*estancia*] in the South" — located to the south of Buenos Aires that belonged to his preferred grandfather (OC 1.562; CF 174). In Chile and Argentina, *casco* can refer to the grounds of a rural property, but in its more common usage, the word refers to forms of protection (skull, helmet, nutshell), from the Latin *quassare*, to hit ("Casco"). Indeed, this house or *estancia* forms a sort of protection against the blows of time and history, including changes to the nation wrought by modernization and immigration and other forms of "discord" and difference that afflict life at both the individual and collective levels. It can be seen as providing a ground for an infinite present (*estancia* is from *estar*, "to be" in a determined state) that links Dahlmann's life to the past and to the idealized figure of the nation. With his purchase of this property, he is on his way to achieving the status of *homo domesticus*, with a "place in some Order" (SNF 503). For years, he does not visit his house in the South, but contents himself (*contentaba*, which is related to containment) "with the abstract idea of possession and with the certainty that this house was waiting for him, at a precise place on the flatlands" (OC 1.562; CF 174). The story can be seen as recounting a gradual movement toward this house, toward the certainty that it is waiting for him in a precise spot, housing his identity and preserving his chosen form of death. The certainty proves elusive, however, as Dahlmann encounters what can be seen as a series of uncanny thresholds.

To begin with, the event that triggers the story's plot takes place on the threshold of his city home. In the stairwell of his apartment building in Buenos Aires, while reading a newly acquired edition of *A Thousand and One Nights*, something brushes his forehead. When he arrives at his apartment, he sees horror "carved" in the face of the woman who opens the door for him, reflecting not a life housed in distanced abstraction, but a frightening encounter with his own alterity. Patrick Dove brilliantly describes how "Dahlmann sees that he is seen from a locus he cannot step into, and this fact of being seen 'from beyond' exposes him to a part of himself that he can neither grasp as his own nor renounce as completely foreign" (*Catastrophes of Modernity* 79). The role of *A Thousand and One Nights* is not incidental, but relates to the rupture of Dahlmann's self-knowledge, with distraction and literature suggesting a mode of knowledge different from the frontal (his *frente* being the site of his wound) forms of certainty and possession.

The wound becomes infected, and he is transferred to a hospital (*sanatorio*), a threshold between life and death, preservation and destruction, *hospis* and *hostis*. If the wound fissured his sense of self as integral whole, his stay at the hospital cracks it wide open and turns it inside out. The description of his arrival sounds more like prison and torture than a place of healing: "his clothes were stripped from him, his head was shaved, he was strapped with metal bands to a table, he was blinded and dizzied with bright lights, his heart and lungs were listened to [*lo auscultaron*], and a man in a surgical mask stuck a needle in his arm" (OC 1.563; CF 175). His insides are plumbed, and he comes to hate himself intensely, especially the vital processes that remind him of his internal alterity, including his "corporal necessities" and the growth of his beard. When he is informed that he had come close to dying, he cries, provoking yet another involuntary emission. Like Ireneo Funes, his feverish insomnia disallows abstraction, including the concept of the passage of time or the fact of mortality: "the unending anticipation of bad nights had not allowed him to think about anything as abstract as death" (OC 1.563; CF 175). Such a menacing abstraction is immediately replaced with the more comfortable one of his house in the South, where he is sent to convalesce.

His apparent departure from the liminal space of the hospital, however, is met with other thresholds. As he departs, he comments on the autumnal air at dawn, a doubly liminal period, and the cityscape is compared to a house, or more specifically, to the vestibular entryways to a house: "the streets were like long porches and corridors [*zaguanes*], the plazas like interior courtyards [*patios*]" (OC 1.563; CF 175). Far from a direct route from illness to health, he seems caught in a vertiginous spin. The word *vertigo*, used to describe his entrance to the hospital, is used again on his exit, and memory and perception seem to have traded places. He remembers things before he sees them, and indeed, he seems to be going backwards: "a few seconds before his eyes registered them, he would recall the corners, the marquees, the modest variety of Buenos Aires. In the yellow light of the new day, it all came back to him [*todas las cosas regresaban a él*]" (OC 1.564; CF 176). The threshold of this backward world has a precise location: It is Avenida Rivadavia, about which Dahlmann used to say that "by crossing Rivadavia one entered an older and more stable world." This conviction requires some selective perception, however: He needs to peer between new buildings to see the (again, vestibular) attributes of this older world ("he sought among the new buildings . . . the arch of a doorway, the long entryway, the almost secret courtyard [*el zaguán, el íntimo patio*]") (OC 1.564; CF 176).

In this liminal zone of the city, Dahlmann remembers (*bruscamente*, this time, not the smooth "remembering before seeing" that he experienced as he moved through the city) a café that has a cat (OC 1.564; CF 176). He buys a coffee and sips it while he strokes the cat. He reflects "that this contact was illusory, that he and the cat were separated as though by a pane of glass, because man lives in time, in successiveness, while the magical animal lives in the present, in the eternity of the instant." David Johnson links this passage to Schopenhauer's belief that what distinguishes human life from that of other animals is humans' ability to "carry about with [them] in abstract concepts the certainty of [their] own death" (qtd. in Johnson 120). That is, unlike humans, animals cannot house themselves through abstraction, incorporating their limit into the infinity of their occupation of the present; as though being (*estar*) were itself already a house or *estancia*. Hence this scene can be read as illustrating Dahlmann's encounter with a limit between his own apparent mastery over existence and the unsheltered being of the cat, which lacks the "abstract idea of [domestic] possession" (Borges, OC 1.562; CF 174). At the same time, Dahlmann considers that the cat already occupies an undivided present, hence is already "home" in a kind of immortality (the cat is described as a disdainful divinity), whereas he is stuck on a journey over endlessly divided thresholds toward his abstract sense of possession, not only of his house in the South, the figure housing his chosen death, but also to his experience of (his *estancia* in) the present moment.

The train journey, which promises to give shape to the successive movement toward his house, provides, rather, a liminal time-space that gives rise to a liminal state of consciousness, as Dahlmann alternates between reading and looking out the window, waking and sleeping, and remembering and anticipating. He feels split in two: "as though he were two men at once," the one moving toward his *estancia* in the South, the other, still imprisoned (*encarcelado*) in his stay (*estancia*) in the hospital, that is, unable to leave behind the constitutive, unmasterable limit of mortality (OC 1.564; CF 176). The landscape is described as *desaforado*, which Hurley translates as "immense," but which also conveys a sense of unboundedness, specifically in the sense of being stripped of its usual structures, laws, and other props of order (OC 1.565; CF 177).[6] The train itself is "traversed and transfigured" by the space and time it traverses.

With the certainties of progression, conveyance, and (self) possession unraveling, Dahlmann arrives at the end of his journey, or at least close to it — he is deposited at a strange station some ways off from his property. He walks to an *almacén*, a rural store that doubles as a restaurant, although the word also evokes a sense of storage (*almacén*, like the English magazine, derives from the Arabic word for storage), which evokes not so much a place of hospitality and restoration, as a jumbled warehouse where things such as repressed memories are kept (OC 1.565; CF 177). And indeed, past events are reenacted in this uncanny space. As he settles down to eat, he feels something brush his face, and he notices that some unruly men (they are described as large boys: *muchachones*) dining at a neighboring table appear to be throwing balls of rolled up bread at him — a dreamlike circumstance that can be linked to an array of associations, including the bullets and lances of the nineteenth-century battles of national expansion, childhood memories of food fights, communion wafers, and even, perhaps, the trail of crumbs in Hansel and Gretel (which is intended to function as an umbilical connection to home, yet is vulnerable to dispersion). The feeling of the bread bits brushing against his face recalls his initial injury (which was described as an unidentified flying object: "something . . . brushed his forehead — a bat? a bird?" [OC 1.562; CF 174]). He is then confronted by one of the men, who "shouted insults at him," transforming the strange sensation into an injury to Dahlmann's sense of self-possession (OC 1.566; CF 179). The man who insults him is described as having an "Indian-looking face [*cara achinada*]," a racialized description that suggests a condition at once autochthonous and foreign. This man seems to double as both the "Indians" who killed Dahlmann's frontiersman ancestor and the woman who opens the door for Dahlmann after his injury in the stairwell, both evoking a feminized "other" that exists within the edifice of the nation and home, and functions as both foil and threat, akin to the Orient for the West in Edward Said's theory of Orientalism.

On this uncanny threshold of past and present, consciousness and dream or fiction, home and foreignness, lies a man:

> On the floor, curled against the bar [*se acurrucaba*], lay an old man, as motionless as an object. The many years had worn him away and polished him, as a stone is worn smooth by running water or a saying is polished by generations of humankind [*o las generaciones de los hombres a una sentencia*]. He was small, dark, and dried up, and he seemed to be outside time, in a sort of eternity. Dahlmann was warmed by the rightness of the man's hairband [*registró con satisfacción la vincha*], the

> baize poncho he wore, his gaucho trousers [*chiripá*] . . . (OC 1.565–66; CF 178)

The man's traditional gaucho attire represents for Dahlmann the manifestation of an ideal of autochthonous authenticity that others believe to have vanished. He appears to embody one of the icons in Dahlmann's collection of Creole memorabilia, thereby confirming the sense of possession that underlies his identity as Argentine. He sees him as a "symbol [*cifra*] of the South (the South that belonged to him)," as if a code to unlock that possession he has had all along, completing a *sentence* that he began when he tied his life to one side of his heritage, his present to a previous *generation*, to use some of the more suggestive words in this striking description (OC 1.566; CF 179).

Nevertheless, the gaucho's garments can also be seen as the wrappings of a mummy, that is, the preservation of material remains through the passage of time, which, nevertheless, cannot be seen as such. Avital Ronnell describes the mummy's wrapping as a "binding around what is not there," linking its twisted casing to the psychoanalytic crypt (qtd. in Marder, *The Mother* 119). Not only is the gaucho's clothing — his *vincha*, *poncho*, and *chiripá*, all forms of wrapping — wrapped around his body, his body is also wrapped around itself (*se acurrucaba*). That is, he is indeed a cryptic figure of the South, but more as a crypt than as a key to a possession. Described, curiously, as ecstatic (*extático*), the crypt can be understood as being both deeply internal — a store within a store, so to speak — and external (OC 1.566; CF 179). As though a repressed image expelled from this internal-external coffer of memory, the gaucho tosses Dahlmann a knife, which, he feels, leaves him no option but to accept a challenge to duel with the man who yelled at him, even as the whole scene continues to waver uncertainly between past and present, stupor and sobriety, and even ferocity and farce.

The challenge to a duel can be read in a number of ways, including as a challenge to the reader to look for dual meanings in the story. Most readers are aware of one duality in this story: the hints that suggest that Dahlmann may never have left the hospital, and is merely dreaming up his chosen death, which he suddenly wants to reconsider — he even thinks "They'd never have allowed this sort of thing to happen in the sanatorium" (OC 1.567; CF 179). But there is another duality behind this one. We know that in 1938, after Borges's father — who had tried unsuccessfully to be a writer — died, Borges had a nearly fatal case of sepsis. He tells how, still feverish, but on the mend, he imagined the figure of Pierre Menard, and when he was better, he wrote "Pierre Menard, Author of the *Quixote*," considered his first "original" fiction, which, not uncoincidentally, addresses the relationship between origin and generation.[7] In a similar vein, "The South" can be read as an exploration — as if life depended on it — of the constitutively divided sense of both *generation*, in the sense of both origin and inheritance (generations), and beginning or creation (to generate), and *sentences* as both determining judgment and linguistic construction.

In addition to the dualities already mentioned, the word designating the end-point of Dahlmann's inheritance and life sentence, *el Sur*, can be seen as harboring its own double entendre, namely the nearly homophonic relation between the Spanish *sur* and the German *zur*, which means "to" + a feminine object.[8] The German dative preposition can be seen as dividing the determinate sense of the Spanish noun, understood as a "precise place on the flatlands" that serves to ground Dahlmann's sense of himself and Argentina (OC 1.562; CF 174). The prepositional sense of a movement *toward* something corresponds to the repetition of the verb *salir* in the final lines of the story. The verb is repeated several times toward the end of the story and appears to refer simply to the act of exiting the *almacén* and going out *to* the plain and the presumptive conclusion of the duel: "'Let's go outside.' They went outside . . . [*Vamos saliendo — dijo el otro. Salieron* . . . ]" (OC 1.567; CF 179). The preterit form is nevertheless followed, in the final sentence of the story, by the present tense of the verb: "and steps out into the plains [*y sale a la llanura*]." This switch to the present can be seen as indicating not a conclusive arrival at a precise site, the end of his life sentence, but as a place where he — or that other librarian with a fondness for some of the lines from *Martín Fierro* — can *leave* interiorizing tropes, including a structure of domestication that purports to contain a sense of life. Reading "sale a la" as "sale *zur*," can suggest a leaving behind of any fixed notion of legacy and telos, proposing instead a moving toward a different relationship to generation and sentences, as though recounting a movement from nationalism toward something like writing or life.

Lest this sound too voluntaristic, an intentional departure from an economy of domestication, let us recall that Dahlmann does not really want to engage in a duel. Prior to the challenge, he was perfectly happy drinking wine and contemplating the characteristics of "the South that belonged to him." It was the gaucho, that external-internal crypt, that compelled him to take up the challenge to duel, exceeding his "slightly willful . . . 'Argentinization' [*criollismo algo voluntario*]" (OC 1.562; CF 174). Furthermore, as Dahlmann reluctantly moves toward the exit, he is not alone in his movement. The sky outside is described as "abierto y acometiendo," an expression that can be seen as suggesting the aggression of an enemy (or a dream or illness), but also as the forceful approach of the sky's openness (OC 1.567; CF 179).[9] The sky in this sense evokes the unboundedness (*desafuero*) of life, time, and relation to others beyond interiorizing tropes such as identity, identity-based inheritance, and the teleological framing of life and collectivity.[10]

Such an incomplete sense of exiting a place toward something indeterminate recalls the structure of *A Thousand and One Nights*, in which every embedded story is left open, to be picked up the next night. This structure of storytelling functions as a mode of survival for Scheherazade, who is at risk of being murdered once she finishes her tales. Analogously, "The South" can be seen as telling a tale not of a dual or a duel death, but of survival, and indeed the generation or creation of a mode of survival — of living on, not circumscribed by domesticating structures — through storytelling, the fictive fashioning of sentences.

Translation is of course also related to survival; and as Sergio Waisman and David Johnson have stressed (in complementary but decidedly different ways), fiction, for Borges, is never far off from translation. *A Thousand and One Nights* is a compilation that can be said to be characterized by translation, bringing together tales from a variety of different cultures, and it is not just any version of this book that appears in the story, but specifically the translation by Gustav Weil into German, that is, the language of the disavowed side of Dahlmann's lineage. In this sense, his initial injury can be seen as a kind of translative return of the repressed that ruptures his monocultural ideal of nation and life. And to the extent that we consider the end of the story as indicating a departure from an idealized ground and telos, perhaps the translator's name, Weil, can be translated to its homophone in English, *while*. (English is Borges's legacy language, after all.) So that rather than life framed by the abstract possession of a house in the South, this story stages the beginning of writing as a stepping out of contained time into the imprecise and boundless "while" of survival.

## *Guarding the House of Judgment*

It is worth considering the relationship of "The South" to "The Man on the Threshold" primarily due to the eponymous liminal figure, who is described in nearly identical terms to the gaucho in the *almacén*. However, other similarities can be noted that bear on the nature of sovereignty, life, and literature. The story describes the struggle for power in British-dominated India, although in the epilogue to the 1952 edition of "The Aleph," Borges explains that this story was inspired by a scene in Buenos Aires, and that he only set it in India "so that its improbability [*inverosimilitud*] might be bearable" (OC 1.671; CF 288). He describes the source of the inspiration as the "momentary and repeated vision of a deep tenement that sits around the corner from Calle Paraná, in Buenos Aires" (translation modified[11]). The description of this glimpse or vision — it is unclear whether it was something he really saw or just imagined — is ambiguous. The word *tenement* (*conventillo*) refers to a building divided into multiple residences, generally for the urban poor. It does not seem coincidental, however, that the national Congress building — a building of multiple chambers, in more ways than one — lies near the corner of Calle Paraná. That is, this description implies a kind of dreamlike superimposition of different houses of power and their temporary, but also repeated, inhabitants.

The story is set in the Punjab, itself a liminal region, around the time of Partition. Following some skirmishes, the British Imperial administration sent in a strongman named Glencairn to "impose order" (OC 1.653; CF 269). Characteristically, this imperial representative is not without some ambiguity. He is described as a cipher (*cifra*) — like the gaucho, a code or inscription — of the mechanisms of Empire; furthermore, he is himself a product of colonization, as a Scotsman with Viking traits (the Vikings colonized Scotland in the Middle Ages) (OC 1.654; CF 270). He appears to succeed in imposing order through "energetic" (read: repressive) means, and this order is said to involve a quelling of ancient conflicts ("had put aside their ancient discords," [OC 1.653; CF 270]). It soon becomes evident, however, that these ancient discords are not ended so much as displaced, with the appearance of peace brought about by the townspeople uniting against a common enemy, Glencairn, who is himself deposed via disappearance.

The narrator of this part of the story, Dewey, is a British representative sent in to investigate Glencairn's disappearance.[12] He is met alternately with silence and with confabulations, until someone leaves him a note that leads him to a house in a poor part of town. It is a low house with a series of dirt patios. On its threshold he sees a man:

> At my feet, on the threshold of this house, as motionless as an inanimate *thing*, a very old man lay curled up on the ground [*se acurrucaba en el umbral un hombre muy viejo*]. I shall describe him, because he is an essential part of the story [*de la historia*]. His many years had reduced and polished him the way water smooths and polishes a stone or generations of men polish a proverb [*o las generaciones de los hombres a una sentencia*]. He was covered in long tatters, or so it looked to me, and the turban that wound about his head looked frankly like one rag the more. (OC 1.654; CF 270–71)

This description, repeated almost verbatim from the description of the gaucho in "The South," can be seen as an indication of a kind of timelessness. The old man on the threshold of this house is described as inanimate and immutable, compared to a stone polished by water, as well as to a sentence, worn down by use and convention. In other words, the river of time has not altered him, or, if anything, it has compressed him down to a kind of core or "essential part" of *la historia* (the story or history), which time or use cannot significantly alter. When Dewey questions him about Glencairn, the old man, who appears to be nearly deaf, or at least nearly deaf to the present (Dewey speculates that the present is only an "indefinite rumor" to him), tells him that his questions remind him of another incident from the early years of the Raj (OC 1.655; CF 271). In this populist tale of resistance, a representative of colonial power is judged ("a judge to judge the judge") and put to death by his subjects (OC 1.656; CF 272). This other incident occurred, the old man notes, in a house "like all other houses" ("*como todas, como ésta*," [OC 1.656; CF 273]). In other words, his sentences tell of a recurrent death sentence, which persists through time, executed by different generations, in different houses, which again evokes Derrida's understanding of a primal, phallogocentric phantasm of mastery over the unmasterable time of life and the otherness of the other (Rottenberg 132). When the man on the threshold concludes his tale, a frenzied jouissance erupts from the house behind him, like the ecstatic discharge of this phallogocentric phantasm. Dewey finds a naked man with a sword and a mutilated body, presumably Glencairn, at the back of the house. The story ends there, with the excretion of the house of judgment, suggesting that sentences and sentences — in the sense of both syntactical coherence and final punctuation — coincide, time and again, through different generations.

The old man appears to be nothing more than an inconsequential pebble on the otherwise smooth threshold of this house of judgment. He is, after all, described as an inert object, condensed to an unchanging core. However, like the gaucho in "The South," he is wrapped like a mummy — both covered in long rags and curled around himself (*se acurrucaba*, [OC 1.654; CF 270]). This layered enfolding suggests that more than an unchanging core, this petrified guardian of the house of judgment is a cryptic manifestation of repressed impulses, which has the potential to be unbound or bound differently by new generations.[13]

The potential for generative unbinding, in which language can serve as something other than a conveyance of a sovereign act, can be seen as evoking the nature of literature.[14] And this may be why, in the story's opening frame, or what we can perhaps think of as its threshold, we find several literary references from different generations, including Juvenal, Kipling, and *A Thousand and One Nights* (OC 1.563; CF 269). Juvenal's satires interrogate the presumed univocity of imperial order, although one of his more famous lines concerning the limits of Rome's reach (*usque auroram*) is misquoted by Dewey, who turns it into a claim for imperial expansion (*ultra auroram*, which appears to combine "non plus ultra" with "the sun never sets on the British empire).[15] Kipling is mentioned in the context of the fictionalized figure of Borges appealing to Allah to reconstruct Dewey's account faithfully ("My text will be a faithful one"), free of exoticizing embellishments such as those provided by Kipling.[16] The play on fidelity and misattribution seems to underscore the fact that "generations of men" do not necessarily polish meaning into an immutable essence, but rather that the passage of time is endlessly generative, transforming ideas and texts. *A Thousand and One Nights*, as we have already seen, exemplarily performs storytelling as endless regeneration from within the house of phallogocentric sovereignty.

# Chapter 5

## Pyramids and Prophecies

### "Funes the Memorious," "A History of Eternity," "The Doctrine of Cycles"

> Mon triste cerveau.
> C'est une pyramide, un immense caveau,
> qui contient plus de morts que la fosse commune.
>
> — Baudelaire, qtd. in Marder, *Dead Time* 92

> The monologue of my singularity deserts itself . . .
>
> — Werner Hamacher, *Premises* 180

Perception, Elissa Marder tells us, is a mode of temporal organization (*Dead Time* 28). This is a central theme in many of Borges's works, but nowhere is it so starkly portrayed as in "Funes the Memorious."[1] The idealist maxim of *esse est percipi* (being is perception) can be considered a fantastic idea, worthy of fictional elaboration. But we do not tend to consider how much our sense of immediacy and presence affects our understanding of what is, and our relationship to what is no longer. Whereas "Tlön, Uqbar, Orbis Tertius" can be seen as exemplifying an extreme version of the idealist maxim in which perception fantastically *creates* being, "Funes the Memorious" stresses perception as constituting a more naturalized unmediated and unmediating relationship to the present.[2] The ideal of an untrammeled access to the living present persists throughout the Western tradition, and there are numerous indications that this story of a Uruguayan adolescent with exceptional memory concerns an enduring trait of metaphysics that pervades things we continue to take for granted today, from the nature of singularity to the modern organizer of singularity and time par excellence, the nation.

The story is structured as a commemorative eulogy to a disadvantaged teenager from rural Uruguay, Ireneo Funes, who lived at the end of the nineteenth century and was endowed with a prodigious, indeed totalizing, memory. The eulogy was purportedly solicited for publication in an edited volume, several decades after Funes's death. It is, in other words, a recollection of another's memory, and begins with a description of some of the differences between the narrator's capacity for recollection and reproduction and that of his subject, whose memory was so acute and capacious that he had no need for writing ("anything he thought, even once, remained ineradicably with him," [OC 1.523; CF 135]). The first sentences perform this in an anaphoric stutter that is disrupted by several disclaimers, as if renouncing the written form in which they appear: "I recall him [*lo recuerdo*] (though I have no right to speak that sacred word [*verbo sagrado*] — only one man on earth did, and that man is dead) . . . I recall him, his taciturn face, its Indian features, its extraordinary *remoteness* — behind the cigarette. I recall (I think) the slender leather-braider's fingers, I recall near those hands a *mate* cup, with the coat of arms of the Banda Oriental" (OC 1.519; CF 131, translation modified). Perhaps in imitation of Funes's own processual perception, the story begins in medias res, the abstract compactness of the direct object *lo* linked, with each repetition, to parts of Funes's body (face, hands, even, figuratively, *mate* and coat of arms[3]), as though trying to reconstruct the subject who, unlike the narrator, possessed the right to "speak that sacred word," *recuerdo* (I remember).

The phrase "sacred word" evokes the Judeo-Christian tradition as described in Genesis and recounted in the Gospel of John, specifically, the divine association between perception, being, and language: "In the beginning was the Word . . . "[4] The term *sacred* suggests an incantatory power, that is, the one who possesses the right to pronounce that word is not necessarily divine, capable of creating through language, but represents that capacity in a direct fashion, like a priest. The narrator makes clear that he does not possess that right: his memory is limited, incomplete, and conveyed by the profane medium of writing. The distinction between a legitimate and illegitimate relationship to originary presence characterizes much of the Western metaphysical tradition, both religious and philosophical, going back to antiquity. Ancient thought makes an appearance in the story in the form of several books in Latin, although the story also evokes ideas that can be traced back to an earlier origin (a secular Genesis, perhaps), namely Plato. The opening of the story, for instance, can be seen as performing some of Plato's ideas about representation and memory, which, as Derrida memorably described in "Plato's Pharmacy," privilege internal thoughts, including memory, and the vehicle of the spoken word. In the *Phaedrus*, Plato describes the mind as the living origin, or father, of thought, and contrasts it with what he considers to be the external, mechanical, and fatherless or illegitimate nature of writing; a distinction that he extends to memory, opposing a vital, internal form of memory to external modes of commemoration, such as writing, that cannot nurture or reanimate their origins or engender memories in another.[5]

Centuries later, Nietzsche caricatures the ideal of limitless perception and memory, characterizing such an ideal as mortifying, rather than vital or generative:

> Imagine the extremest possible example of a man who did not possess the power of forgetting at all and who was thus condemned to see everywhere a state of becoming: such a man . . . would see everything flowing asunder in moving points and would lose himself in the stream of becoming . . . It is altogether impossible to live at all without forgetting . . . To determine the boundary at which the past has to be forgotten if it is not to become the gravedigger of the present, one would have to know exactly how great the plastic power of a man, a people, a culture is: I mean by plastic power the capacity to develop out of oneself in one's own way, to transform and incorporate in oneself what is past and foreign, to heal wounds, to replace that which has been lost, to recreate broken moulds. (Nietzsche, "On the Uses and Disadvantages of History for Life" 62; as quoted in Marder, *Dead Time* 28)

In this passage, Nietzsche describes the hypothetical case of a man with a limitless memory, in which his perception of the endlessly emerging present overcomes him, making it impossible to live. Perception without forgetting becomes a gravedigger and buries its bearer. As Marder points out, life requires forgetting, a name for a constitutive, internal division of consciousness, which Freud called the unconscious (*Dead Time* 28). The opposite of forgetting, then, corresponds to a defensive operation of consciousness, which affirms its unbounded presence, even while disregarding the spatio-temporal process on which it is based, which includes the filtered emergence of memory traces.[6] In order to live, Nietzsche affirms, it is necessary to attend to the boundaries of our perception, which allows us to acknowledge and develop our sense of self in relation to the existence of loss, rupture, and "past and foreign" elements. The "plastic power" he describes is not restorative or unlimited creativity, but rather something like survival (*sur-vivance*), or life through exposure to finitude.

Funes can be seen as a parodic and even more extreme version of Nietzsche's man who lacked forgetting. In keeping with Borges's tendency to situate philosophical and religious ideas in conjunction with historically specific, everyday elements, the story sets the fantasy of originary plenitude that recurs throughout the Western metaphysical tradition in the psychic theater of a poor, disabled teenager being raised by a single mother in the outskirts of Western modernity. Like a kid who, feeling himself marginalized from the churn of dominant society, becomes consumed with a virtual sense of omnipotence through video games, alt-news platforms, or mastery of sports trivia (or any other variety), Funes overcomes such limitations by perceiving *himself* as "the extremest possible example of a man who did not possess the power of forgetting."

Seen this way, we can compare the account of Funes to that of Juan Dahlmann in "The South," which more explicitly addresses the slippage between perception and memory, or the perceptual organization of time more generally. Also more explicit in "The South" is the link between family and nation, or more precisely, an overcoming of a perceived imperfection in one's ancestry through ardent nationalism. For Dahlmann, this was simply a division that he considered discordant in the split origin of his patrimony. He resolves this split by disavowing one side and structuring his life around the other — although, as we have seen, he can never really escape the split. For Funes, the division is more extreme, since he lacks any knowledge about his father: "some people said his father was a doctor in the salting house (an Englishman named O'Connor) others said he broke horses or drove oxcarts for a living over in the department of Salto" (OC 1.520; CF 132). His memory, which is apparently infallible, cannot recover one crucial piece of information — a lack that can be seen as resonating on different levels, symbolic as well as practical. As an adolescent, he is emerging into adulthood, where his mother's care will no longer be able to protect him from his lack of a legitimate name. Without a legitimate paternal name, he does not exist in society; the singularity of his existence is not socially validated. Earlier, before his accident, one of his peculiarities was to remember everyone's full name, which is to say, fore-, middle, and surname — in traditional Hispanic culture, this corresponds to given name, paternal surname, maternal surname — as though practicing the difference between himself and others.[7]

This includes especially, in this story with two protagonists, his difference from the narrator. Unlike Funes, the narrator has a father, who is mentioned both as the motivation for his visits to Funes's town and for his departure. The fact that both boys are described as riding on horseback to the Estancia San Francisco indicates early on that there is a certain doubling at work, a peculiar fraternity evoked by the name of the town, Fray or Friar Bentos. One of the two, the one with the family and the name, returns happy and singing, and the other is thrown (*volteado*) from his horse and becomes incapacitated (*tullido*) (OC 1.520; CF 132). The accident seems in fact to invert (*voltear*) their fortunes, since Funes's incapacitation turns out to produce an exceptional capacity, as is suggested by the word *tullido*, whose Latin root *tollere* means simultaneously to destroy or take away and to raise up (a notion that has strong philosophical resonances).[8] And whereas Funes goes from a fatherless state to a capacity for perception and memory that effectively constitutes its own origin and provides its own legitimacy — namely, the "right" to pronounce the sacred word, *recuerdo* — the narrator's father falls ill, an event that precipitates the central encounter of the two characters.

Although the narrator's name is not given, and although the dates included in the story precede Borges's birth, there are numerous autobiographical elements that link the narrator to Borges. The more explicit details include the names of the Haedo family, with whom Borges's family vacationed on several occasions in Fray Bentos, Uruguay, and the fact that the narrator is a writer from Argentina. But there are two subtle, almost secret, details that concern paternal origins: Borges was reported to have been conceived at his family's vacation house in Fray Bentos, and the date given for the telegraph that the narrator receives that informs him of his father's decline is February 14, 18__, and Borges's father died on February 14, 1938.[9]

The latter fact brings this story into relation with the story of Borges's entrance into fiction writing as I describe it in the chapter on "The South": After the death of his father, who was an unsuccessful writer, Borges had a brush with death, and while he was in the throes of a fever he dreamt the figure of Pierre Menard, which he developed into his first "original" work of fiction. I observed in the previous chapter that "The South" can be seen, among other things, as staging the possibility of writing as a departure from contained, domesticating structures of the temporality of both life and history. The subterranean autobiographical details in "Funes" can be seen as indicating a similar relationship between writing, time, life, as well as the relations between self and other, and totality and singularity. Whereas "The South" is more about fixing the *end* of life — as life sentence — "Funes" concerns an anxiety about origins, with Funes's unknown paternity and the narrator's father's mortality explicitly featured in the story, and the details of Borges's conception and his father's death secretly folded in. The figure of the origin is often viewed as constituting a ground for identity, not only guaranteeing the subject's place in society and (patrilineal) history, but also providing a basis for self-knowledge. The father figures as an origin, which should be impervious to time, but in this story it is marked by finitude. The time of conception, although constituting a biological beginning, is not, strictly speaking, an origin. It precedes the subject and relates to the contingency of beginnings, including the fact that we might not have been and that there is a part of "us" that is beyond us.[10] This anxiety can be seen as setting off a kind of shared, or doubled, hallucination, in which Funes — impaired, illegitimate, without any relation to time other than the slow progression of the clock and a fan-like zeal for national heroes that helped birth the still-emergent Uruguayan nation — appears to become capable of autogenesis, his perception constituting its own origin, with no need for any other. Although the narrator presents himself as a witness to Funes's extraordinary abilities, perhaps as projection of self-sufficiency relating to the disavowal of his father's fragility, and, thereby, his own, he also allows us to see cracks in the fantasy, providing the possibility of imagining a different perception of time, difference, and representation.

## *Origin Stories*

As I have already suggested, this fantasy or fiction has antecedents in a long metaphysical tradition, from the divine pronunciation of the sacred word in Genesis, to Plato's sense of the paternal dimension of the mind, including memory, which is legitimately passed on through the spoken word. In what follows I will read this story in relation to Borges's idiosyncratic account of the history of metaphysics in "A History of Eternity," centering on two of Funes's apparent namesakes, Irenaeus and Friedrich Nietzsche. This account of philosophical antecedents concerns not only the nature of perception as (self) origin, but also the nature of singularity and its relationship to time.

In "A History of Eternity," Borges observes how the concept of eternity has held generations in thrall throughout history. He notes that modern thinkers tend to focus on the "jarring, urgent" problem of time, but suggests that we have not fully managed to resist the appeal of eternity, a concept devised by "[r]emote, . . . bearded, mitred men" "in order to staunch in some way the flow of hours," which has proved surprisingly persistent through the ages (OC 1.135, 387; SNF 123, 135). He enumerates several versions of eternity, focusing primarily on two primary types, the Platonic and the Christian, which correspond to categories that will reappear throughout his work: "Realism," which privileges the general over the singular, and "nominalism," which privileges the singular over the general.

Although he mentions Plato, Borges begins this conceptual overview with the Neoplatonist Plotinus, who, he avers, "amplifies" in crepuscular fashion the Platonic legacy (SNF 125).[11] Plotinus's universe is characterized by plenitude and immutability, in which every aspect of the material world is a mere reflection of the "truer Reality":

> Whatsoever man is filled with admiration for the spectacle of this sensible universe . . . let him next lift up his thoughts to the truer Reality which is its archetype. There let him see all things in their intelligible nature, eternal not with a borrowed eternity, but in their proper consciousness and their proper life; their captain also he shall see, the uncontaminable Intelligence and the unreachable Wisdom, and the true age of Kronos, whose name is Fullness. For in him are embraced all deathless things, every intelligence, every god, every soul, immutable forever. It is well with him: why should he seek to change? He has all things present to him: whither should he move? ("Historia" OC 1.377; SNF 125, translation modified)

The universe thus conceived becomes a "motionless and terrible museum" with no life or death, only presence (OC 1.377; SNF 126). It effectively rules out representation, which is rendered tautological or pleonastic, or what Derrida will call, thinking of Plato, unproductive expenditure, "life going out of itself beyond return" (qtd. in Naas, *Plato and the Invention of Life* 120).

Borges observes that such atemporal categories live on in the structure of the proper noun and the broader notion of species. He avers that Miriam Hopkins "is made up of Miriam Hopkins," not the physical elements that constitute the film through which her image is projected; simpler examples include categories (*géneros*) such as birds, lions, and tables, in which variation is subjected to the "primacy of the species and the almost perfect nullity of individuals" ("History" OC 1.378; SNF 127). He claims — here, as he does elsewhere — that despite the persistence of categorical thought, including the very use of nouns and even proper names, few modern thinkers recognize themselves as Platonist or Realist. Nominalism, on the other hand, is so universal that we barely notice it — "we all do nominalism *sans le savoir*, as if it were a general premise of our thought, an acquired axiom" ("Historia" OC 1.387; SNF 135). Note the heavy dose of irony that describes the generalization of attention to the singular, and, indeed, undoes the apparent opposition between the categories of generality and singularity, as well as the idea that these questions are as antiquated and remote as they may seem.[12]

Borges uses Plotinus to represent the putative dusk of Platonic eternity in the third century CE. The dawn of what he here calls the nominalist version of eternity he places earlier, in the hands of Irenaeus, a second-century bishop who was instrumental in the standardization of Christianity at a time where variations abounded. A Greek by birth, Irenaeus is a poster child for the turn from philosophy, as exemplified by the Greeks, to Rome as metonym of imperial reason. His principal work is *Against Heresies*, which elaborates a strong distinction between orthodoxy and heterodoxy, primarily Gnosticism. Borges, who professed a persistent intellectual curiosity in religion, wrote on both Gnosticism and Irenaeus, in which he describes his interest in the construction of systems of belief. He mentions Irenaeus several times, in each case underscoring the calculated nature of his writings, born of a drive for power.[13] Irenaeus essentially Christianized imperial telecommunication, using doctrine as a conveyor of truth from Rome.

In addition to advocating geographical connection under the sign of empire, Irenaeus amalgamated time. Irenaeus "decreed" a "coercive eternity," which Borges affirms was "much more than a vain priestly adornment or an ecclesiastical luxury: It was a solution [*resolución*] and a weapon" (OC 1.381; SNF 130). He locates its force in the mystical structure of the Trinity, which today may seem a mere superstition, or nightmare, or "a useless theological Cerberus." The strangeness of the Trinity consists not only in the apparent paradox of three-in-one, or one-in-three, but also the question of their relationship: Did one, for instance the Father, engender the others, for instance the son? Irenaeus proclaimed that any belief in such natural, temporal sequentiality (professed by some of the Gnostics, for instance), was heresy, and that Christian orthodoxy was based on a simultaneity of the three. By extension, the simultaneity of the Father, Son, and Holy Spirit consumes those categories that insufficiently describe time: past, present, and future. This is achieved thanks to a superb (*soberbia*) sleight of hand by Irenaeus, who attributes the simultaneity of creator and creation to a divine Word or *Logos*, a mutilated "Time-word" that lies beyond time ("a mutilated *zeitloses Zeitwort*," [OC 1.383; SNF 131]). In this Word all things are written, "not only real things, but also those that are merely possible" (OC 1.385; SNF 133). One can almost hear Borges's chuckle at the irony of theologians declaring such absolute priority for the Word, and then searching the Bible for justification, as he so acidly puts it here: "The Scriptures were scoured for a passage that would allow for this infinite supplement."

The three-in-one structure that encompasses past, present, and future is just as totalizing as Plotinus's "motionless and terrible museum," "more impoverished than the world" (OC 1.377, 381; SNF 126, 129), but it is much more agile. It does not reserve eternity for ideal forms and discard the rich variety of the material and temporal world. The eternal divine is infused into everything, in all time. Borges illustrates this idea with several quotations (which seem to resonate with a number of his texts): "I am the Alpha and Omega"; Boethius's declaration from prison, possibly on the eve of his execution: "*Aeternitas ist interminabilis vitae tota et perfect possessio*" and, more to Borges's liking, Hans Martensen's "almost voluptuous" formulation, "*Aeternitas ist merum hodie, est immediata et lucida fruitio rerum infinitarum*" (OC 1.384; SNF 132).[14] This expansive present encompasses not only what is, but also what is thought — remembered or imagined — in the present. It "seeks to gather up all the details of the universe in a single second," resulting in a multiplicity that exceeds the very category of universe: Irenaeus's "precise and combinatory eternity is much more copious than the universe" (OC 1.386; SNF 135, 134). Borges wonders dryly if this may be too much, even for God, and says it runs the risk of resembling the final chapters of James Joyce's *Ulysses*.

In a different essay published in the same volume, "The Doctrine of Cycles," Borges considers another version of eternity from the opposite extreme of the Western tradition: Nietzsche's exposition of the eternal recurrence. Although at first glance this essay appears to be a straightforward critique of Nietzsche, it is in fact more subtle and ironic than it might seem (perhaps, one might even speculate, as a cover-up for how Nietzschean Borges's thought was becoming[15]). Although the bulk of the essay is dedicated to describing the idea of eternal recurrence with fantastical detail and mock horror, Borges eventually acknowledges that Nietzsche's invocation of this "most abysmal thought" (Nietzsche, *Zarathustra* 174) concerns the idea that the very possibility of return unsettles metaphysical certainty. It appears as an extension of an acceptance of what is, in minute singularity, as what might return, which Borges describes with another literary analogy: "Nietzsche wanted to be Walt Whitman, he wanted to fall minutely in love with his destiny" ("Doctrine" SNF 120). This is clearly different from Irenaeus's nominalism: For Nietzsche, there is no God, and therefore no divine Logos to contain or pre-scribe the infinite singularity of the universe. Furthermore, the literary analogy — both analogies, in fact — imply that the engagement with singularity comes about in relation to writing (and, in the case of Joyce's *Ulysses*, rewriting), whereby the singular is marked as something that can return.[16]

Nietzsche is fervently opposed not only to the idea of divine guarantee, but to the idea of any kind of priestly function implying a connection to anything smacking of divinity, including the structure of the concept. He rails against philosophers, including Plato, for their tendency to enclose and preserve the flux of things and thought into concepts, which he calls a mummification or entombment of becoming.[17] He links this tendency of philosophy to a metaphysical dimension of language itself, which appears to confirm the relationship between naming and being, an assumption that both grounds and is grounded in the affirmation of an "I": "the ego is taken for granted, the ego as Being, and as substance, and the faith in the ego as substance is projected into all things . . . I fear we shall never be rid of God, so long as we still believe in grammar."[18] The notion of the eternal recurrence is understood to shatter this grounded sense of being and move it beyond a historical syntax that buries the living present, as he insinuates in the passage quoted earlier from "On the Uses and Abuses of History."

Despite his radical challenge to a defensive and conservationist structuring of self, concept, and history, in his performative engagement with Nietzsche's (performative) thought in "The Doctrine of Cycles," Borges suggests that Nietzsche's thought falls short in the end. Observing that Nietzsche denied that the eternal return had anything to do with memory, he invokes the theory — clearly Freudian, and yet attributed to his translator and friend Néstor Ibarra — that perception always involves an element of memory, and that there is an abyssal threshold between the two which, when triggered, provokes an involuntary and uncanny sense of return or déjà vu ("Doctrine" OC 1.417; SNF 121). At the opposite pole of this is the "atrocious lucidity" of insomnia, in which the threshold of consciousness is stubbornly elusive and the sleepless subject either loses himself in the stream of becoming, like the man who doesn't forget, or imagines himself as transcending time. Borges accuses Nietzsche, chronically afflicted by this malaise (like Borges, and, not surprisingly, Funes), of allowing the unrelenting gyration of sleepless nights to infect his theory of recurrence, in which he could imagine his consciousness to be eternal. Furthermore, Borges notes that the idea of recurrence was not an original idea, and asks, acerbically, if "Nietzsche, the Hellenist" (OC 1.415; SNF 119) could have been unaware of this fact. He points out that even though Nietzsche was a prolific reader, he appears to erase any precursors, and depicts the notion of recurrence as starting with him, which he stages before a "vast pyramidal block . . . 'six thousand feet beyond men and time,'" where Nietzsche claims that the idea first came to him: "Immortal the instant in which I engendered the eternal recurrence. For that instant I endure the Recurrence" (qtd. in "Doctrine" OC 1.415; SNF 119).[19] Borges suggests that the theatricality of this eureka moment demonstrates registers of conceptual and linguistic security resonant with religious transcendence of time, both past and future; a prophet born before a pyramid, as it were: "My key to this mystery is grammatical, almost syntactical . . . for a prophet, the only grammatical person is the first." No wonder, then, that Nietzsche neglects to mention precursors: "The prophetic style does not allow for the use of quotation marks, nor the erudite attestation of books and authors." Borges massages this omission into absurdity: "If my human flesh can assimilate the brute flesh of a sheep, who can prevent the human mind from assimilating human mental states? Because he rethought it at great length, and endured it, the eternal recurrence of things is now Nietzsche's and does not belong to some dead man who is barely more than a Greek name. I will not insist; Miguel de Unamuno already has his page on the adoption [*prohijación*] of thoughts" (OC 1.415; SNF 119). If I eat lamb, it becomes part of me; why not, he dryly suggests, assume that reading involves a similar process of internalization? He cites Miguel de Unamuno as a more recent instance of such assimilation, describing it as a form of *prohijación*, or adoption, with the parental metaphor resonating with Nietzsche's use of the word *engendered* (*zeugen*).[20] Borges suggests that Nietzsche, following — indeed, *repeating* — a long line of writers and thinkers, performs a kind of immaculate conception, in which, in rejecting structures of paternal authority (God, philosophy, etc.), he also erases history and becomes his own origin, at once paternal womb and pyramidal tomb. This is, of course, especially ironic since the idea that Nietzsche engenders before the pyramidal block is the idea of recurrence, the reemergence of elements beyond the protective, self-present figure of the I. Throughout his work, Borges will play with the tension between thought and recurrence in ways that are ultimately quite Nietzschean, although, unlike Nietzsche, he stresses the returns of reading and memory in ways that undermine any sense of immaculate conception or recuperation of paternal authority.

## *Infallible Perception*

Not without a hint of cruelty, Borges caricatures the onto-theological tradition by combining the icons of its dawn and dusk, Irenaeus and Nietzsche, in the figure of Ireneo Funes (we could say that the figure of Funes pokes fun at FN). Even after the supposed death of God, and at the extremes of an incipient peripheral modernity, eternity lives on, infinite details gathered every second in the perception and memory of this illegitimate, disabled teenager, confined to his room in a dusty Uruguayan town; a nobody or everyman turned superman. As we observed earlier, Funes can be seen as a version of Nietzsche's man without forgetting, whose defensive structure of memory is based on a disavowal of "what is past and foreign," including time, and the fact that it is preceded by things it cannot know or master, including the contingency of conception. In Funes's case, this is exacerbated by the fact that he does not know who his father is, a lack that he is forced to bear in his social "standing." The character of Funes also conjoins Irenaeus's trinitarian Logos, in which infinite phenomena of past, present, and future are gathered together into the divine One, to Nietzsche's mortal and terrestrial overman.

In addition to resonating within Funes's names, Irenaeus and Nietzsche are also invoked in the first paragraph of the story. This appears most directly in the quotation of a Uruguayan critic who called Funes "a maverick [*cimarrón*] and vernacular Zarathustra" (OC 1.519; CF 131). (Note that the very fact of this quotation marks the narrator's difference from the self-engendering "I" that Borges ironically associates with Nietzsche.) The qualification of "vernacular" in its most basic sense means local as opposed to central or standard, hence the soft sh's of the Uruguayan dialect, as opposed to the (supposedly) most philosophical of languages, German.[21] It also marks a distinction from sacred discourse, such as the Irenaean logos or Latin, implying that the figure of Zarathustra from which the Uruguayan one derives represents a kind of sacredness or secure and securing universality, which is, of course, quite the contrary to what Nietzsche intended. Etymologically, the word *vernacular* comes from the Latin root *verna*, denoting a slave born at home, and it subsequently evolved to refer to domesticity and nativity, or nationality more generally, all of which has some resonance with the housebound character of Funes. In the context of Uruguay, the word *cimarrón* refers to *yerba mate*, the regional tea of the Río de la Plata area, hence it would seem to reinforce this emphasis on autochthony. However, it can also mean wild or even rebellious, often in the sense of a slave that has escaped captivity. There are several allusions to Funes's life as one of imprisonment (he is called an "eternal prisoner," a condition exaggerated by the bars on his windows, [OC 1.520; CF 133, translation modified]), but it is implied that his physical limitations are overcome by virtue of his extraordinary mental capacities. Nevertheless, the fact that both adjectives are ghosted by shades of imprisonment begs the question of whether he does in fact escape.

Irenaeus, along with the Christian orthodoxy that he initiated, is evoked in the opening sentence: "I recall him (though I have no right to speak that sacred word — only one man on earth did, and that man is dead) holding a dark passionflower in his hand, seeing it as it had never been seen, even had it been stared at from the first light of dawn till the last light of evening for an entire lifetime" (OC 1.519; CF 131, translation modified). Immediately a distinction is made, as we have already observed, between the illegitimacy of the narrator's memory, and Funes's right to pronounce the "sacred word" *remember*, which in the Irenaean sense of *logos* can be understood as holding together the past and the present. This first description of Funes, furthermore, conjures him as absorbed in the "*immediata et lucida fruitio rerum infinitarum*," a nominalist who encounters eternity in the particular ("History" OC 1.384; SNF 132). The choice of object is far from insignificant: The passionflower was used as a pedagogical instrument for Spanish missionaries to teach the Christian Passion to the native peoples of Latin America, suggesting that more is at stake than simple absorption in the intricacies of nature. First, like Borges's joke about nominalism being so universal that we barely notice it, the particular object in this case allegorically represents a particular version of universality, complete with resonances of imperial logic.[22] Second, in its allegorical use, the reproductive components of the passionflower were used to represent the end of Jesus's life, that is, the transitory moment at which he presumably was folded back into the Trinity, the absolute multiple-in-one. Finally, this *dark* passionflower evokes the Biblical description of seeing through a glass darkly (*The English Bible*, Corinthians 13:12), perhaps setting up a distinction between Funes, who seems to possess divine perception, and others, including the narrator.

The narrator, stuck in the dark, reveals the mechanisms underlying the "grammatical person" that absorbs the past into its present. From half a century away, the narrator struggles to remember Funes, not with one sacred word — a "mutilated *zeitloses Zeitwort*" ("History" OC 1.383; SNF 131) — but with many words, beginning with the repeated *recuerdos* that open the story. The narrator describes his account of Funes as "not the least impartial," a triple negative that suggests both an effort to praise Funes's remarkable qualities, and an admission that his narrative is comprised of parts (OC 1.519; CF 131, translation modified). His recollection does not manage to make things singularly present, as perhaps Funes's memory did, but keeps them "singularly remote," an effect that appears to have occurred while he was in Funes's presence, as well: "I recall him — his taciturn face, its Indian features, its extraordinary *remoteness* [*singularmente remota*] — behind the cigarette" (OC 1.519; CF 131). The allusion to indigenous features in Funes's face evokes a history that (even more than his paternal lineage) is largely forgotten, even by this man who apparently forgets nothing; and whose erasure, furthermore, was a direct effect of history as represented by the passionflower that Funes contemplates with such absorption in the opening sentence.[23] That is, certain elements are "singularly remote" for Funes, as well.

For the narrator, the distance from Funes has only grown, including the half century that has passed since his last encounter. He describes himself as arriving, "now" (*arribo, ahora*), which is to say, again, half a century later, at the "the most difficult point in my story [*relato*]" (OC 1.522; CF 134).[24] There is a subtle joke in this sentence, which is that the "point" of his story is presumably self-contained in space and time, with no extension, dimension, or duration, and therefore cannot be represented by the sequential and iterative nature of language. The "most difficult point" is that the present (*arribo, ahora*) is always divided and involves a return (*re-lato*). Since Funes's words are said to be "now . . . irrecoverable" (they cannot be punctually recovered, taken back to an undivided now) the narrator explains that he will not reproduce Funes's words, but will rely instead on the indirect structure of summary. He acknowledges that this involves a sacrifice — a separating off of the sacred (word) — and beseeches his readers to compensate for this separation or loss with their imaginations. Oddly, however, what he asks his readers to imagine is not fullness or presence, but separation: "Indirect discourse is distant and weak; I know that I am sacrificing the effectiveness of my tale. I only ask that my readers try to hear in their imagination the broken and staccato periods [*entrecortados períodos*] that astounded me [*me abrumaron*] that night" (OC 1.522; CF 134). It seems moreover that Funes's articulation of the "sacred word" was not seamless. He, too, stammered, and did so over time, his *zeitloses Zeitwort* broken as he paused to catch his breath or thoughts. Or, perhaps, it was the time-words themselves that were intermittent, or half-cut periods (*entrecortados períodos*), since this is what the narrator describes as having overwhelmed or astounded (*abrumar*) him that night. The description recalls the rhythm of smoking, in which the smoker's pauses alter the flow of speech and produce a cloud (*bruma*) of smoke. The temporality of cigarettes also involves a phoenix-like recurrence of disintegration, the ephemeral nature of which the narrator describes in the moment he first hears Funes's voice emerge from the darkness. He notes that he didn't see his face until dawn, but thinks he remembers the "momentary glow of his cigarette" (OC 1.522; CF 134).

Prior to the account of the "enormous conversation of that night" that constitutes the center of the story, the narrator recounts other "staccato periods" of his memories of Funes, including the first time he saw him, when he learned about his accident, and an epistolary exchange that leads up to their final encounter (OC 1.521, 522; CF 134). The narrator observes that there is something of Funes's story that has the quality of a dream, referring to the way that the "staccato periods" of their first encounter resonates with the news of his accident. The first time he saw Funes, he was running along a high wall above the narrator and his cousin, cutting a figure against a "limitless" storm cloud ("nubarrón sin límites," OC 1.520; CF 132). When he returns three summers later, he learns that Funes had become paralyzed after being thrown from a horse. His fall from the horse disabled his body ("estaba tullido"), but intensified his mental abilities, to the point that "now his perception and his memory were perfect [*infalibles*]" (OC 1.520, 522; CF 132, 135). It is as though the limitless cloud has descended on him, to cushion his fall and engulf him in a dream (or cigarette) cloud of infallibility.

The narrator mentions that he had recently begun studying Latin. Somewhat pretentiously, as though to confirm the epithet of literary frou-frou (*literato, cajetilla*) that he imagines Funes would level at him (OC 1. 519; CF 131), he takes his textbooks with him on his vacation to Uruguay. Word reaches Funes of these books, and shortly thereafter he writes the narrator a letter to request a short-term loan. This letter is easy to gloss over as a mere passage to the tantalizing description of Funes's incredible memory, but there are some elements in it that are worth examination.

The primary motive of the letter is to request the loan of one of the narrator's Latin books, together with a dictionary, "for a full understanding of the text, since I must plead ignorance of Latin" (OC 1.521; CF 133). Funes promises to return the books "in good condition, and 'straightaway' [*en buen estado y casi inmediatamente*]." The letter is written in a phonetic style promulgated by Andrés Bello (i for y, j for g) and in a perfect script ("the penmanship [*la letra*] was perfect"). The narrator derides the idea that someone could master a language as complex as Latin with nothing but a dictionary, and sends him the hardest book in his possession, Pliny's *Natural History*, which, he admits "exceeded (and still exceeds) my modest abilities as a Latinist." Funes's assumption that he could learn Latin (acquire a "full understanding of the [original] text") based on a quick read of the dictionary — which he apparently did, along with other Romance languages and the more recent imperial language, English (OC 1.524; CF 137) — suggests that from the limitless cloud of his newfound cognitive abilities, he can overcome linguistic difference. This, together with the description of the perfection of his handwriting and the phonetic spelling, suggests a similar return of writing to its putative source, that of speech, which underlies a mode of communication that presumes a transparent and direct link to another. His infallible condition enables him to return everything, all difference, to a kind of originary state — in good condition and *almost* immediately, as he says of the book loans (OC 1.521; CF 133).

As prelude to the request for the books, the letter also recalls (*recordaba*) the first encounter of Funes and the narrator. The letter can be read as an externalized form of Funes's memory. The style is described as "flowery and ceremonious," which at first glance seems far from the ideal of direct communication I have just described (OC 1.521; CF 133, translation modified). The word *ceremonious* derives from the Latin, *caerimonia*, which refers to religious ritual and the notion of sanctity more generally. Hence this letter is a manifestation of Funes's pronunciation of the "sacred word," *remember*, that is, a form of remembering that secures its contents. The modifier *flowery* can be seen as reflecting an effort to instill life into the dead letter of writing, which, with the phonetic spelling, endeavors to be as close to the spoken word as possible. Since this description follows shortly after a reference to artemisia (*santonina*, [OC 1.520; CF 133]), a medicinal plant traditionally used as an antiparasitic purgative, it can also be seen as contributing to the purported sanctity of memory. The "parasite" against which this flowery style is applied in the pleasantries about the narrator is the nature of time, described as "lamentably ephemeral," a fugacity that, furthermore, has just claimed the narrator's uncle. Funes tries to fix this fugacity in the form of a date, naming with his characteristic precision the day on which he and the narrator first crossed paths — remembering, as it were, his previous distinctive capacity for remembering, which is to say, remembering his own memory.

The reference to the narrator's uncle reinforces the effort to counteract temporal dispersion. In the letter, the narrator describes how Funes "dwelt briefly, elegiacally [*ponderaba*], on the 'glorious services' that my uncle, Gregorio Haedo, who had died that same year, 'had rendered [*prestado*] to his two motherlands [*las dos patrias*] in the valiant Battle [*jornada*] of Ituzaingó'" (OC 1.521; CF 133). Like a mortuary monument, this ponderous mention endeavors to tie together the "lamentably ephemeral" nature of time, which has recently claimed the uncle's life, to a historic day (the word *jornada* means both day and military excursion), sixty years prior. The word *prestado* [loan] stands out, especially since it is in the next clause of the same sentence that Funes requests the loan of the narrator's Latin books. This repetition implies that, just as Funes promises to return his loan "in good condition," which also resembles his claim to a seamless form of linguistic acquisition or translation ("a full understanding of the [original] text"), the uncle's "loan" of "glorious services" will also be paid back or redeemed in the secular form of the glory of national heroism, represented here by Funes's ponderous praise.

The historical event to which Uncle Gregorio loaned his service was a conflict in the civil wars that plagued the Río de la Plata region for much of the nineteenth century after the wars of independence from Spain. At the Battle of Ituzaingó (1827), newly independent Argentina attempted to annex Uruguay by wresting it from Imperial Brazil, and ended by providing the basis for Uruguayan independence, which was established in 1828 (although civil wars continued for decades). In other words, the narrator's uncle contributed to the birth of the Uruguayan nation-state, rejecting the inheritance of imperial rule (itself reproducing in the Americas, with the Empire of Brazil replacing Portugal), and replacing it with a structure nominally based on self-determination. Gregorio "loaned his services" to the birthing of Uruguay, not as a father, linking a patricidal band of brothers, but as an uncle, helping to produce a cousinly bond of patriotism that exceeds biological inheritance and even, possibly, a strict demarcation between the two emergent countries in the Río de la Plata region. Funes praises Gregorio's contribution to his two mother or fatherlands (*patrias*), a slightly odd formulation that implies a shared experience of national self-determination against imperial invaders, but also intimates an uncanny sense of doubling — like that between Funes and the narrator — between Uruguay and Argentina, two countries that were previously one, and which are both united and divided by a river.

The allusion in Funes's letter to the inception of the Uruguayan nation resonates with other allusions to Uruguayan nationalism throughout the story, which are not as pivotal as Juan Dahlmann's patriotic proclivities in "The South," but they are recurrent enough to take seriously. Unlike Dahlmann, whose patriotism intensified and idealized the preferred half of his lineage, Funes's patriotism can be understood as replacing and compensating for his unknown father and consequent illegitimacy. He may not know his father, but he knows his *patria*, and he can celebrate its autogenetic beginnings, in which the founding fathers made history begin with them, throwing off a repressive colonial legacy and almost entirely obliterating any indigenous inheritance, although, as we see with Funes's indigenous features, they were not entirely successful.

There is an unspoken challenge to the self-determination represented by the national forefathers (or fore-uncles) that concerns the more recent history of the town where this story takes place. The town was formerly known as Villa Independencia but was renamed Fray Bentos in the 1860s after the British meat-packing company that was established there, and whose name became nearly synonymous with a kind of canned meat pie sold in Britain.[25] The renaming of the town from one celebrating Uruguayan independence and self-determination to the name of a British (that is, imperial) company repeats and reinforces Funes's lack of a legitimating paternal last name. His nationalism can be seen as a response to this, as can his extraordinary memory, which can be thought of as resembling the company's product of preserved and tinned meat.

The figure of the letter is thought to construct a link between writer and reader by means of written language, in this case described as phonetically structured, and with perfect script (*letra*). This letter, furthermore, requests a loan of books in an unknown language, to whose "original text" Funes will easily access, and which he promises to return in good (original) shape and "almost immediately." Analogously, the reference to the narrator's uncle seeks to link past and present and refers to a founding moment — supplanting more recent experiences of foundational loss, including the names of Funes's father and his town — of one of the modern figures of linking par excellence, the nation. And all these economies of relation can be seen as resembling Funes's mind, which "infallibly" gathers and preserves impressions, keeping them safe from loss, dispersion, and unfortunate fugacity.

The description of Funes's letter is followed directly by the description of a telegram from Buenos Aires informing the narrator that he must return because his father was unwell (OC 1.521; CF 133). Unlike Funes's letter, this telegram does not purport to embody an ideal, unifying form of telecommunication, but rather delivers, as it were, distance and division. To begin with, of course, it informs the narrator of his father's frailty, which, perhaps symbolically, is located far from the narrator, back home in Argentina, perhaps implying that origins — fathers and "home," or any situated sense of belonging in time or space — are always characterized by finitude and distance, located across a wide "river" (of time), such as that which separates his two mother or fatherlands (*las dos patrias*), Uruguay and Argentina. The telegram informs the narrator that his father is not well, and urges him to "return home immediately," which recalls Funes's promise, stated just a few lines before, to return the books he is requesting "in good condition and 'straightaway.'" The narrator, however, cannot return immediately, because he needs to pick up his loaned books. In doing so, he encounters Funes, whose mind appears to function without mediation and constitutes its own origin and end, and it is this embodiment of immediacy that paradoxically mediates the narrator's return to his ailing father.

But even before he goes to receive the *almost* immediate return of his books, the narrator finds himself stuck in mediation. As a kind of "distraction" from his pain, he fixates on the telegram's syntax, which awkwardly claims that his father "was 'not at all well' [*no estaba 'nada bien'*]" (OC 1.521; CF 133). The narrator ponders what he calls "the contradiction between the negative form of the news and the absoluteness of the adverbial phrase." The quotation marks call attention to the fact that there is not one just adverb, but two ("nada bien"), a doubleness that resonates with other forms of doubling in the story. While the "nada" can function as an intensifier, stressing that the father is not at all well, taken separately, the phrase can also be read as suggesting that nothing (that is, the substantive form of *nada*) is well, that is, with the father unwell, nothing is "en buen estado," implying that returns (to origins, the past, etc.) will always be mediated.

Following this syntactical and emotional disjuncture in the face of the news of his father's illness, the narrator goes to Funes's house for what can perhaps be thought of as the return of the letter — that *letra perfecta* that promised the return in *buen estado* of his Latin books. Upon entering the house, he hears Funes's voice before he can see him: "suddenly I heard Ireneo's high, mocking voice. The voice was speaking Latin; with morbid pleasure, the voice emerging from the shadows was reciting a speech or a prayer or an incantation. The Roman syllables echoed in the patio of hard-packed earth; my trepidation made me think them incomprehensible, and endless [*indescifrables, interminables*] . . ." (OC 1.521; CF 134). Funes's voice, emanating from the darkness, enacts a startling return of the *letra perfecta*, bringing a dead language back to life, returning its written form "in good condition," in the near immediacy of spoken language (OC 1.521; CF 133).[26] There is no distraction from *this* resonant (call to) return. Unlike his reaction to the urgent news regarding his father, the narrator's emotion is now so immediate that it acquires agency. At first it is only the sound of the disembodied "Roman syllables" resonating in the darkness that troubles him, appearing indecipherable and interminable, as though this language of empire possesses an unlimited immediacy of sense to which the narrator has no access, which will always "exceed [his] . . . abilities as Latinist," or in other words, marking him as one who always struggles with dead letters or the life-death of language. The narrator later learns that Funes was reciting from memory a chapter on memory from Pliny's *Natural History.* Pliny's expansive work is considered an ur-text of encyclopedias and can be seen as linking the political sovereignty of Rome to that of knowledge, its empirical fact-gathering extending to the farthest reaches of the empire, a secular precursor to Irenaeus's mystical *logos*.

Funes's recitation concludes with the final phrase from Pliny's chapter, which is included in the text: *ut nihil non iisdem verbis redderatetur auditum* (OC 1.522; CF 134). This can be translated as "nothing that can be heard can be repeated with the same words," although there is in the Latin a double negative that does not translate directly into either English or Spanish, a fact that performs the impossibility of exact repetition in translation, that operation that for Funes is a mere "almost" in his perception of an object. It also resonates with the curious syntax in the telegram about the narrator's father, whose double negative also emphasizes difference in repetition, or put differently, the unreliable relation between *no* and *nothing*. Although these words initially strike the narrator as indecipherable, they are in fact deciphered a few lines later, with no negative, when Funes describes the subject of Pliny's chapter as the art of "repeat[ing] what [one] had heard, though it be but once." Funes, "with obvious sincerity [*evidente buena fe*]," dismisses such an art as unremarkable compared to his own natural, spontaneous ability to recall things. His extraordinary powers of perception and memory elide the difference between original and reproduction, nature and techne. His faith is in himself alone, beyond any artifice or technique — "The prophetic style does not allow for quotation marks" ("Doctrine" OC 1.415; SNF 119) — unlike the narrator, whose perception and recollection are invariably marked as mediated.

Following the recitation of Pliny's chapter on memory, the narrator recounts, in his "indirect discourse," Funes's account of his abilities (OC 1.522; CF 134). He says that before his accident, he was "blind, deaf, befuddled, and virtually devoid of memory [*miraba sin ver, oía sin oír, se olvidaba de todo, de casi todo*]." The narrator reminds him of his clock-like sense of time and memory for proper names, but Funes scoffs at this. His abilities before the accident can be seen as enumerating objects in the "motionless museum" of Neoplatonic eternity ("History" OC 1.377; SNF 126). In contrast to the sensory details of the memory of the narrator's first encounter with Funes (the color of the storm clouds, the trees bending before the wind, the conflicting emotions of fear and hope, the sound of "almost secret" footsteps), Funes appeared to reduce the world around him to proper names, akin to what Borges describes as the Neoplatonist sense of the "primacy of the species and the almost perfect nullity of individuals," in which a bird is a bird, a table, a table, and Miriam Hopkins "is made up of Miriam Hopkins" ("History" OC 1.378; SNF 127).

With his fall from the horse, he was rendered physically incapacitated (*tullido*), but his perceptual and mnemonic abilities were "infallible": "the present was so rich, so clear, that it was almost unbearable [*el presente era casi intolerable de tan rico y tan nítido*], as were his oldest and even his most trivial memories" (OC 1.522; CF 135). It is as though his fall took him from a Neoplatonic eternity to an Irenaean-nominalist one, hence not really a fall, but an awakening to a storm of singular sensations, in which the most distant and inconsequential memory was experienced as orgasmically vivid and present: "the most trivial of his memories was more detailed, more vivid than our own perception of a physical pleasure or a physical torment [*tormento*]" (OC 1.524; CF 137). That is, his "infallible" perception constitutes a secular transcendence of the Christian Fall, a kind of negation of negation that also recalls philosophical transcendence (his condition as *tullido* recalling the Hegelian term *sublation*).[27] More importantly, his perception, described as simultaneous and infinitely varied ("multiform, momentaneous, and almost unbearably precise") recalls Irenaeus's "mutilated *zeitloses Zeitwort*," *logos*, which seeks to encompass and deny time in the same stroke (OC 1.524, 383; CF 137; SNF 131). The descriptions of Funes's memory also recall Nietzsche's description of the extreme example of "a man who did not possess the power of forgetting . . . and who was thus condemned to see everywhere a state of becoming" (Nietzsche, "On the Uses and Disadvantages of History for Life" 62). As I suggested earlier, this hypothetical lack of forgetting can be understood as a defensive mode of remembering that blocks out the porous nature of consciousness, replacing it with a perception that is almost fetishistic in its intensity, disavowing loss, rupture, and "past and foreign elements." And yet, in Borges's sardonic mashup of Irenaeus and Nietzsche, we find Funes awakening from a Christian and Neoplatonic slumber to a post-theological nominalism planted firmly in a first-person singular capable of subjecting past and present to the prophetic embrace of eternity, recalling Borges's description of Irenaeus's eternity as "a solution and a weapon" ("Historia" OC 1.381; SNF 130).

Not including the opening description of Funes's contemplation of the passionflower, the first example of his perceptual powers is of glasses of wine, a symbol with both Irenaean and Nietzschean resonances. The narrator explains that where "we" — that is, people with normal perception — perceive three glasses of wine on a table, Funes sees "every grape that had been pressed into the wine and all the stalks and tendrils of its vineyard [*todos los vástagos y racimos y frutos que comprende una parra*]" (OC 1.522; CF 135). This example neatly lays out how Funes's perception collapses time into a sensory present. Whereas a person with normal perception observes wine and forgets the process that preceded it, Funes sees the entire process of production in one glance. It is perhaps not insignificant that the word *wine* does not appear. What "we" perceive may not even be the wine, but the category, or containers of the singularity of this wine: glasses on a table. Funes, on the other hand, has no need for these fragile containers; he has already imbibed the contents of these three cups, which like the Eucharist, connects him to the trinitarian extensions of time.[28] Or perhaps like Nietzsche, he has no need to drink wine, since the water of inner experience is sufficiently intoxicating. Such intoxication does not, however, imply a lapse in consciousness, since he apparently has no lapses in consciousness. Even his dreams, he insists, are like normal peoples' conscious perception ("My dreams are like other people's waking hours" [OC 1.523; CF 135]). And yet is it a coincidence that Funes begins his description of his mnemonic abilities with the word *vástago*, which refers to the beginning of wine production, but also means offspring or child? His infallible trinitarian (Cerberean) perception devours the past, including, by implication, his own germination. His consciousness produces its own wine, as well as its own production. He no longer has need of the father he does not know.

As with the wine glasses, many of the other details provided about Funes's memory contrast the extreme singularity of his memory with structures that evoke the "Platonic" variety of eternity. For instance, the narrator explains that whereas "we" can perceive geometrical shapes fully ("son formas que podemos intuir plenamente"), Funes is capable of such full intuition with "the stormy mane of a young colt, . . . a flickering fire and its uncountable ashes, and the many faces of a dead man at a wake" (OC 1.523; CF 135). Whereas we can fully and simultaneously perceive a triangle, Funes perceives infinity and difference — not only multiplicity and movement (for example, the storm-tossed mane), but also transformation, decay, and trace — in the trinitarian instant of the many in one and the one in many.

Such infinite and eternal multiplicity recalls Borges's dry observation that Irenaeus's "precise and combinatory eternity is much more copious than the universe," an abundance that risks overwhelming syntax, such that a description of it would resemble the final chapters of Joyce's *Ulysses* ("History" OC 1.386; SNF 134). And indeed, Funes says that he experimented with reconstructing an entire day, but "each reconstruction had itself taken an entire day," which can be read as a good-humored dig at Joyce's novel, which, of course, verbosely recounts a single day (OC 1.523; CF 135).[29] Yet in the capacity for full intuition represented by Funes's mind, the details of perception do not overwhelm syntax, but appear to be fully contained by an expansive, internalizing "I." In "A History of Eternity," Borges describes the recurrent drive to eternity as a greediness of "magnanimous appetites . . . for all the minutes of time and all the variety of space" ("History" OC 1.387; SNF 136). Funes can be seen as embodying such an appetite. The description of a memory that can reconstruct the experience of a stretch of time, whether a day or an entire life cycle, recalls the map in "On Exactitude in Science," as another instance of representation that matches its original point for point. However, such a representation would be derided as far too general for Funes's intricate memory.

He tries to adapt other forms of representation to his perception, including names and numbers, those signifiers that were his forte before his fall. The narrator recalls John Locke's speculative invention of a language capable of corresponding to the singularity of the world, in which "each individual thing — every stone, every bird, every branch — would have its own name" (OC 1.523; CF 136). He explains that Funes considered even that idea too general, since for him not only was every tree different, but every leaf on every tree was also different from every other, and even the same leaf was different each time he perceived or imagined it. Names, including species names, are useless given the dizzying and endlessly changing (although simultaneously grasped) nature of his world. He experiments with limiting his memories of each day to a set of memories, "which he would later define by numbers [*cifras*]" (OC 1.524; CF 136).[30] Analogously, he also tried to reinvent a system of numbers, which, inversely, turns numbers into names.

The origins and details of this project are somewhat obscure, but I want to suggest that they reveal an important factor in Funes's voracious memory. The narrator speculates that the project of inventing a new numbering system was inspired by Funes's frustration that the so-called *treinta y tres Orientales* ("thirty-three Uruguayan patriots") relied on a number that required two signs (that is, 33) and three words (*treinta y tres*) (OC 1.524; CF 136). Thirty-three Orientals is a name given to a group of men whose resistance to the Brazilian empire and whose negotiations with Argentina led to the birth of the Uruguayan nation (*República Oriental del Uruguay*). Funes's desire to invent an original system of numbers was inspired by his concern that a group that effectively fathered the unifying structure of the nation did not have a single word and sign ("una sola palabra y un solo signo") to designate their set, or the unifying category that brings them together. In a funny play on the Trinity (33-in-one), Funes circuitously resolves to replace the number that names these founding fathers with a single and distinctive name or sign ("un signo particular"), which we can perhaps understand as relating to his own lack of a legitimating paternal surname. Furthermore, although we are not told what the number thirty-three is renamed, the other examples of name-numbers included in the story are elements that could be taken from a history book of the Río de la Plata region, including topographical features, material culture, and historical actors, great and small: a Uruguayan river, a kettle (used for mate, the traditional drink of the region), a cut of meat, natural resources (whales and gas), a local satirical periodical, and historical figures such as the Thirty-three Orientals, Napoleon, and an Uruguayan jurist.[31] That is, just as he renames the group of founding fathers, his whole "system" of numbering consists of an enumeration of national attributes, bringing together disparate "minutes of time and . . . variety of space" under an unnamed name, that of the nation, which, like the Irenaean logos, is a capacious structure understood to unite things in their singularity ("History" OC 1.387; SNF 136).

Another similar, albeit less "systematic" approach appears in a description of Funes's association of disparate images. We read, "He knew the forms of the southern sky [*las nubes australes*] on the morning of April 30, 1882, and he could compare them in his memory with the veins in the marbled binding of a book he had seen only once, or with the feathers of spray lifted by an oar on the Río Negro on the eve of the Battle of Quebracho" (OC 1.522; CF 135). These images appear at first glance to simply demonstrate the intricate singularity of his perception and memory in which, like Irenaeus's logos, Funes's "precise and combinatory eternity is much more copious than the universe" ("History" OC 1.386; SNF 134). But the associations between such disparate scenes also suggest that Funes's perception, like the structure of the nation as well as the Irenaean logos, can bring together radically disparate things, including the historically momentous and the ephemeral. The final term is the most ephemeral and arcane: the foamy wake of a random, anonymous movement on a river in the south of Argentina on the evening of the Quebracho, a battle in 1846 over national sovereignty on a river in the north of Argentina — which also concerned Uruguayan sovereignty, and even the very question of national sovereignty.[32] The association between a random movement on one river and a defense of sovereignty recalls D.F. Sarmiento's description of Argentina's rivers as the arteries of an organically unified body of the nation (Sarmiento 58). Although Sarmiento's emphasis was on economic and cultural circulation, the description of Funes's mental prowess stresses how a movement, however small and anonymous, in one part of the nation, can be understood as happening in the same corpus as an important historical event happening in another part. And Funes's memory retains them both, like a national archive that houses pictures of presidents along with ephemera otherwise lost to the swirling currents of time.

At the same time, the examples may be too polarized to really make sense. Does the foamy wake of an oar far from a historic battle really constitute part of the same entity? Do these two terms perhaps challenge the question of what constitutes a nation and (its) history? Perhaps Funes's nationalist number-names can be seen as an attempt to counteract this dispersion, gathering different aspects of existence within a nation's parameters under the sign of the One ("una sola palabra y un solo signo"). That is, the infinitely finite nature of existence is subjected to a larger unifying structure, in this case, both Funes's mind and the ideal of the nation, capacious enough to include historical battles and seemingly insignificant and transitory movements. Although, just as the Battle of Quebracho (like much of the nineteenth century) strains the ideal of unified national sovereignty in the region, this detail strains the integrity of Funes's perception, since it refers to something that evidently preceded his birth by several decades.

The nature of this memory may provide a hint to this "extremest example" of remembering (Nietzsche, "On the Uses" 62). A foamy wake can be read as evoking a memory trace that is not fully processed by consciousness. A foamy wake left by an oar manned by an unknown rower before Funes's birth can perhaps, without too much of a stretch, be connected to the unknown circumstances of his conception. The linking of this anonymous movement to a celebrated historical action can be seen as an effort to compensate for that unknown element of his personal past with a known and celebrated historical event. Like the number-names, perhaps we can surmise that Funes's hyperbolic perception of singularities is an expression of feeling that his own singularity is not recognized since it is not legitimized by a paternal surname, without which it is as ephemeral as foam on a river. Singularity in this sense is, like Irenaeus's nominalism, understood to be in-dividual: contained within a unified and unifying structure and determined by a phallogocentric structure of inheritance. Such a sense of sanctioned singularity is in effect another version of Neoplatonism, since the individual is considered a privileged extension of the species: "Miriam Hopkins is made up of Miriam Hopkins" ("History" OC 1.387; SNF 127). Funes's infallible powers of perception and memory seem to provide him with a singular, auto-generated form of individuality that derives from nothing but itself, like so many claims to intellectual and aesthetic originality.

## *Rocked and Negated*

There are several indications that Funes's infallible individuality is not, in fact, truly unified or self-sufficient. The strongest hints are, perhaps not unsurprisingly, linked to water. To begin with, in addition to the foamy wake, there are the other terms in the memory collage, including clouds, which are drifting clusters of evaporated water. Although the word used to describe the marbled veins in a book is *vetas*, which refers to strata like mineral veins, such a figure is ultimately an aqueous design that can be seen as mimicking the unstable weave of text and the hidden currents embedded in every book.

In another oft-overlooked image, there is the "vague painted lake scene [*vago paisaje lacustre*]" that is described as appearing in the window of Funes's house, although it is unclear whether the landscape is one found outside the window or represented on the blind (OC 1.519; CF 131). Hurley opts for the latter, translating the phrase as "a yellow straw blind with some vague painted lake scene," but this choice, while perhaps inevitable, obscures an important ambivalence. The word *vago* corresponds to the English word *vague*, but it also refers specifically to an indefinite style of painting, which is presumably what inspired Hurley's interpretation. It also has a number of other meanings, most of which revolve around indeterminacy, as well as another set of meanings that denote emptiness, including a specifically Argentine use which refers to a "solar vacío," with *solar* referring to a family-owned estate, or family lineage.[33] Not only is this local sense of the word extremely suggestive in the context of this story, the very vagueness of the word *vago* seems to underscore the fact that we cannot be certain whether the "lacustrine landscape" is painted or real, inside or outside, like all of the details of Funes's perception and memory.

Furthermore, this reference to a self-contained body of water contrasts with the rivers that flow through the heart of this story, including the Río de la Plata, which divides Uruguay and Argentina. The narrator traverses this fluid border several times on his visits to Uruguay and again, presumably, the morning after the nocturnal colloquy with Funes. The fact that the boat the narrator will take is named *Saturn* (*El saturno*) suggests that the river also doubles as a figure for timelessness, and its crossing as potentially a kind of (eternal) melancholic return (OC 1.521; CF 133).[34] The commemorative essay that serves as the pretense for the story also appears to traverse both the river and the half century since the narrator knew Funes, and can be read as a kind of saturnine return to a fantasy of immediacy and fullness, although there are indications that the narrator is cognizant of the river-like flow of time that separates him from such a lacustrine landscape.

Finally, a river is mentioned as an antidote to Funes's persistent insomnia. The narrator observes that "To sleep is to take one's mind from the world [*distraerse del mundo*]," and Funes's "inexhaustible" sense of reality renders such distraction elusive (OC 1.524; CF 137).[35] In his efforts to fall asleep, he would lie on his back and "picture every crack in the wall, every molding of the precise houses that surrounded him." Although the experience of staring at the cracks and features of one's room is familiar to anyone who has ever spent a sleepless night, Funes's "picturing" of the cracks and frames of the houses that surround him suggests a defensive reaction to the loosening of consciousness that occurs as one nears sleep. His first antidote to such an experience is to turn toward a tract of new houses, described as intact, unfurnished, and made of "homogeneous shadow," phantasmatic domiciles for the *homo domesticus* of a burgeoning modernity. His other method is to abandon the domestic and lacustrine structure of containment altogether and imagine himself "at the bottom of the river, rocked (and negated) by the current [*mecido y anulado por la corriente*]" (OC 1.524; CF 137). In this image, Funes imagines himself rocked like a child no longer (or not yet) driven by defensive mechanisms, and he allows his voracious consciousness to sink beneath a flow he does not control. This current can be thought of as a dimension of consciousness fundamentally different from the defensive modality that characterizes the waking mind, which in Funes's case embodies the fantasy of an "I" capable of housing a totalizing perception as well as its full recurrence. No lacustrine landscape painted on the window of the eye, this river is a force that alters and divides, like the Río de la Plata flowing through *las dos patrias*, exposing internalizing structures to an infinite and differential singularity that can never be unified or contained. "Singularity" in this sense would not involve a legitimating surname or sovereignty over one's own thoughts and perceptions, but a vulnerability to what comes (including from our own unconscious), which necessarily exceeds any and all unifying structures. Unlike nominalism, which Borges suggests is simply another version of the effort to "staunch . . . the flow of hours" ("History" OC 1.387; SNF 135), this sense of singularity is fundamentally temporal, and can be said to run beneath the story, and indeed beneath all of Borges's writing.

This distinction recalls Nietzsche's description of the relationship between life and forgetting that we considered at the beginning of this chapter. Funes can be seen as an extended portrait of the "extremest possible example of a man who did not possess the power of forgetting," and hence as a "gravedigger of the present" (Nietzsche, "On the Uses" 62). Yet in the crevices of the depiction of this extreme subject, whose magnanimous appetite seems to internalize everything it touches into an eternal present, there are suggestions of a different relationship to singularity that could transform the pronominal "I" from a structure of sovereignty, which Nietzsche associates with death, to a "plastic" engagement with loss, rupture, and difference, which is also a form of life or survival. For instance, Funes perceives transformation, including decay and decomposition — "the quiet advances of corruption, of tooth decay, of weariness" — including his own: "His own face in the mirror, his own hands, surprised him every time he saw them" (OC 1.524; CF 136).[36] Although on the one hand this seems to correspond to more entries in the "precise and combinatory eternity" of his mind ("History" OC 1.386; SNF 134), the fact that such transformation provokes surprise suggests that the very structure (or at least its corporeal frame) of the perceiving "I" is marked by change, that is, his lacustrine memory cannot contain itself. For the most part, however, engagement with loss, rupture, and difference is limited to the character of the narrator, that is, the one who does survive, and does so acknowledging his limits: his profane and limited memory, his tendency to distraction, his indirect and imperfect writing.

## *Bronze Monument*

The story ends with a scene that recalls Nietzsche's description of his encounter with the idea of the eternal recurrence. At the end of the nocturnal encounter between Funes and the narrator, the dawn breaks, and the narrator describes his vision of Funes thus: "I saw the face that belonged to the voice that had been talking all night long. Ireneo was nineteen, he had been born in 1868; he looked to me as monumental as bronze — older than Egypt, older than the prophecies and the pyramids" (OC 1.525; CF 137).[37] The figure of Funes towers before the narrator like the "vast pyramidal block" that Nietzsche describes coming upon while hiking in the lacustrine landscape of the Swiss Alps, which triggered the conception of the eternal recurrence: "Immortal the instant in which I engendered the eternal recurrence. For that instant I endure the Recurrence" (qtd. in "Doctrine" OC 1.415; SNF 119). The breaking of dawn is a pseudo-Zarathustrean moment in which the narrator sees Funes as more than human, and yet also not quite alive, as though a dream image that merges the pyramidal block of Nietzsche's eureka moment and the bronze death mask that was made of him after his death. Funes's abilities appear as the manifestation of a capacity for preservation and sanctity that is older than the pyramids, those lavish structures designed to preserve and protect that Nietzsche rejected as foundational structures of "Western" metaphysics.

What is older than such ancient ruins of architectural efforts to contain or resist time, or the discursive structures that anticipate what is to come, if not the retroactively conceived structure of the cosmographic origin story, which in the Judeo-Christian tradition is recounted in Genesis, and later retold in the Gospel of John? There, the divine Word (*verbo sagrado*) creates the world out of chaos and is free of any difference between word and thing. Irenaeus interpreted this generative Word as a structure that contained all time, an extreme form of prophecy and preservation. The narrator of "Funes the Memorious" thereby concludes his testimony of the only man on earth who had the right to utter the sacred word *remember* as though he were seeing the light in the embodiment of *logos* in a "maverick [*cimarrón*] and vernacular" superman (OC 1.519; CF 131), a logos that he acknowledges he cannot replicate, due to his fallible memory and writing. In this sense, the narrator can be seen to perform *another* version of Nietzsche's encounter with the eternal recurrence, a more Nietzschean one, in which the sedimented structure of the pyramidal block (the entombing figure of idealist capture) is exposed to the turns and returns of time and thought, an engendering that is more degenerative and disseminative — that is, a form of survival — than foundational.[38]

Furthermore, this "maverick and vernacular" wonder is set not in the Swiss Alps, "six thousand feet beyond men and time," but in the mind of a poor, fatherless, disabled teenager in rural nineteenth-century Río de la Plata. Funes's life is exposed to marginalization, ostracization, degradation, and historical change, including even the renaming of the town from Villa Independencia to the name of a British meat-packing company. His extraordinary mental capacities can be read as a fantasy — shared, at least partially (or not the least impartially) by the narrator, especially as he faced his own father's demise — of overcoming these conditions, preserving "*immediata et lucida fruitio rerum infinitarum*" in a salvational structure that is both pyramid and prophecy, and thereby dispelling the need for a paternal figure ("History" OC 1.384; SNF 132). This personal fantasy situated on the global periphery can be seen as an extension of the transhistorical, collective effort to deny or compensate for finitude and the lack of an authoritative "father" that goes by the name of metaphysics — a tradition that Nietzsche, who himself lost his father at a young age, spent his life critiquing.

In the story's final scene, such forms of compensation for finitude are joined by another, namely the ideal of a realization of logos through technology. There are allusions throughout the story to different forms of recording technology. When the narrator arrives at Funes's house, it is pitch black and he hears Funes's voice emanating from the darkness, seeming to him "incomprehensible and endless" (OC 1.521; CF 134). This description corresponds at once to the ancient foreignness of Pliny and the recent and equally alien invention of the phonograph, a technology that ostensibly captures and reproduces the voice "in good condition [*en buen estado*]," surpassing the indirectness of writing and ensuring the present's access to the past in the form of eternal returns (OC 1.521; CF 133). Visually, the darkness of the night of the "enormous dialogue" is broken only by "the momentary glow of [Funes's] cigarette" (OC 1.521, 522; CF 134), which can be seen as evoking the flickers at the beginning of a film reel, especially given the cinematic description of daybreak at the end of the story and the emergence of his face. Not only does his face tower like a bronzed movie star in a technicolor talkie (a new technology at the time of the story's writing), the peculiar syntax of its appearance — "I saw the face that belonged to the voice that had been talking all night long [*vi la cara de la voz que toda la noche había hablado*]" — evokes the way the recent advent of sound film linked voices to visual images.[39] New recording technologies, already mentioned as a possible mode of verification of Funes's extraordinary recall (OC 1.523; CF 135), can be seen as a screen onto which collective fantasies of atemporal capture and perfect repeatability are projected, like the more pedantic tradition of metaphysics and the ominous rise, in the years in which this scene is narrated (the late 1930s), of monumental leaders promoting national ideals of ahistorical totality and autogenesis.

# Chapter 6

# Unearthing the Archive

## "The Aleph," "The Zahir"

Like the stories discussed in the preceding chapters, "The Aleph" is structured around an ideal of sovereignty associated with the subject and some of its most exemplary extensions, including the house, family, nation — and, more pronounced in this case, love and technology, including the "technics" of memory and writing. This ideal culminates with the onto-theological premise of the Aleph, a point that contains all points, a site of absolute presence, which appears to constitute, *in nuce*, "that secret, hypothetical object whose name has been usurped by men but which no man has ever truly looked upon: the inconceivable universe" (OC 1.667; CF 284).

The story's epigraphs from Hamlet and Hobbes can be seen as indicating the fact that sovereignty, "usurped" under onto-theological or household names, always has a political dimension:

> O God, I could be bounded in a nutshell, and count myself a king of infinite space
> (*Hamlet* II, 2)
>
> But they will teach us that Eternity is the Standing still of the Present Time, a *Nunc-stans* (as the Schools call it); which neither they, nor any else understand, no more than they would a *Hic-stans* for an Infinite greatness of Place.
> (*Leviathan* IV, 46 [OC 1.658; CF 274])

The epigraph from Hobbes comes from part IV of *Leviathan*, which concerns the "kingdom of darkness," in which darkness refers to ignorance and misunderstanding. Hobbes attributes ignorance to superstition and misinterpretations of Scripture. As part of his effort to delineate between civil and religious sovereignty, he takes special issue with the question of time. He endeavors to distinguish between the "Kingdom of God," understood as something *to come*, and the temporal present of civil sovereignty. As a corollary of this, he insists on the distinction between the material and mortal nature of human existence and immortality, which, he says, pertains only to divine resurrection and not to present existence. He describes how the mishmash of misguided biblical exegesis and Aristotelian metaphysics, spawned in the convoluted new structure of the university, produced errors such as that of the eternal present or "standing still of the present time," a realm crowded by ghosts, magic, and hellfire, which is governed by priestly authority at the expense of civil governments. The *nunc stans* and all that is purported to inhabit it is, Hobbes avers, an effect of faulty hermeneutical skills in readers who cannot distinguish between a figural and literal or predicative sense. His intent, of course, is to conjure such intrusions from the human realm and defend an ideal of sovereignty in which the sovereign has infinite power over the finite lives of the governed.[1]

Hobbes purports to conjure ghosts, including the specter of eternity, from the exercise of governing mortals, who live in earthly time. Hamlet lives in earthly time, although, in response to the murderous usurpation of his family and kingdom, he fantasizes (articulated as a prayer to a God he is clearly not relying on) about withdrawing to a microcosmic universe in which he could reestablish his sovereignty, likely the nutshell of his own mind. Nevertheless — and this is left out of the epigraph or left latent in it — he has bad dreams: "Hamlet: O God, I could be bounded in a nutshell, and count myself a king of infinite space, were it not that I have bad dreams. Guildenstern: Which dreams, indeed, are ambition; for the very substance of the ambitious is merely the shadow of a dream." (Shakespeare, *Hamlet* Act 2, scene 2, 251–59). His interlocutor, Guildenstern, misunderstands his exclamation, assuming that his dreams reflect an intact desire to regain political sovereignty. However, Hamlet's description can be understood as referring to something more radically unsettling, namely the finitude that lies at the heart of all sovereignty.

"The Aleph" stages efforts to conjure away bad dreams associated with temporal existence and impose a unified sovereignty. Ghosts, including some of the same ones that afflicted early modern conceptions of sovereignty, haunt modern efforts to affirm certainty and control in the face of finitude. As though to stress the long and varied history behind these efforts, the story mingles numerous allusions, including Jewish mysticism and Dante's *Divine Comedy*. In a kind of dreamlike mash-up, the Hebrew-named Aleph is located in what can be understood as a purgatorial space between loss and possession, recalling the fact that, as Borges observes with an almost perverse satisfaction, Dante's poem describes the southern hemisphere as being occupied only by Mount Purgatory ("Nine Dantesque Essays" SNF 269). The two protagonists, Carlos Argentino Daneri and the narrator, named "Borges" (I will write his name with quotation marks to mark his fictional nature), perform similar but slightly different versions of subjective sovereignty. They can be thought of as doubles, rivals, guide and guided, like Virgil and Dante — or maybe all three. They are both writers and seekers, Ulysses-like Dantes pursuing different objectives.[2] In Argentino's case, it is literary recognition (he enjoyed the attentions of Beatriz, the story's love interest, along the way), in the narrator's case, it is Beatriz's attention (he is already a recognized writer).

## *Nutshell Sovereignty*

The story opens with the narrator reflecting on the death of his beloved, Beatriz Viterbo. The morning of her death is described as candescent (*candente*), glowing with heat, evoking the heat of summer in Buenos Aires as well as the heat of hell and the light of possible redemption that will flicker illusively throughout the story in various forms (OC 1.658; CF 274). This candescence is represented furthermore in the glow of cigarettes in the new advertisement that appears on the billboard at Constitution Plaza. The narrator recognizes the advertisement as a marker of infinite change, which he rejects, as a form of domination of his place in the ("inconceivable" [OC 1.667; CF 284]) universe: "the vast unceasing universe was already growing away from her, and . . . this change was but the first in an infinite series. *The universe may change, but I shall not*, thought I with melancholy vanity" (OC 1.658; CF 274). Following this reflection, he retreats from the burning pain of loss and the conflagration of change represented by the city's billboards to a kind of nutshell sovereignty where he believes that he has some control over his circumstances. He acknowledges that this retreat constitutes a peculiar improvement over his courtship of the living Beatriz, who, it turns out, was exasperated by his "futile devotion [*vana devoción*]": "now that she was dead, I could consecrate myself to her memory — without hope, but also without humiliation" (OC 1.658; CF 274).

The temple for this melancholic consecration ends up being Beatriz's family house, where her portraits, unchanged, continue to be displayed. Whereas during her lifetime, he brought "modest offerings" to the altar of her images (including books whose pages she never cut, much less read), after her death, he is free to indulge in acts of vain eroticism (*vanamente eróticos*) that seem to have more to do with himself than with her (OC 1.659; CF 275). The living room where her portraits are displayed is described as *abarrotada*, which means bursting, filled to the brim, and yet also implies a kind of prison, from *barra, barrote* (OC 1.658; CF 274).[3] The word suggests that the living room of the paternal house functions as a kind of reinforced archive that holds time still. In his melancholic refusal to accept change in the wake of Beatriz's death, the narrator locks himself into a timeless present, a *nunc stans* — one that is reminiscent of Dante's poetic elaboration of medieval Christian cosmology, crowned by the phantasm of another dead Beatriz (Beatrice). The narrator's archive remains intact for twelve years, during which he visits Beatriz's house annually on her birthday, to visit with her father (who is not described in the story) and her cousin, Carlos Argentino Daneri, who has similarly constructed an archive in relation to the family house.

## *A World in the Basement*

Carlos Argentino describes how, when he was a young child ("before I ever attended school"), someone said there was a world in the basement (OC 1.664;

CF 280). Although his aunt and uncle had declared the basement off-limits, he decides to explore it anyway, and falls (literally rolled, *rodé*) down the proscribed steps. When he opens his eyes, he sees what he calls the Aleph, "the place where, without admixture or confusion, all the places of the world, seen from every angle, coexist [*están*]" (OC 1.664; CF 280). He later learns that the description of a world in the basement referred to a trunk (perhaps referring to a "world" of old possessions, or artifacts and souvenirs of world travel), but he nevertheless clings to the discovery of this world, creating, in effect, his own *nunc stans*. In other words, Argentino's discovery of the Aleph corresponds to the epigraph from Hobbes, in which, due to an inability to distinguish predication from figure, which names its inability to name, sovereignty is haunted by ghosts that it does not recognize as such. It also corresponds to the epigraph from Hamlet, in that the Aleph becomes, for Argentino, a source of nutshell sovereignty, from which he banishes any "bad dreams." The fact that Argentino discovered the Aleph as a young child invites a psychological reading, in which he challenges the paternal (or in this case avuncular) prohibition and turns his own lack — his unfamiliarity with the "world" in the basement, and his subsequent discovery of the non-correspondence of language and objects — into a fetish or phantasm of absolute possession.[4] This can also be understood as a distorted version of the fable of Babel, in which the "forbidden steps" (*escalera vedada*) lead to a Godlike perspective.

Not understanding the tropic nature of language, Argentino gives it his own spin (*rodé*) and embraces metaphor as a proper noun. It is not, of course, coincidental that the object that he spins in such a way is "the world," a noun that is, perhaps, the exemplar of figuration, since what we tend to understand as world is hardly a single, stable thing. The very notion of world tends to ignore or disavow its own spinning nature, not to mention its vastness, variety, and mutability.[5] In his adult life, Argentino translates his secret childhood vision into other registers, beginning with his "*apologia* for modern man":

> "I picture him," he said with an animation that was rather unaccountable, "in his study, as though in the watchtower [*torre albarrana*] of a great city, surrounded by telephones, telegraphs, phonographs, the latest in radio-telephone and motion-picture and magic-lantern equipment, and glossaries and calendars and timetables and bulletins . . . ."
>
> He observed that for a man so equipped, the act of traveling was useless; our twentieth century had upended the fable of Muhammad and the mountain — mountains nowadays did in fact come to the modern Muhammad. (OC 1.659; CF 275–76, translation modified).

As though he were a mechanized being, as though technology — or maybe just the cognac he had just imbibed — spoke through him ("an animation that was rather unaccountable"), he describes a modern Muhammad, situated in a Babel-like watchtower, equipped with numerous devices of tele-technology capable of connecting, dominating, and standardizing time and space. Modern technology is celebrated as achieving the infantile or premodern ideals of totality and timelessness, bringing close that which is far in time or space, a secular version of the *nunc* and *hic stans* of the Hobbes quote. It is as if Argentino were proclaiming, like the narrator of Kafka's "On Building the Chinese Wall," that the Tower of Babel had at last been perfected, although the specific kind of tower that is mentioned, a *torre albarrana* ("watchtower"), is significantly different from the tower in the Biblical fable. The term *torre albarrana* refers to a tower that is located outside a walled fortification and derives from the Arabic word for foreign or outside (*al-barrana*). Unlike the Tower of Babel, which was a symbol of linguistic and social unity, the "tower" of technology can be understood as using disunity to protect unity, a prosthesis to supplement human sovereignty over the world.

## *Literary Extractivism*

Something about Argentino's description reminds the narrator of literature. He is apparently referring to the pomposity of his "vindication," but Argentino agrees that there is a similarity between tele-technology and literature, which he is developing in a poem that he has worked on for years, titled "The Earth" ("*La Tierra*"). The narrator describes it as an endeavor to "versify the entire planet," in which the verb conveys not only the formal quality of poetic verse, but also stresses a resonance between the turning or tropic dimension of poetic language and the roundness of the earth (OC 1.661; CF 277). In a sense, this lifelong poetic project can be seen as reversing Argentino's early fall down the stairs, or suturing together the turning movement of the fall with both the turn of phrase that led him to explore the basement and the sphere that he encountered there. If Argentino's discovery of the Aleph is understood as phantasmatic compensation for linguistic incompletion, and specifically the figural turn toward the object that it cannot possess outright, his poem can be seen as an anxious effort to master that which eluded him in his youth, using figural language to follow the turn of what is real or true, which he believes he possesses in the recesses of his house. His use of figural or poetic language to represent his own sovereign truth is similar in this sense to the *torre albarrana*, using that which is exposed to the other — the non-correspondence of word and object — to bolster the fortified sense of a total truth.

Although the narrator, "Borges," is acidly disparaging of Argentino's poem, there are suggestions that this lengthy section of the story is in fact an exercise in self-parody. The narrator's description pans Argentino's poem for traits that can be associated with Borges's own writing. He mentions erudite references ("to include within the space of four lines three erudite allusions spanning thirty centuries of dense literature" [OC 1.660; CF 276–77]); unusual adjectives, including neologisms ("Verbal ostentation was the perverse principle that had guided his revisions: where he had formerly written 'blue,' he now had 'azure,' 'cerulean,' and even 'bluish'" [OC 1.662; CF 279]); enumeration ("a technique whose lineage may be traced to Scripture — that is, enumeration, congeries, or conglobation" [OC 1.660; CF 276]); as well as a claim of humor ("truly *modern* art demands the balm of laughter, of *scherzo*" [OC 1.660; CF 277]). However, there are several details that distinguish this parody from his "real" work. As many critics have noted, enumeration is a common technique in Borges's work.[6] The enumeration of synonyms of enumeration in this story — "enumeration, congeries, or conglobation" — seems to pose the question of whether this technique adds up to a unifying "conglobation," whose root, *globo*, suggests the totalizing pretensions of Argentino's poem and its subterranean source, or leans more toward the side of a jumbled amassing (congeries), as it might be said to do throughout Borges's work. In a similar fashion, Argentino appears to include references as a way of claiming literary inheritance and legitimacy: He describes how he places poetic fathers (namely Homer and Hesiod) on the facade of the "dazzling new edifice" (*flamante edificio*, which can also mean burning building) that is his poem, and affirms that this earns (*granjea*) the approval of academic experts (OC 1.660; CF 276). Borges's allusions to other writers, on the other hand, can be understood as invoking an understanding of tradition that unsettles claims to originality, authority, or direct genealogy.

Of special significance in the context of the story, Argentino claims that his literary techniques may be extravagant, but underneath it all, his poem demonstrates "scientific rigor — 'because that broad garden of rhetorical devices, figures, charms, and graces will not tolerate a single detail that does not accord with its severe truthfulness'" (OC 1.663; CF 279). Argentino's description of scientific rigor insists that, like the imperial map in "On the Exactitude of Science," the representative quality of his poem corresponds, no matter how floridly, to the unadorned ground of truth. The metaphor of the poem as a garden, furthermore, resonates with other allusions to domestic space, including the description of his poem as a "dazzling new edifice" said to earn (*granjea*) academic approval, considering that the verb *granjear* derives from *granja*, farm or country property, and its tertiary and quaternary meanings involves caring for and making a profit from cultivated lands and possessions.[7]

Indeed, Argentino makes several associations between writing and economic value. In a particularly revealing analogy, he complains about literary critics, who "possess neither precious metals nor even the steam presses, laminators, and sulfuric acids needed for minting treasures, but who can *point out* to others the *precise location* of a treasure" (OC 1.662; CF 279). This analogy suggests that, in contrast to criticism, literary production constitutes a kind of extraction and minting of precious metals. Argentino gestures toward this analogy on several other occasions, as well, including a passing description of how a particular verse is "a good 24 karats [*muy subidos quilates*]" (OC 1.662; CF 278). In reference to his discovery of the Aleph, he reflects that "The child could not understand that he was given that privilege so that man might carve [*burilara*] out a poem" (OC 1.664; CF 281), in which the verb *burilar*, which means to carve metal, recalls the earlier analogy of minting money, and makes quite explicit that the resource that he is extracting is related to the Aleph.[8] When the narrator asks how the Aleph is visible in the darkness of the basement, Argentino responds, "Truth will not penetrate a recalcitrant understanding. If all the places of the world are within the Aleph, there too will be all stars, all lamps, all sources [*veneros*] of light" (OC 1.664; CF 281). The word *venero* means source or origin, and also, in the context of mining, it refers to the veins or concentrations of valued resources.[9] The resonance between illumination and buried precious metals, both common figures for truth, suggests that the Aleph, buried in the basement of Argentino's family home, constitutes a source of truth that grounds his florid poem-garden, which is also a form of cultivation or production of exchangeable currency.

## *Inalienable Aleph*

In a dramatic moment of the story — which is relayed over the telephone, as if to stress the vulnerability of technological connectivity — Argentino tells the narrator that the proprietors of the neighboring café, Zunino and Zungri, have threatened to raze his house so as to expand their business. He blusters that his house is "*indispensable*" (another word that has an economic connotation) because there is an Aleph in the basement that he needs to complete his poem (OC 1.664; CF 280). Before he mentions the Aleph, the narrator is sympathetic to his defense of his domestic sovereignty, because his own nutshell sovereignty is rooted in the house, as well.

The mention of the Aleph, however, disrupts the tele-communicative connection, so to speak, since the narrator has no idea what he is talking about. Argentino's claim to ownership of the Aleph — "*It's mine, it's mine* . . . Lawbook in hand, Zunni will prove that my Aleph is *inalienable*" — cannot be shared, since Argentino's footing in the *torre albarrana* of his mind appears to be firmly outside the precinct of shared reason (OC 1.664; CF 280–81). The narrator hangs up and hurries over — "inmediatamente," that is, without mediation, distance, or delay — to see in person what Argentino is talking about.

Before discussing the narrator's arrival and experience of the Aleph, I want to comment on the ostensibly marginal details of the threat to Argentino's house. The characters Zunino and Zungri are often overlooked in the lead-up to the viewing of the Aleph, understandably enough, but, like other glimpses of modernization in Borges's stories (between the buildings in "The South," for instance, and toward the east in "Funes the Memorious"), they indicate a new and encroaching register of sovereignty that is both similar to, and slightly different from, the figure of totality explored in the story.[10] Zunino and Zungri are first mentioned when Argentino invites the narrator to the new neighborhood café, developed by Zunino and Zungri, who are also the owners of his family house. Argentino displays a pride in this new business almost as though it were an extension of his house, or at least a sign of progress (*progresismo*) that serves to level the differences between his and the neighborhoods of the established elites ("it must be that you recognize that this place is on a par with the most elevated heights of Flores" [OC 1.662; CF 278]). In other words, he views the architectural modernization of his neighborhood as similar to modern technology in its ability to reduce or erase distance and difference, even while reaffirming its own distinction.

He theatrically admires ("fingió asombrarse de") an aspect of the café's lighting, even though the narrator assumes he has already seen it. This detail suggests a commonality with his family home, which harbors "all sources of light" in its depths; that is, his false astoundment (*asombrarse* comes from the word *sombra*, shadow — he is cast into the shadow of surprise by the light fixture) performs a claim to truth that he shares with his landlords. The narrator overhears other café patrons talking excitedly about the money invested by Zunino and Zungri in the establishment, "the sums invested . . . without a second's haggling [*las sumas invertidas sin regatear*]." As with his family house and its hidden resource, the modern café is distinguished by light and wealth, although in this case the wealth is not extracted but invested, marking a change from an old economic model based on territorial sovereignty and resource extraction to a new one of capital investment.

Furthermore, Zunino and Zungri's investments enact a kind of turning (*in-vertir*) that is similar to Argentino's "versification," although the detail that theirs is an investment without bargaining may mark an important difference. We can understand the restitutive efforts through which Argentino has endeavored to transform his childhood misunderstanding of figural language by cultivating an overgrown garden of tropes that does not "tolerate a single detail that does not accord with its severe truthfulness" as a kind of bargaining or exchange, as well as, perhaps, his relentless substitution of adjectives in the effort to haggle down to a truer description of his objects: "where he had formerly written 'blue,' he now had 'azure,' 'cerulean,' and even 'bluish.'" (OC 1.662–63; CF 279). But what I think is most suggestive is that embedded in the etymology of *regatear*, as indeed in that of the English "bargain," is the sense of hiding something (OC 1.662; CF 278).[11] In other words, the ostentation of Zunino and Zungri's new café-bar turns around an economy that is out in the open, without a secret haggling over limits; its light fixtures and value are there for all to see. On the other hand, Argentino's source of value is hidden; his florid tropes are visible, but the putative source of truth that underlies them is not.

As I have already mentioned, Argentino vows to resist their "unlimited" expansionism, which threatens the ground of his domestic sovereignty, with the law:

> Dejectedly and angrily he stammered out that that now unstoppable pair [*esos ya ilimitados*] Zunino and Zungri, under the pretext of expanding their already enormous café [*desaforada confitería*], were going to tear down his house. "The house of

> my parents, my house, the old and deeply rooted [*inveterada*] house on Calle Garay!" he repeated, perhaps drowning his grief in the melodiousness of the phrase . . . "*It's mine, it's mine* . . . Zunino and Zungri shall never take it from me — never, *never*! Lawbook in hand, Zunni will prove that my Aleph is *inalienable* [*inajenable*]." (OC 1.663–64; CF 280–81, translation modified)

He will use the law to fight that which is outside the law — *desaforada* reinforces the sense of limitlessness (*ilimitados*), but also connotes a sense of operating beyond jurisdiction — without understanding that the law is on their side, as suggested by the alliterative resonance of the lawyer Zunni's name with the café proprietors, and also by the inescapable fact that, for whatever reason, Zunino and Zungri already own Argentino's family home. In other words, although Argentino claims that the Aleph is inalienably his, it is, in fact, undeniably strange or foreign (*ajeno*). The tension over the claim to territorial sovereignty can be understood both historically, as relating to the tension between nationalism and expropriation related to capitalist expansionism, and also as an intrinsic foreignness that exceeds all borders, including the subjective, the domestic, and the national.

## *Seeing and Being*

Argentino calls the narrator "Borges" in as an arbiter, perhaps since as an already established writer, his authority may lend some weight in his effort to defend the inalienable source (origin, originality) of Argentino's writing. When the narrator arrives at Argentino's house, he is asked to wait, and, as he has for the twelve years since Beatriz's death, he waits in the *abarrotada* living room and looks at the photographic portraits of Beatriz. Out of what he calls a "desperation of tenderness," he approaches the large "*intemporal*" portrait of her on the piano and says, "Beatriz, Beatriz Elena, Beatriz Elena Viterbo . . . Beloved Beatriz, Beatriz lost forever — it's me, it's me, Borges" (OC 1.665; CF 281). Just as at the beginning of the story he declares that he will not change despite changes in the universe, as represented by the cigarette billboards that are updated on the day of Beatriz's death, here he repeats the sentiment in the face of the threat of demolition of the archival space of melancholic ritual that affirms and reinforces his nutshell sovereignty. The narrator's assertion that he is himself, he is Borges, contrasts with the multiple iterations of the name of Beatriz, who is, as he acknowledges, lost forever — he is I, he is Borges, whereas she is "Beatriz, Beatriz Elena, Beatriz Elena Viterbo . . . Beloved Beatriz, Beatriz lost forever." The almost liturgical repetition of her name emphasizes the sound "Be," which is also reinforced by the initials of her first and middle name, BE, which resonates with the first two letters of her last name, "Vi," which means "I saw" in Spanish (and is also homophonic with the

English "be"). In other words, in a twist on the Berkeleian premise that "being is perceiving" (*esse est percipi*), his own present being is reflected in the portrait of the dead Beatriz, the archival preservation of that which is lost.

His wait is due to the fact that Argentino is in the basement, which the maid understands to be a photographic darkroom, explaining that "Sr. Daneri [*el niño*] was in the cellar, as he always was, developing [*revelando*] photographs" (OC 1.665; CF 281). This apparent misinterpretation is, in fact, quite apt. Her description of the middle-aged Argentino as a child astutely connects his spatial descent to the basement to a temporal return to childhood (via a spatio-temporal descent to his subconscious), related to his infantile confusion over the nature of language and his subsequent turn to literature as a space where he can manage its deficiencies, rooting its tropic turns in the ground of truth, which provides "all sources of light" (OC 1.664; CF 281). His descent to the basement, like Dante's descent to hell, furthermore, resolves in "revelation" (the Spanish word for developing film) and a kind of light writing (photo-graphy), whereby language does not provoke clumsy falls into darkness, but rather serves as an inert medium for the light of truth. Such revelation constitutes a kind of ideal production of being through perception (*esse* as *percipi*), thanks to a suturing of difference and distance (both temporal and spatial), like the narrator's idealization of Beatriz's photographs and Argentino's idealization of modern technology.

When Argentino arrives, his description of the Aleph reiterates the figure of revelation in relation to the mystical registers of Kabbalah and alchemy, structures of belief that involve an appeal to the human form as microcosm for the universe, as well as an uncovering of an absolute truth or value from base matter (the metallurgical dimension of alchemy resonates, furthermore, with the motif of value extraction from the Aleph). Borges's characteristic use of bathos is in full display here, since the lofty ideal of a definitive unveiling is situated in the rodent-filled darkness of the basement and described in Argentino's alternately folksy and pretentious diction. His description of the method for viewing the Aleph effectively repeats his childhood experience in a deliberate fashion, as the controlled fall of lying down just so, experiencing fear (in this case of rodents), and then, after a short pause, seeing the Aleph.

Before leading him to the basement, Argentino gives the narrator a glass of the Argentine cognac ("A glass of pseudocognac [*seudo coñac*]") that the narrator had brought to the house earlier that year (OC 1.665; CF 281). Argentino calls the cognac false (*pseudo*) because it is produced in Argentina, rather than the eponymous, hence legitimate source, the Cognac region of France. He deems it "interesting" (OC 1.659; CF 275), perhaps indicating the interest that he seeks to extract from the apparatuses of totality that promise to surpass old grounds and models of legitimacy. The fact that his first taste of the *coñac* sets off his exaltation of modern technology earlier in the story, and he calls for a cup of it before leading the narrator to the basement to see the Aleph, suggests that there is a connection between it and the vision of totality associated with both modern technology and the Aleph. It is perhaps his perception that domestic *coñac* can pass for French cognac that inspires his panegyric to transmissibility, connectivity, and communicability in his "vindication of modern Man." It can perhaps be thought of as a "spirit" of translatability, which overrides differences and distances without remainder.

The spirit of translatability culminates in the mystical apparition of connectivity that is the Aleph, a point "that contain[s] all points" (OC 1.664; CF 280). This apparition can be understood not only as a mystical version of technology, but also as a fictionalized version of idealism, which, as Borges says in "Avatars of the Tortoise," produces the "world" as "hallucinatory" in which one's perceptions are taken for reality (OC 1.273; L 208 [see my discussion of this in the next chapter]). In "Avatars of the Tortoise," such a hallucinatory understanding is compared to phantasmagoria, which resonates with Argentino's evocation of magic lanterns and cinema, among other devices of modern connectivity and reproducibility that are said to bring the world to Mohammed. However, in "The Aleph," "Muhammad" or the secular-prophetic "modern Man" is not a neutral base of terrestrial convergence, but an arrogant and fallible character with a fair amount of baggage stashed in his basement. Among other things stored under the surface of Argentino's consciousness is his childhood trauma of discovering that the fact that the word "world" did not actually mean "the whole world," and his defensive hallucination that sutured this disjuncture, in which, among the bottles, bags, and perhaps a trunk, he finds a full receptacle, the world contained in a point, which he subsequently transcribes into a poetic versification of the earth, with which he seeks to translate the turnings of both language and world.

When the narrator follows Argentino to the basement, he looks around for the trunk that figuratively contained the world, as though archaeologically searching for the source of Argentino's childhood confusion. He sees only empty bottles and bags, which implies that the basement is a space of discarded containers for things, including, perhaps, outgrown perceptions and understanding (OC 1.665; CF 282). He has a sudden fear that, Poe-like, Argentino has trapped him in a pit after feeding him poison (OC 1.666; CF 282). The idea of poison, of course, refers to the cognac, which, like the Platonic *pharmakon*, bears a slippery linguistic difference in its recesses, of the sort that Argentino has spent his adult life denying. The pharmakon's slippage includes the meanings of both poison and remedy, implying perhaps that what works for Argentino as a remedy may constitute a poison for the narrator. Furthermore, this poison/remedy (*cognac/coñac*, or the virgule between the two) concerns writing, which is a primary point of difference between the two men. Writing for Argentino is a remedy, what I have been calling a suturing of difference and disjuncture, although it is a remedy concocted as a response to a perceived poisonous effect of language, in which words do not mean what they appear to say and the world is not where it is said to be, cannot be re-presented, and may not be "present" at all (*hic* or *nunc stans*).

## *Unearthing the Archive*

In the damp, dark basement, contemplating the underside of Argentino's sanity amidst the empty containers of his various remedies, the narrator descends to his own depths, which he tries to distinguish from those of his host's ("I felt a vague discomfort, which I tried to attribute to my rigidity, not to the operation of a narcotic" [OC 1.666; CF 282]). This is when he sees the Aleph. In contrast to Argentino's reaction of suturing a world — although it is unclear whether the Aleph is the same for both, if indeed it is anything (external) at all — the vision, which includes the remnants and cryptic containers of his own psychic basement, provokes the narrator to de-suture the atemporal archive he created after Beatriz's death to offset the changing universe.

Whereas for Argentino writing about the Aleph constitutes a pharmacological remedy, a seamless mode of converting the "world" that he extracts from his basement into a coin-like poem, for the narrator it is a source of desperation. He begins his account thus: "I come now to the ineffable center of my tale; it is here that a writer's hopelessness begins [*Arribo, ahora, al inefable centro de mi relato. Empieza, aquí, mi desesperación de escritor*]" (OC 1.666; CF 282). The acknowledgment of the limited nature of language before an extraordinary vision is a common conceit in literature, including the end of the *Divine Comedy*, in which the narrator Dante mentions every few cantos that he cannot possibly do justice to the divine radiance that he is beholding (he does not have so many concerns as he slogs through the horrors of hell). Although the scene of the narrator's viewing of the Aleph evokes the *Divine Comedy* in a jumbled and profane way, there is an important difference. Whereas the narrator Dante struggles to convey divine glory, hence, using language as slippery supplement to the unquestioned One, for the narrator "Borges," the impossibility of adequately describing the Aleph paradoxically reveals the intrinsic dis-unity that underlies the hallucinatory projection of unity.

What does the narrator see when he sees the Aleph? It is probably best not to reduce it to a single interpretation, since it is, precisely, not single. Moreiras describes the vision of the small iridescent sphere, described several times as a "point," as a prick or punctum in which the narrator encounters "the real": "It is a punctum, in the Latinate sense that Barthes emphasized: a place in which the trace of presence is painfully felt as a lack that convokes presence, a site of mourning, a private place" (Moreiras, *Tercer espacio* 140, translation mine). The vision certainly seems to confront the narrator with something beyond his earlier resolve to resist the "vast unceasing universe" through an archival structure contained by Beatriz's family home and anchored by her atemporal photographs (OC 1.658; CF 274). What he sees is an underside of those portraits and his resolve to resist change, or rather, he perceives the ways in which the "vast unceasing universe" is part of him and he part of it. Far from the static photographs of the above-ground archive, this subterranean space is infinitely finite. From the "populous sea" to "all the ants of the earth," it is a tempestuous pullulation of images, which he can only recount in snatches in an exceedingly long sentence punctuated by the repetition of the word *vi* ("I saw") (OC 1.666; CF 283).[12]

What he sees does not reflect him, his own *be*-ing, as it did with his earlier apostrophe to Beatriz (*Vi*-terbo). On the contrary, like a fun-house mirror, he sees "all the mirrors on the planet (and none of them reflect[ed] me)" (OC 1.666; CF 283). Each thing, furthermore — and the example given is a mirror's glass — is infinite things, because, he says, "I could clearly see it from every point in the cosmos [*desde todos los puntos del universo*]" (OC 1.666; CF 283). Reflection gives way to refraction, exploding any ground of subjective comprehension or objective structure. Indeed, any stable sense of ground recedes into the soft spaces of memory like an Escher drawing: He sees floor tiles of different houses that he remembers, presumably from different times of his life ("[I] saw [*vi*] in a rear courtyard on Calle Soler the same tiles I'd seen twenty years before in the entryway of a house in Fray Bentos" [OC 1.667; CF 283]), and a plot of earth where a tree used to be ("[I] saw a circle of dry soil within a sidewalk where there had once been a tree"). He sees efforts to represent the world, including a globe, which is situated in a cabinet between two mirrors, its spatial representation both contained and exploded; and a volume of Pliny's *Natural History*, of which he can see every letter on every page, resulting in a totalizing jumble reminiscent of the library of Babel.[13] He sees scenes from global catastrophes, including London as a broken labyrinth (an imperial seat fractured into uncertain pathways), and survivors of a battle writing postcards, shattered mirrors from the front of global destruction (these oneiric images providing a kind of shattered reflection of the destruction taking place during the story's composition during the 1940s).

Amidst the shards of efforts to exert sovereignty over self and world, he sees scenes of his love life: his desire for a woman with "violent" hair, a "haughty" body, and a cancer in her breast — like a dream image of inaccessible love, as though an inversion of the Petrarchan blazon, which enumerates parts of the beloved's body like so many (possessable) riches (OC 1.667; CF 283). This glimpse of inaccessible desire is followed by the appearance of hidden recesses that reinforce that inaccessibility, in the form of "obscene" and "detailed" letters that Beatriz had written to Argentino, stashed in a desk drawer.[14] Like the mirrors that do not reflect the viewer, these letters unsettle any sense of the narrator's self-sovereignty: The *letra* (handwriting or letter) of these letters addressed to another make him, and the archival structure in which he barricaded himself, tremble ("the handwriting [*la letra*] made me tremble"). These cryptic missives lurking beneath the consecrated memories of an unrequited love give way to Beatriz's sepulcher and its decayed contents ("[I] saw the horrendous remains of what had once, deliciously, been Beatriz Viterbo"), and the incessant change that he is ultimately unable to exclude or protect against: "[I] saw the circulation of my dark blood . . . the alterations of death . . . [I] saw my face and my viscera, [I] saw your face, and I felt dizzy, and I wept, because my eyes had seen that secret, hypothetical [*conjetural*] object whose name has been usurped by men but which no man has ever truly looked upon: the inconceivable universe" (OC 1.667; CF 283–84).

The anaphoric repetition of the word *vi* (I saw) ends in a concluding statement that endeavors to syntactically tie up what he has just seen with the effect of affect and reason: "I wept, *because* . . . " (OC 1.667; CF 284). The gush of emotion may be a better response than the effort to reason, however, since the narrator has explained that normal syntactical or sequential language is not capable of grasping what he saw. This extremely long sentence, front-loaded by a stammering effort to gather some of it ("Something of it, though, I will capture" [OC 1.666; CF 283]) concludes by putting into question what it was that he saw, which he calls an object but also admits that it is a conjectural object, with the root *jacere* (throw) suggesting a relational action with an uncertain end more than a static thing-in-itself. There seems to be an implicit disjuncture between seeing, understanding, and representing, since this secret, conjectural object appears to be nothing less than a porthole onto "the inconceivable universe" (OC 1.666; CF 284). The word *inconceivable* (*inconcebible*) to describe an "infinity [*conjunto infinito*]" (conjunto can mean whole, but, etymologically, suggests something more like an ensemble or assemblage — that which is brought together) recalls Borges assertion in "Avatars of the Tortoise" that infinity ruins (*corrompe, desatina*) all concepts ( OC 1.666, 1.268; CF 282; L 202). What the narrator sees in the Aleph exceeds and unsettles any definitive sense of conceptual bringing-together. He slips into this clunky conclusion the fact that such inconceivability does not, however, prevent people — men — from trying to "usurp" it by claiming for it a name.

In the postscript of the story, the narrator speculates on how Argentino came up with the name of the Aleph. He reflects that for the Kabbalah, *Aleph*, the first letter of the Hebrew alphabet, "signifies the En Soph, the pure and unlimited godhead," and also that the letter has "the shape of a man pointing to the sky and the earth, to indicate that the lower world is the map and mirror of the higher" (OC 668; CF 285). This Kabbalistic belief in the capacity for human language to signify divine unity reflects a Babelic desire to overcome finitude and linguistic difference and deferral. The fact that *Aleph* is also the symbol for transfinite numbers, in which the total is no bigger than any of its parts, resonates with the Kabbalistic (and alchemical) belief in a microcosmic dimension of the individual human being. David Johnson points out that the letter *Aleph* is also the first letter of the Biblical words *anokhi*, "I," as in "I am God," and "I am," as in *Eyhey asher Eyhe*, I am that I am, or I will be what I will be (Johnson 180). Although these associations suggest a bridge between human comprehension and the absolute, Johnson notes that such an interpretation or translation is not universally accepted. He refers to Gershom Scholem's view that in the opening statement of the Ten Commandments (I am the Lord thy God), all that was initially heard was the sound of the Aleph, which was assumed to be the beginning of the word *anokhi*. Scholem writes, "to hear the Aleph is to hear next to nothing: it is the preparation for all audible language, but in itself conveys no determinate, specific meaning" (qtd. in Johnson 180). Johnson aptly describes this as a "stuttering at the origin," in which that which is presented as a foundation for faith is incomplete in itself and subject to interpretation, so that "what ought to be universal, univocal, is ruined by the singularity of its articulation" (Johnson 180).

Argentino's decision to give the name of Aleph to the vision in his basement makes him one of the men who usurp the name of the inconceivable universe, overriding such a "stuttering." After the narrator has cried over what he has seen in the "secret and conjectural object" of the Aleph, Argentino "jovially" (like Jove) affirms, "you'll never repay me for this revelation" (OC 1.667; CF 284). Like God, he descends from on high — although it is only the top of the basement stairs — to receive praise for his revelation, although he frames it not (only) as praise or admiration, but as an unpayable debt. This claim of the narrator's indebtedness reinforces the idea that Argentino sits on an invaluable treasure that he extracts and mints into literature, which exceeds the narrator's literary resources.

Distinct from Argentino's self-congratulatory claims of originality and ownership, the narrator performs something much closer to a stuttering at the origin. The repetition that structures his account of the Aleph is fundamentally different from Argentino's translative economics. The "vi . . . vi . . . vi," suggests a starting over, a chasing after the memory of what he saw, relating to the sense of the Aleph as a pro-blem ("the central problem . . . is irresolvable" [OC 1.666; CF 282]), from the Greek "throwing forward, ahead of, through." Whereas Argentino's experience of the Aleph and his poetic production can be seen as a defense mechanism devised to protect him from the trauma, first experienced as a young child, of language's non-arrival at "the world," in the narrator's experience of the Aleph, the defense mechanism that he had established in the wake of Beatriz's death breaks down, and he encounters the palimpsest of his psyche and the markers of mortality, including the illness and decomposition of Beatriz and his own face, blood, and guts, amidst the "vast unceasing universe" (OC 1.658; CF 274), which he cannot, in the end, escape. He encounters both finitude and the corrosive effects of infinity, which affect both the spherical globe, reflected infinitely in the mirrors, and the spherical Aleph, repeated infinitely in itself: the Aleph in the earth and the earth in the Aleph, and so on. His description, "[I] saw the Aleph from everywhere at once [*vi el Aleph, desde todos los puntos*]," indicates that the point seen from all points is not a single, all-encompassing point (OC 1.667; CF 283).

## *Hospitable Returns*

Perhaps because the vision that he experiences in Argentino's basement underscores the fact that "the vast unceasing universe" (OC 1.658; CF 274) changes perpetually, the narrator is willing to allow the Aleph and the house in which his defensive archive had been located to be destroyed. Or rather, it is not strictly a matter of will. When Argentino interrupts his viewing of the Aleph, the narrator responds, as if from some internal drawer of his psyche ("The indifference in my voice surprised me" [OC 1.667; CF 284]), as though he had seen nothing, which leads to the destruction of the house and its hidden Aleph. This, perhaps, is his "payment," in which he invokes the destructive, poisonous side of the pharmakon against the self-deluded remedies that both men have concocted in relation to the structure of the Viterbo-Argentino family house. As he takes his leave from Argentino, he thanks him for the "hospitality" of his basement — a word that, like the pharmakon, has a forked root that invokes both friend and enemy, welcome and hostility — and suggests that he seek remedy for his ills by leaving his house behind ("the country . . . was the very best medicine one could take" [OC 1.668; CF 284]), knowing full well that such departure marks a definitive end.

As the narrator returns to the streets of what he had just termed the "pernicious . . . metropolis" (as opposed to the hospitality of the house and the recuperative properties of the country), he says that for a time, "Out in the street, on the steps of the Constitución Station, in the subway, all the faces seemed familiar" (OC 1.668; CF 284). The double sense of the word *familiar* implies not only that he has already seen "all the faces" from the miraculous peephole of the Aleph, but also that they have been domesticated within figures of familiarity. It is interesting that the description of the city seems to repeat the description of his last visit to Argentino's house: He mentions stairs and the underground. The return to Constitución (constitution, furthermore, relates to the sense of a setting up, making firm, from Latin *con-statuere*), where Borges vowed at the beginning of the story to retreat from the changing universe, suggests that the entire story can be read as an elaboration of that retreat into a stabilizing structure of memory. In the end, however, he notes that after several days of extreme familiarity, cognition and recognition again become finite: "forgetfulness began to work in me again" (OC 1.668; CF 284), in which a structural porosity ("Our minds are permeable to forgetfulness" [OC 1.669; CF 286]) effects an unworking of domesticating figuration.

In the postscript we learn that Argentino's house has been demolished — not just a family house but an *inmueble*, a term that has both economic connotations, like property, and derives from the Latin root *immobilis*, which means immobile. In other words, the underground foundation for Argentino's dream of the world as immobile (*nunc* and *hic stans*) is destroyed. Its translation into poetry persists, however, and its minted value is recognized with a second-place prize in the national literary competition, while the narrator's work — titled *Los naipes del tahúr (The Gambler's Cards)*, indicating a different economy, one that is open to chance — does not receive a single vote. It is not Argentino's whole poem that is recognized, but selections of it, which are chosen and published by the *Editorial Procusto* as "Argentine pieces" (*trozos*), suggesting that literature conceived through a nationalist lens is, like the unfortunate victims of the mythical metalsmith Procrustes, stretched or cut to fit a preestablished frame (OC 1.668; CF 284). This dig at national literary preferences fictionalizes the 1942 Argentine literary competition, which passed over Borges's "The Garden of Forking Paths," noting that it did not sufficiently reflect Argentina, and which apparently inspired him to write "The Argentine

Writer and Tradition," in which he interrogates the relationship between writing and nationality (Spagnuolo 54–56). More important than the autobiographical element, however, is the resonance between nationalism and universalism, which is echoed in a footnote in "*Deutsches Requiem*" that describes Germany and its literature as the mirror of the world (OC 1.618; CF 230). In a similar way, the *Editorial Procusto* extracts sections pertaining to Argentina from "The Earth" (the title of Argentino's poetic project) as independent representatives of the whole.

## *Falsifying and Losing*

The narrator distinguishes himself from Argentino in several ways, primarily as a loser — of both Beatriz and the national literary prize — and in his acknowledgment of loss more generally, including the impossibility of mastering time and space, as well as the secret and inconceivable dimensions of himself. Although at the beginning of the story he entrenches himself in relation to a domesticating archival ritual that is intended to guard against the changing universe, his encounter with the Aleph leads him to accept that difference and change are fundamental parts of life itself, which presumably informs his decision to invite the Aleph's destruction and welcome its forgetting.

Nevertheless, at the end of the story, the narrator slides back into a longing for certainty and containment. He indulges in some odd speculations about the veracity of the Aleph. He first questions its name: "Did Carlos Argentino choose that name, or did he read it, *applied to another point at which all points converge*, in one of the innumerable texts revealed to him by the Aleph in the house?" (OC 1.669; CF 285). The latter hypothesis would suggest that the source of the name of an ab-solute source was derivative, characterized by finitude and deferral, the "point that contains all points" divided by another point.

Based on this thought, the narrator dismisses the Aleph in Argentino's house as a false one and introduces the idea that there is another, true Aleph. He bases this theory on the authority of a recovered manuscript penned by a representative of the British Empire (the convergence of the many in the one being central to the ideal of Empire), who dismisses a series of legendary objects that rely on vision as "mere optical instruments," and contrasts them with an Aleph that can be heard inside one of the columns of a mosque in Cairo: "The faithful who come to the Amr mosque in Cairo, know very well that the universe lies inside one of the stone columns that surround the central courtyard . . . No one, of course, can see it, but those who put their ear to the surface claim to hear, within a short time, the bustling rumor of it" (OC 1.669; CF 285). Although the narrator does not affirm that this other Aleph exists, his inclusion of the account at the end of his narration implies that he would like it to be true.

It recalls, furthermore, his earlier description of the telephone, in which he expresses his indignation at the fact that the telephonic receiver, from which "Beatriz's irrecoverable voice had once emerged might now be reduced to transmitting the futile . . . complaints" of Argentino (OC 1.663; CF 280). This remark reflects a belief that the *techne* of the telephone is capable of producing the unique presence of a voice, thereby reducing distance and difference, as Argentino says of the different forms of telecommunication and mechanical reproduction, indicating that the narrator is in fact much closer to his rival than he admits. Having realized that his reception of Beatriz's irrecuperable voice was even less successful than he was previously aware, the narrator now pins his hopes on the Aleph in the mosque column, whose phonocentric superiority, like a divine telephone, delivers the universe to the ears that approach it. Although its location in a mosque column suggests that it forms an integral part of a structure dedicated to the intemporal consecration of the proper, not unlike the foundation of a family house, a final comment in the quoted manuscript reflects that this structure includes an element foreign to its *re-ligio*. The manuscript ends with the observation that the mosque dates from the seventh century, but the columns came from pre-Islamic temples, since, as Ibn-Khaldun said, "In the republics founded by nomads, the attendance of foreigners is essential for all those things that bear upon masonry" (OC 1.669; CF 285–86). This incorporation of foreigners in the construction of the proper is like an inverted image of the *torre albarrana* that Argentino referred to in his celebration of tele-technology. Whereas the *torre albarrana* suggests that the idea of technology as that which reduces distance and difference is situated in foreign territory, outside the structure of the proper, the column in which the telephonic Aleph is located is itself of foreign origin vis-à-vis the structure of consecration that it upholds.

The final sentences of the story, in which the narrator contemplates whether such an Aleph exists, reveal the reason that he longs for such a device: "Our minds are permeable to forgetfulness; I myself am distorting [*falseando*] and losing, through the tragic erosion of the years, the features [*rasgos*] of Beatriz" (OC 1.669; CF 286). Our finite, porous, temporal minds constitute a foreign element or exteriority in every attempt to conceive the totality of the world, every effort to deny difference, distance, and time. The narrator closes with the acknowledgment that this internal foreign element results in an irreparable loss of his memory of the image of Beatriz, leaving intact his longing for phonological redemption in the form of the auditory Aleph, without placing too much stake in it.

Incidentally, "The Aleph" contains subtle but significant differences from its partner story, "The Zahir." The two stories feature small round objects that seem to approximate a connection to absolute knowledge, and which appear following the death of the narrators' unrequited love interests. Whereas the narrator of "The Aleph" creates an archive and ritual to protect his memories of Beatriz from the incessant changes of the universe, the narrator of "The Zahir" reflects that his beloved, Teodelina Villar, sought to dominate time through fashion, pursuing "perfection" through an assiduous attention to the shifting dictates of style, with the rigor of doctrinally determined ritual ("Teodelina Villar would make her entrances into orthodox places, at the orthodox hour, with orthodox adornments, and with orthodox world-weariness" [OC 1.630; CF 243]). At her wake, the narrator considers that Teodelina managed to achieve in death the perfection that she doggedly pursued throughout her life: "My thoughts were more or less these: No version of that face that had so disturbed me shall ever be as memorable as this one; really, since it could almost be the first, it ought to be the last. I left her lying stiff among the flowers, her contempt for the world growing every moment more perfect in death" (OC 1.631; CF 243). This defiance of time leaves its mark on him and, "Drunk with an almost impersonal piety," he buys a drink at a corner store and receives a small coin in exchange, an apparently normal twenty cent coin with the letters NT — recalling the word *ente*, or being — scratched into it (OC 1.631–32; CF 244, translation modified). The coin, which comes to be associated with the "superstition of the Zahir" (OC 1.634; CF 246), soon exercises a strange effect on him, triggering strings of associations that all seem to return to the same idea, just as his perambulations that night mysteriously lead him back to the corner store where he received the coin. The exchange of the coin for the memory of Teodelina's embalmed face sets up an analogy between memory (or more generally, the relationship between consciousness and the temporality of existence) and the structure of a closed economy, where representation returns full circle to the ground of value or meaning.

In addition to the apparent transformation of the memory of Teodelina into the Zahir, the association between memory and money is evoked in a story that the narrator writes in order to distract himself from the obsessive thoughts of the coin.[15] The story retells the Norse myth of Fafnir, a man metamorphized as a serpent who guards an infinite treasure, who soon will be killed by a sword named Gram (OC 1.633; CF 245). Moreiras astutely observes that this story within the story can be seen as representing the threat of writing (Gram) to the economic guarding of memory (*Tercer espacio* 143).

In "The Aleph," the description of Argentino's poetic production as a kind of minting of riches that he has extracted from the Aleph suggests that his writing aspires to resemble Fafnir's guarding of the treasure against a Gram-like threat. The narrator is like Fafnir with respect to Beatriz, but the Aleph seems to have a Gram-like effect on him, shattering his archival trove and leaving him "permeable to forgetfulness" (OC 1.669; CF 286). Indeed, the opposition between guardian and threat is blurred as his permeable memory "falsifies" Beatriz's features (*rasgos*) as though counterfeiting a coin face, distorting the intact and transmissible value it presumedly represents. Interestingly, the word *rasgo* primarily refers to physiognomic features, but it also connotes writing and derives from the verb *rasgar*, which signifies rupture or tearing ("Rasgo"), suggesting that any effort to fix singular features into a prosopopoeic face may always already be subject to a Gram-like threat.

Although the narrator of "The Zahir" tries to resist the coin's power by writing the fable of Fafnir and Gram, by the end of the story he is on the verge of succumbing to its closed economy, gradually losing the ability to perceive any *rasgos* other than those of the Zahir. In the story's final sentence he fantasizes that the loss of his mind may result in a return, indeed, he hopes for nothing less than the absolute return of divine redemption: "Perhaps by thinking about the Zahir unceasingly, I can manage to wear it away; perhaps behind the coin is God [*Quizá yo acabe por gastar el Zahir a fuerza de pensarlo y de repensarlo; quizá detrás de la moneda esté Dios*]" (OC 1.636; CF 249). The double play of *gastar*, which means both to spend and to wear away, implies that loss may lead to a kind of exchange, whereby the wearing away of the coin's *rasgos*, along with all other singular features of the world, may allow him to trade in singularity for divine knowledge and presence.

# Chapter 7

# Throwing the Race

## "Avatars of the Tortoise, "The Perpetual Race of Achilles and the Tortoise," "The Nothingness of Personality," "Death and the Compass"

Borges stages the tension between eternity and infinity throughout his work. Although the terms may seem synonymous, the former corresponds to unity and immutability, while the latter concerns uncontainable multiplicity and division, or infinite finitude. Sovereignty tends to appeal to eternity in its different modes, from Shih Huang Ti's efforts to erase China's past and protect its future with giant walls, to the ideal of absolute meaning sought by librarians and protected by anonymous officials in the Library of Babel, to the structure of order, whether personal, political, or combinations of the two, as depicted in "*Deutsches Requiem*," "The South," and "Funes the Memorious," among others. Such efforts seek to "usurp," in Borges's words, nothing less than the inconceivability of the universe and the "unlimited dimensions" of possibility ("The Aleph" OC 1.667, CF 284; "The Library of Babel" OC 2.502, CF 115). As we have seen, his works repeatedly explore how such "unlimited dimensions" cannot, in fact, be usurped or mastered, whether at the level of individual cognition, or social, political, or ideological control. Infinity, in other words, cannot be beat, as his recurrent invocations of Zeno's paradox of Achilles and the tortoise would seem to demonstrate. This chapter begins with a deep dive into two essays that Borges dedicated to this paradox, which I affirm need to be read *as* essays, which is to say, as nuanced and performative explorations of their subject. I then turn to consider how Borges connects the disruption of eternity to two extremes, the nature of individuality on the one hand, and law on the other.

### *Pursuing the Jewel of Conceptual Capture*

Borges dedicated two essays to Zeno's paradox of Achilles and the tortoise, and subsequently sprinkled references to Zeno throughout his work. What was it about Zeno's paradoxes that intrigued him so? The first sentence of "Avatars of the Tortoise" provides a clue: "There is a concept which corrupts and upsets all others [*el corruptor y el desatinador de los otros*]" ("Avatars" OC 1.268; L 202). Borges avers that this concept is not Evil, but the infinite. The distinction is emphasized through the use of the capital letter in the former term, *el Mal*, although the very fact of the distinction introduces a kind of association — indeed, the substantivized participles, "el corruptor y el desatinador de los otros," sounds a bit like Satan. But, Borges affirms, the infinite exceeds the ethical realm, understood as a schema to distinguish good from bad. Indeed, the infinite "upsets," or more specifically alters, ruins, and disturbs (*corromper, des-atinar*) any path toward certainty. Is it therefore an über-concept, a long shot that nevertheless wins the race, or does it also upset the racetrack and its own designation as concept? Borges's fascination with Zeno's paradox seems to stem from the fact that it stages this question in support of a foregone premise, namely that change cannot happen — the race of truth has always already been won — and yet, in order to do so, he leaves his runners midway on the track, perilously exposed to the unsettling influence of infinity. Moreiras observes that Borges presents Zeno's paradox as an "absolutely resisting instance of epistemic articulation," which, nevertheless, is paradoxically "reconceptualized . . . as epistemic truth" (*Exhaustion* 138). In his twin essays dedicated to this paradox, Borges traces some of the efforts by subsequent thinkers to close the gap and win the race of certainty. In what follows, I will consider how he questions such efforts and claims a role for aesthetics as a mode capable of indicating the impossibility of victory.

It is not lost on Borges that the paradox of Achilles and the tortoise was intended as a parable to prove the impossibility of change: "Its inventor, as is well known, was Zeno of Elea, disciple of Parmenides, who denied that anything could happen in the universe" ("The Perpetual Race of Achilles and the Tortoise" OC 1.257; SNF 43). Elsewhere Borges says of Parmenides, "he denies difference, denies multiplicity, denies time and makes of the intricate universe an immobile sphere" ("Nota Preliminar" 9, translation mine). Parmenides famously argued that the universe is characterized by a principle of unity and immobility, in contrast with his contemporary, Heraclitus, who sustained that change and difference were inevitable.[1] Heraclitus is a recurrent reference in Borges's work, but he is never (so far as I am aware) mentioned in direct reference to the recurrent mentions of Zeno. However, I want to suggest that the distinction between static unity and temporal change and disunity, associated with the ancient polemic between Parmenides and Heraclitus, underlies Borges's interest in the paradox of Achilles and the tortoise.

Moreover, Parmenides and Heraclitus are early representatives of a polemic that has persisted in different forms throughout history, between thinkers who believe that they have a firm grasp on the nature of the universe — "that the universe is, in some way, a cosmos and an order [*orden*]" ("Nota Preliminar" 9, translation mine) — and those that do not.[2] The description of "a cosmos and an order," published in 1945, resonates with other invocations of the word *order*, as I have described in earlier chapters, as well as with contemporary conflicts over world order. The etymology of the word *cosmos*, furthermore, also implies an imposition of order: It comes from the Greek *kosmos*, meaning "order, good order, orderly arrangement," and the verb *kosmein*, which primarily means to dispose or prepare, but includes military and political meanings of arranging troops for battle and establishing a government or regime.

Zeno's paradox of Achilles and the tortoise describes a footrace in which the tortoise has a head start on the fleet-footed warrior, who nevertheless cannot catch up with it, because when he runs ten meters, the tortoise runs one; "Achilles runs that meter, the tortoise runs a decimeter; Achilles runs that decimeter, the tortoise runs a centimeter; Achilles runs that centimeter, the tortoise, a millimeter; fleet-footed Achilles, the millimeter, the tortoise, a tenth of a millimeter, and so on to infinity" ("Avatars" OC 1.268; L 202–03). The scenario appears to have been concocted in order to demonstrate how the appearance of movement in reality gets nowhere, or in Borges's description, "the hero's course will be infinite and he will run forever" ("Perpetual Race" OC 1.258; SNF 44). Since infinite unity is always already there, the triumph is more that of the Parmenidean cosmos than the runner's (although the notion of an infinite trajectory is indeed intrinsic to the figure of heroism, which seeks to preserve an event, in conjunction with a person and a name, throughout history).

Borges delights in the fact that Zeno's "desperate persecution of both immobility and ecstasy" is based on the figure of infinity, which is more destabilizing — *desatinador* — than he seems to have realized ("Perpetual Race" OC 1.258; SNF 44). Far from achieving the ecstasy of immobility and unity, the infinite divisibility of the track implies an unsettling shrinking of both time and space: Achilles "will run forever, but he will give up before twelve meters, and his eternity will not see the end of twelve seconds . . . the runners diminishing, not only because of perspective but also because of the singular reduction required by their occupation of microscopic places" (OC 1.258; SNF 44). Intended to disprove the possibility of movement and change in support of the infinite One, the paradox sets up an absurd situation in which the runners not only do not advance, but also, along with their chances at "ecstatic" immobility, begin to disappear. This affects not only the runners but also the philosopher on the sidelines who has set up this race in the first place. As Achilles's eternity shrinks, so does Zeno's, along with the certainty that this impossible race proves an ecstatic immobility.

This defeat does not, however, discourage future philosophers from attempting the same course. On the contrary, it inspires a series of would-be heroes to try their hand at mastering the disruptive effects of infinity. Borges recounts some of these in what he dryly calls a "mobile history" and "biography" of infinity ("Avatars" OC 1.268; L 202). He describes a series of refutations, passing through fundamentally different philosophies, as well as religion and poetry, that grapple with the paradox of infinity articulated by Zeno. This biography of infinity includes several key names in the transhistorical polemic of whether the universe can be represented as "a cosmos and an order," with an emphasis on the singular articles (*a*, *an*), that is, whether the uni-verse turns around the One. Central to this is his description of Aristotle's use of the disruptive effects of infinity as described by Zeno to refute Plato's theory of universal forms. Aristotle argues that if we consider the idea of an eternal form that transcendentally grounds individual temporal appearances, we need a third category for thinking the relation between the two, and a fourth for thinking those three, and so on. Borges includes a footnote from Plato's *Parmenides* in which Plato argues in kaleidoscopic fashion that unity does indeed consist of many parts, but all the parts are one ("Plato expounds a very similar argument to demonstrate that the one is really many" ["Avatars" OC 1.270; L 204]). This gesture is repeated by Aquinas, who acknowledges the radically contingent nature of existence, but affirms nonetheless that God brings it all together. "Such is the cosmological proof; it is prefigured by Aristotle and Plato" ("Avatars" OC 1.271; L 205).

Nevertheless, Borges affirms that the question posed by Aristotle affects the very ability to posit such a cosmological premise: Who is to say that my ability to affirm a unified theory of the universe is not a *part* of a fundamentally contingent and multiple universe? Infinity unsettles all conceptual certainty. When we believe that we have engendered (*engendrado*) it in a conceptual casing, Borges posits that infinity "explodes and annihilates it," like a dragon emerging from its egg ("Perpetual Race" OC 1.261; SNF 47). He suggests that the possibility of a *regressus in infinitum* "is perhaps applicable to all subjects. To aesthetics: such and such a verse moves us for such and such a reason [*motivo*], such and such a reason for such and such a reason . . . To the problem of knowledge: cognition is recognition, but it is necessary to have known [*haber conocido*] in order to recognize, but cognition is recognition . . . " ("Avatars" OC 1.272; L 207). The intractability of infinity undermines any claim to authority or originality: unity cannot be unified, divinity cannot be absolute, aesthetic judgment exceeds subjective autonomy, critical judgment lacks firm ground. Although he calls this fundamental uncertainty a dialectic ("How can we evaluate this dialectic?"), it is important to note that there is no synthesis to resolve the division and divisibility of each affirmation, not even the notion of infinity. Infinity does not win the race or become a new principle. The participle *regressus* is misleading, suggesting a completed or total action, whereas the effects of infinity not only do not win the race, but, in fact, ensure that the race is unwinnable and ongoing.

"How can we evaluate this dialectic?" How do we judge the validity of our own propositions when we know they are subject to infinite divisibility, rather than guarantors of cosmological order? Like other thinkers throughout history who considered the idea of cosmological order "an error or a fiction of our partial knowledge" ("Nota preliminar" 9), Borges avers that "It is venturesome to think that a coordination of words (philosophies are nothing more than that) can resemble the universe very much" ("Avatars" OC 1.272; L 207). In a sense this can be seen as the big claim of these essays, although it is important to stress the way they stage its fictive and divisible nature. The construction of the above sentence can be seen as undermining its propositional nature, starting with the timid predication, "it is venturesome [*es aventurado*]," which implies both doubt and risk, in the sense of confronting that which arrives (L. *advenire*), implying something different from what is or what is already known. The parenthetical phrase divides the assertion like possibility infinitely divides the actual, and the sentence as a whole reminds us of the fictive and contingent nature of any effort to explain the universe, constructed out of linguistic units that bear little resemblance to it, much less constituting a reliable map or guide to its order.

At this point, Borges takes up the adventure that he proposes for himself, daring ("me atrevo," which Irving aptly translates as "I venture") to consider whether any "illustrious" coordination of words might come closer — "at least in an infinitesimal way" — to resembling the universe than any other ("Avatars" OC 1.272; L 207). The interjection suggests that even if one philosophical postulation were to resemble the universe more than any other, it is still not free from the corruptive influence of infinity, which would undermine its lead over the others, in what amounts to a philosophical version of Zeno's famous footrace.

Borges "ventures" that only in Schopenhauer's work has he "recognized some trait [*rasgo*] of the universe" ("Avatares" OC 1.272–73; L 207).[3] Although it might appear that the conclusion of this essay amounts to a full-fledged embrace of Schopenhauer's philosophy, and indeed has been read as such, careful inspection of this passage reveals that this "coordination of words" does not win the philosophical race or break free of the "dialectical" divisibility that conditions all understanding.

Like Borges does in these pages, Schopenhauer also confronted the radical contingency of existence, discarding the assurances provided by previous cosmological concepts.[4] However, Borges implies that he also establishes a ground for understanding based not on a map of the universe as a whole, but on the authority of the individual philosopher-subject and his powers of perception. Borges describes his philosophy as the "doctrine" — a word with distinct theological overtones — that "the world is a fabrication [*fábrica*] of the will." The word *fábrica* means both fabrication and factory, the former echoing divine creation, the latter stressing human construction and techne. This sense of onto-theological fabrication is then compared in the next few sentences with artistic creation: "Art — always — requires visible unrealities. Let it suffice for me to mention one: the metaphorical or numerous or carefully accidental diction of the interlocutors in a drama . . . Let us admit what all idealists admit: the hallucinatory nature [*carácter*] of the world. Let us do what no idealist has done: seek unrealities which confirm that nature. We shall find them, I believe, in the antinomies of Kant and in the dialectic of Zeno" ("Avatars" OC 1.273; L 207–08). The example of the theatrical dialogue appears incidental, but in fact it indicates a theatrical staging of the relationship between art and philosophy.

Following the dramatic pause delivered by the ellipsis, we can discern an encounter — metaphorical or numerous or carefully accidental — between an *us* ("Let *us* admit") and a *them,* while an *I* flickers in and out of the shadows like a stagehand. The topic of the dramatic dialogue is "the hallucinatory nature (or character) of the world." The OED defines *hallucinatory* as "The apparent perception (usually by sight or hearing) of an external object when no such object is actually present."[5] In its extreme form as caricatured by Borges, idealists take their understanding for reality, or as a fabrication of it. They believe that their illustrious coordinations of words resemble (*se parecen*) or even create the universe. The first-person plural appears to refer to artists, or those who create things that are not really there (such as this dramatic dialogue), but without the philosophical claim on reality. Borges's admission here of "what all idealists admit" does not support idealism so much as alter it, unmooring it from philosophical certainty and pushing it closer to realms such as art and (psychological) fantasy, which allow him to stress the contingencies and limitations of such "hallucinations."

He illustrates this with a reference to Novalis: "The greatest magician (Novalis has memorably written) would be the one who would cast over himself a spell so complete that he would take his own phantasmagorias as autonomous appearances. Would this not be our case?" ("Avatars" OC 1.273; L 208).[6] The term with which Novalis is perhaps most widely associated, magical idealism, would seem to be in line with the notion just described of taking one's understanding of the world for reality, with the magic seeming to be something like an aesthetic enhancement of philosophical conceptualization or a glorification of philosophy's ability to create. However, Novalis is more interesting than that. Christopher Warnes reads Novalis in light of Fredric Beiser's identification of a "struggle against subjectivism" within German Idealism. Warnes distinguishes Novalis's thought from "absolute idealism," associated primarily with Fichte, which is rooted in the subject's apprehension of the world. Novalis's notion of *magical* idealism, on the other hand, relying on a Romantic aesthetics of exposure to the unknown, is concerned with "undoing the antinomies between language and the world and between subject and object" (Warnes 488–89).[7] Far from endowing the philosophical subject with an unlimited and seamless power of creation, magical idealism undermines philosophical claims to the grounds of truth, including both the knowability of the world and the capacity for knowledge of the subject. The first-person plural in the Novalis quote, "would this not be our case?," is thereby already divided between one who sees himself as a magician believing in the autonomy of the phantasmagorias he has created, and one who, in observing this contradiction, does not.

The reference to phantasmagorias is particularly interesting in this context. Phantasmagoria describes a genre of horror theater, popular in the eighteenth century, in which ghosts and demons were projected onto walls or screens via magic lantern. The "magical" dimension of idealism in this anecdote is not so much an artistic enhancement of ideas, as an uncanny enlivening of the dead or supernatural. As part of his theatrical show, the magician-philosopher disavows the uncanny element and invites the spectators to take the unreal as real, the dead as alive. Since he has also bewitched himself, he has repressed his awareness of the technological mechanisms that he uses to produce this show. Philosophy tends to be conducted through the technology of language, rather than magic lantern, but the dependence on a prosthetic supplement is quite similar, including the articulation of the first-person pronoun as a ground for reality.

Borges follows Novalis's ironic question, "would this not be our case?," with a phantasmagorical projection that both mimics that of Novalis's magician and draws attention to its material support: "I conjecture that this is so. We (the undivided divinity operating within us) have dreamt the world. We have dreamt it as firm, mysterious, visible, ubiquitous in space and durable in time; but in its architecture we have allowed tenuous and eternal crevices of unreason which tell us it is false [*pero hemos consentido en su arquitectura tenues y eternos intersticios de sinrazón para saber que es falso*]" ("Avatars" OC 1.273; L 208). The theatrical declamation of the first-person plural — no longer divided between an *us* and a *them*, but now speaking as one, the royal *we* of a hero assured of his victory in the grand contest of understanding the world — expresses certainty in both itself and the eternal and ubiquitous truth of its oneiric projection of the world. Nevertheless, like Zeno's racetrack, the syntax of the declamation divides the very affirmation of unity, the parenthetical description of an undivided divinity dividing the first-person plural, and the repetition of the morpheme *div* reinforcing the divisions that the statement disavows: "We (the undivided divinity operating within us ) . . . " Another division appears at the end, when the same pronoun that affirms the eternal unity of both itself and the world that it dreams allows that there are gaps in that same world: "we have allowed [*consentido*] tenuous and eternal crevices [*intersticios*] of unreason which tell us it is false." The words *con-sentido* and *inter-sticio* imply a division of sense and standing, respectfully, and add to the acknowledgment that neither "we" nor "the world" that we dream is as integral — "firm, mysterious, visible, ubiquitous in space and durable in time" — as we would like to think.

Amidst the multiplicity of this histrionic dialogue, including an internal division that undermines the speaker's claim to indivisibility, it is hard to discern where Borges's own perspective lies. It is almost as if there is no room for any perspective other than the idealist one, an idealism that, furthermore, seems to take on political-theological overtones, decreeing both the unassailability of its own authority and of the cosmic order it ensures. Interestingly, in the polemic between those who believe in the possibility of affirming a general map of the universe and those who question it, the idealists fall in the latter camp. If individual perception fabricates the world, there can be no general and complete map of the universe, since the universe would change depending on the perspective. Nevertheless, the idealists — the bombastic Schopenhauer prime among them — effectively turn (*their*, that is, the final *Nosotros*) individual perception and their own "coordinations of words" into a generalizing ground. This is neatly parodied in "Tlön, Uqbar, Orbis Tertius," a phantasmagorical world created by idealists that rejects any kind of system, but which firmly establishes "the subject of knowledge" as "one and eternal" (Tlön" OC 1.469; CF 76). Indeed the "We" at the end of "Avatars of the Tortoise," resoundingly certain of the truth of its phantasmagorias, resembles the fictional personae of stories such as "The Library of Babel" and "The Lottery in Babylon."

However, as with those stories, the construct of authority is undermined by an excess it cannot contain. At the end of "Avatars of the Tortoise," another *we*, a divided and dividing *we*, is there to observe it. This *we* emerges from the other one, separate but connected, as indicated by the semi-colon and *pero* ("We have dreamt it as firm . . . ; but [*pero*] . . . we have allowed . . . "), stressing, perhaps, that in the instability of dreams we are never completely in possession of ourselves (OC 1.273; L 208). Despite the spell that we cast over ourselves that allows us to take our own projections as autonomous truth, there are cracks in the phantasmagorical setup that remind us that philosophical claims to truth are dependent on "coordination[s] of words," limited and contingent efforts to contain that which by nature cannot be contained, namely the unconditional and infinitely finite nature of existence.

This returns us to the earlier *we*, the *we* associated with art, which was distinguished from the *they* of idealist philosophy. Indeed, buried in the phantasmagorical conclusion of this essay, it is possible to discern the subtle articulation of a kind of thinking and writing that undermines onto-theological efforts to assert a "cosmos and an order" of the universe. This kind of thinking is associated with aesthetics, which traffics in unreality and thereby never claims to "resemble . . .. the universe." In Borges's hands, this aesthetic component calls attention to the technical apparatus of the philosophical phantasmagoria, including the finite and contingent nature of both language and the structure of the subject, amplifying hallucinatory glitches in the projected "ecstasy of immobility." Its ultimate objective, however, is not only to stress the incompleteness of epistemic articulation, to use Moreiras's term, but also the *fact* that things resist it — that the universe, including ourselves, exceeds and unsettles our efforts to explain it. Infinity is the name that Borges gives this excess, calling it a concept that evades conceptualization, as it "corrupts and upsets [alters, ruins, disturbs] all others" ("Avatars" OC 1.268; L 202).

Although infinity might make us think of inanimate cosmic matter and mathematical formulae, Borges repeatedly connects infinity to the nature of life. "The Perpetual Race of Achilles and the Tortoise" opens the association of Zeno's paradox with the figure of a jewel (*joya*), which is described as a "precious little thing, delicate though not necessarily fragile, easy to transport [*traslación*], translucency that can also be impenetrable, ageless flower" (OC 1.257; SNF 43). This description suggests something that endures without change, something that can be seen but not plumbed, something that should be mortal (that is, a flower) but is not. This tiny talisman of immutability, furthermore, is said to endure through both time and *traslación*, which can translate as both movement and translation. Borges says that the paradox's endurance through the ages makes it possible to "declare it immortal [*saludarla inmortal*]," literally greet as immortal, which is a translative speech act in which a mortal being is hailed as immortal, such as the moment of bestowing royalty.[8] The expression effectively forms its own paradox, since the act at once bestows a symbolic mantle and acknowledges the need for its bestowing. Furthermore, *saludar* is a form of greeting (or leave-taking) that involves a wish for health, which implies that health is not guaranteed. In this context, Borges's proposal to revive or literally relive Zeno's paradox — "Let us revive it once more [*vivámosla otra vez*]" — can be seen not as an innocent turn of phrase, but rather an affirmation that this supposedly immortal paradox is in fact intimately related to life.

The association with life is implied also by the fictional title "Biography of Infinity," which Borges mentions in "Avatars" as the title of a project that, ironically, (his) life does not allow him to complete: "life forbids me that hope" ("Avatars" OC 1.268; L 202). His reliving of Zeno's paradox through its "avatars," or repeated incarnations, can be seen as a kind of *traslación* that, far from confirming its immortality or merely enumerating its articulations through the ages, puts into movement the recurrent impulse to capture the nature of existence in immobile and translucent form. The "biography" is a "mobile history" of recurrent efforts to achieve the "ecstasy of immobility" of philosophical conceptualization. Perhaps we can think of this movement in relation to Heraclitus, such that the "perpetual race" names a perpetual coursing of change, rather than a racecourse to immobility.

At the end of "The Perpetual Race of Achilles and the Tortoise," life is named as a site where such coursing is felt, in tension with the idealized "ecstasy of immobility": "existence in a physical body, immobile permanence, the flow of an afternoon in life, are challenged by such an adventure [*aventura*]" ("Perpetual Race" OC 1.261; SNF 47).[9] The experience of standing still or of the creep or flow of clock or calendrical time is challenged by a different kind of flow, one that cannot stand still or be contained in a single physical body or period of time. As with its use in "Avatars of the Tortoise," the word *aventura* can be understood in relation to its etymological sense of exposure to what comes, which cannot be known beforehand. This adventure alarms a certain experience of life but is not antithetical to life itself. In fact, in "The Perpetual Race of Achilles and the Tortoise" it is described in terms of life, as well: "Such decomposition is effected by the mere word *infinite*, troubling word (and then concept) that we have recklessly engendered and that once accepted into a thought, explodes and kills it" ("Perpetual Race" OC 1.261, translation mine).[10] Infinity "decomposes" our very understanding of life, altering even our belief in our ability to (re)produce — to serve as origin or ground for the concepts we beget, including that of infinity. Such gem-like concepts seek to trap life, time, the universe, etc., like an insect in amber or a still-born egg, but infinity bursts out, killing this contained version of life and making room for a form of life that goes "outside of itself beyond return . . . [an] irreducible excess" (Derrida, quoted in Naas, *Plato* 119–20).

This sense of life as adventure, or unprotected exposure to what comes, is implied by the word *pullulation* in the peculiar conclusion of the essay. Like the histrionic end of "Avatars of the Tortoise," Borges concludes "The Perpetual Race of Achilles and the Tortoise" with a theatrical formulation that appears to grant the final word to idealism, but ultimately undermines that gesture: "Zeno is incontestable, unless we admit the ideality of space and time. If we accept idealism, if we accept the concrete growth of the perceived [*crecimiento concreto de lo percibido*], then we shall elude the *mise en abîme* of the paradox [*la pululación de abismos de la paradoja*]" ("Perpetual Race" OC 1.261; SNF 47). The coral-like "concrete growth of the perceived," a version of the world as "fabrication of the will," is presented as, effectively, winning the race set in motion by Zeno; and yet at the same time, its putative victory merely constitutes the most vivid phantasmagoria of absolute mastery, while "infinity" — that which resists absolute mastery — seeps through the structures conceived to contain it, pullulating in their interstices.[11]

## *The Race of Life*

One of the most important structures of phantasmagoric mastery is that of the subject, which Borges acerbically critiques in "The Nothingness of Personality," an essay that denounces the existence of an integral self, punctuated with the refrain, "There is no whole self [*No hay tal yo de conjunto*]."[12] In a remarkable passage, Borges writes that attempts to express "oneself and . . . the whole of life constitute a kind of race akin to Achilles's race with the tortoise: "A strenuous, panging dash between the prodding of time [*el envión del tiempo*] and man [*el hombre*], who, like Achilles in the illustrious conundrum formulated by Zeno of Elea, will always see himself in last place" (*Inquisiciones* 100; SNF 6–7). The affirmation of selfhood is described as a race with time that can never be won.[13] The figure associated with Achilles is described as "el hombre," which can be understood as "the man," that is, the runner who is trying to outpace "the prodding of time," but it also, as Esther Allen astutely translates, suggests Man in general, or an understanding of humanity based on the integrity of the classical subject, capable of knowing himself and the world. Like the description of "we" and "the world" at the end of "Avatars of the Tortoise," this man/Man pursues the "ecstasy of immobility," but is thwarted by time, described here as both a contender in the race and as a force that pushes the runners, and even conditions the course (the word translated as "prodding," *envión*, comes from *enviar*, sending or sending on one's way, derived from *via*, way). Borges describes such a pursuit in religious terms, as a quest for redemption ("the Calvary toward which idolaters of themselves are on a fatal course"), and describes literature as the quasi-secularized form that preaches it (*Inquisiciones* 100; SNF 6). However, he also frames this essay as a search for a different aesthetic, one that is not based on the metaphysical pursuit of subjective presence and representation. Rather than a literature that equates self-expression with outrunning time, and specifically, the time of life ("to try to express oneself and to want to express the whole of life are one and the same thing"), this essay proposes a mode of writing that acknowledges the inevitable defeat of the race against time, and which traces the entanglements of both life and time, rather than denying them. This is illustrated by an autobiographical section in which Borges describes how, in a symbolic moment of departure from Europe to Argentina, after a number of years away, he realizes that there can be no real return, either to another person (he describes wanting to bare his soul to his friend, and leave it with him, palpitating) or, by implication, to a home or place of origin (*Inquisiciones* 99; SNF 6). Against this quasi-erotic, quasi-sacrificial ideal of self-presence, a kind of personal Calvary, he is struck with the thought that "never would one full and absolute moment [*un instante pleno*], containing all the others, justify my life, that all of my instants would be provisional phases, annihilators of the past turned to face the future, and that beyond the episodic, the present, the circumstantial, we were nobody." That is, he realized that life was not a race against time to arrive at the present (the ecstasy of immobility in "un instante pleno"), but rather that the *enviones* of time are themselves the condition of possibility of life itself.

## *Infinite Dissymmetry*

"Death and the Compass" can be read as a version of the concerns associated with Zeno's paradoxes transposed into more modern and political registers. The story is constructed around a central antagonism and pursuit, which corresponds to a larger pursuit of political domination based on a structure of enmity, a symmetrical division in the race to assert a unified sense of order. A reference to Zeno at the end of the story suggests an alternative to this racetrack in which all roads purportedly lead to Rome.

In the prologue to *Artificios*, the volume in which it was published, Borges makes two important comments about the story. The first is that "in spite of the German and Scandinavian names," the story takes place in an oneiric Buenos Aires, and he proceeds to link placenames in "Death and the Compass" to real sites in Buenos Aires as well as to the fictional site of an event in "Tlön, Uqbar, Orbis Tertius" (OC 1.517; CF 129). The second is that he has imagined an amplification of the story in both time and space, in which vengeance would be inherited, that is, enmity would endure through time, and would extend to include the entire earth. Written in 1944, it is hard not to think of this as an allusion to the Second World War, including both its geographical scope, its violent refashioning of inherited hatred, and the ways in which its divisions were perpetuated in other parts of the globe, including Argentina. The use of French names to describe a "Buenos Aires of dreams" can perhaps be read as a jab at Argentina's neutrality during most of the war (until January 1944), and at the common pretension that Buenos Aires is the Paris of the Americas, which in the early 1940s meant something decidedly not neutral. Furthermore, the war was both distant and close, as I have already observed. The reference to German names, of which Scharlach's might be one, can be seen as strengthening this association, as can the allusion to "Tlön, Uqbar, Orbis Tertius," in which the idealist world described in that story is compared to "any symmetry . . . with an appearance of order," including Nazism and anti-Semitism (OC 1.473; CF

81). That "Death and the Compass" concerns the murder of Jews can be seen as clinching the association with Nazism, although the fact that Scharlach, the crime boss who is behind the murders, is himself Jewish might be said to complicate that a little.

The figure of enmity in the story is structured like a detective story. The detective genre always relates, ultimately, to efforts to impose a single, unified law of the land. The criminal is defined as someone who has transgressed this law, and needs to be either banished or killed, or made to submit to a judicial structure based on equivalence. Police logic is itself at times divided — Sherlock Holmes and Scotland Yard, for instance — but ultimately the internal differences are subsumed into the imposition of sovereignty: the independent detective who comes close to being an outlaw to solve the case slinks back into the shadows once order is restored. In "Death and the Compass," police logic is directed by the police commissioner, Treviranus, whose Roman-sounding name suggests that he is the ultimate guardian of legitimacy and order, a representative of the unifying structure of Rome against illegitimate pretenders. The story is set in a time in which the rule of a single law is not a given. The series of crimes occurs in a landscape in which there is more than one law, and law itself is embattled: the urban center, represented by the police, is surrounded by warlords (*caudillos*) that rule the periphery. The word *caudillo* harks back to nineteenth-century Argentina, when rural landowners fought to maintain territorial power against the drive to establish national unity in relation to universal ideals of law. The ongoing tensions depicted in the story between center and periphery, legitimate law and caudillo rule, can be understood as suggesting that despite the nineteenth-century victory of the former over the latter, the tensions are ongoing. In the story, they concern a fight for sovereignty over the city, and by extension, a place in modernity and a claim to its riches, whether monetary or symbolic.

The legacy of nineteenth-century tensions is symbolized by the color red, which served as a marker of allegiance to the leader of the Argentine caudillos, General Juan Manuel de Rosas, and is evident in both protagonists' names, Erik Lönnrot and Red Scharlach. The root of the former contains the word *rot*, German for red, and Scharlach's nickname is nothing other than *Red*, while his last name falls somewhere between the color scarlet and the name of the Shakespearean character Shylock.[14] In a story whose title announces death, the color red evokes blood, although it is not necessarily limited to the blood that flows out of a body after death, but also that which flows through the living, including that of the two protagonists, emphasizing a kind of virtual fraternity, or a shared experience of living, even in enmity. Nevertheless, enmity wins out as the logic of the land, in which both sides seek the other's blood as a key to their own victory, or at very least their survival. The word *red* also relates to the detective genre term, "red herring," referring to a false lead, not unlike the one that the tortoise has over Achilles. Furthermore, while following the red herrings that Scharlach uses as bait to lure his adversary, Lönnrot unwittingly falls into his net (in Spanish, *red*).

Once this entrapment is revealed, Scharlach explains that the elaborate ruse was designed as an act of revenge for a police sting led by Lönnrot, in which his brother was imprisoned, and he himself sustained a bullet wound. He managed to retreat to a villa south of the city to recuperate from his wound. During his convalescence, he entered a delirium dominated by symmetry, which was enhanced by his fever and the "maniacal" symmetries of the mansion, which includes a sculpture of Janus. The description of Scharlach's delirium suggests that the figure of symmetry is not just architectural, but legal, based on a Talionic principle of equivalence that structures the relationship between outlaws and the representatives of the law. In supposed exchange for a past crime or the lack of adherence to a single civic law, Lönnrot and the police attacked Scharlach and his brother, placing him in a prison that is described as quadrangular (*cárcel cuadrangular)*, and leaving Scharlach to recover in the "desolate symmetrical villa [*quinta*]" of Triste-le-Roy (OC 1.542; CF 154).

Although the quadrangular symmetry of the brother's punishment seems to dictate that he must avenge the wrong and attack the attacker, an obligation that is reflected in the dreamscape of the villa, the word *quinta* suggests that this place of convalescence could also mark the possibility of a break from logic of symmetry. The word, meaning "fifth," came to refer to the house and property of a large landowner, deriving from the fifth part of earnings paid by the peons living on the land. Hence it is a name that indicates a fundamental asymmetry of power and privilege built on a structure of equivalence. And nevertheless, this *quinta* lies in ruins on the border of a socio-political sphere in transformation. If *quintas* such as this one once represented the ground of power of a ruling class in Argentina, which relied on both a symmetrical structure of the law and an asymmetrical privilege, such a role has been lost, and, although caught between sovereign orders (law and outlaw) that both rely on symmetry, it can be seen as constituting a liminal space that might allow a departure from such symmetry. The fact that it lies to the south of the city, furthermore, evokes, as in "The South," an association with that which lies beneath consciousness and control, the domestic structures housing not a firm sense of identity but uncanniness and uncertainty.

Wounded by a police bullet, Scharlach agonized at the boundary of life and death in this *quinta* for nine days and nine nights.[15] From the depths of his fever, the outskirts of his consciousness responded with horror to the dominance of symmetry, personified by the statue of the two-faced Janus, but clearly related to the rein of duality and equivalence that structured his world: his brother's imprisonment in a "quadrangular prison" as punishment for an unnamed crime, and the presumed obligation to avenge it. He comes to hate symmetry so much that he perceives the symmetrical aspects of his own body as monstrous: "I came to feel that two eyes, two hands, two lungs are as monstrous as two faces" (OC 1.542; CF 154). His Irish caretaker presents Christianity as a path to salvation: "he would repeat, over and over, the goyim's saying [*sentencia*]: All roads lead to Rome. At night, my delirium would grow fat upon that metaphor: I sensed that the world was a labyrinth, impossible to escape — for all roads, even if they pretended to lead north or south, returned finally to Rome, which was also the quadrangular prison where my brother lay dying, and which was also the Villa [*quinta*] Triste-le-Roy" (OC 1.542; CF 154, translation modified). The word *sentencia*, as I discuss in chapter four, refers both to a semantic structure and theological-juridical finality. In the context of the conflict between law and outlaw, it takes on the latter resonance, and in Scharlach's state of delirium and vulnerability, prompted by his pharmacological caretaker, it takes on an absolute quality, absorbing all difference, including all dualities — North and South, law and outlaw, Jewish and Christian, ancient and modern, crime and revenge, sacrifice and salvation — into a single order, metonymically linked through the name of Rome. This sentence or verdict proclaims that there is no escape from this centripetally totalizing logic, no path that is not determined by its inevitable destination, which becomes a form of incarceration. Following Paul North's distinction between mazes and labyrinths (*The Problem of Distraction* 102), this carceral convergence corresponds not to a labyrinth, but to a maze, in the sense that the structure dictates an order that is observable from above, although not always discernible from the ground. Scharlach refuses his caretaker's effort to convert him to Christianity but appears to accept the inevitability of its structure. Swearing to multiple gods, including Janus ("I swore [*juré*] by the god that sees with two faces, and . . . all the gods of fever and mirrors"), he vows to weave a similar maze around the man who had incarcerated his brother (OC 1.542; CF 154–55). Since there seems to be no escape from the logic of equivalence and totality that his adversary thrust upon him with the imprisonment of his brother, he will simply turn this same structure against him. In this he resembles his namesake Shylock, who similarly became a villain by merely following the equivalential law of the land.

Although a vow (*juré*) implies a structure of exchange, similar to that of revenge, and the gods to which he vows appear to reflect the same syntax of divided sameness, which is to say, split unity, it is possible to discern a slight difference from the logic of totality conveyed by the *sentencia* pronounced by his caretaker. The god "that sees with two faces" can be seen as representing the apparent inescapability of symmetry, equivalence, and totality, especially during Scharlach's feverish recovery. However, Janus Bifrons is fundamentally different from the Christian monotheistic paradigm. Rather than a convergence of difference into a single political-theological order ("Rome"), Janus represents divergence and divisibility. He is a god of beginnings, passages, limits, and transitions, both spatial and temporal. Furthermore, the gods of fever and mirrors can be seen as introducing an element of distortion and difference, more evident in relation to fever, but also arguably present in mirrors, as well. Scharlach appears to buy into the logic of equivalence in his determination to exact revenge on Lönnrot, sentencing him to the same fate as his brother since it seems there is no escape from the "rectangular prison" that is the logic of equivalence and unity. At the same time, his vow — a message that might not arrive at its destination, a buy-in to an exchange that may not be reciprocated — can be seen as holding out hope of something different, a different kind of labyrinthine path than the one that leads to Rome.

As though a response from the gods of feverish mirrors, it is Lönnrot, trapped by Scharlach's web, who proposes such a different path:

> "There are three lines too many in your labyrinth," he said at last. "I know of a Greek labyrinth that is but one [*única*] straight line. So many philosophers have been lost upon that line that a mere detective might be pardoned if he became lost as well. When you hunt me down in another avatar of our lives, Scharlach, I suggest that you fake (or commit) one crime at A, a second crime at B, eight kilometers from A, then a third crime at C, four kilometers from A and B and halfway between them. Then wait for me at D, two kilometers from A and C, once again halfway between them. Kill me at D, as you are about to kill me at Triste-le-Roy." (OC 1.544; CF 156)

On the one hand, Lönnrot proposes a simple subtraction: instead of the four-pronged ruse that Scharlach used to catch Lönnrot, which reflects or doubles the "rectangular prison," only one line is needed (OC 1.542; CF 154). Although this sounds like a reduction and a convergence, akin to that of "all roads lead to Rome," since it evokes infinity, it is in fact the opposite. Although both Lönnrot and Scharlach seem to agree that it would be possible for a fatal encounter on that line, between A and C, the infinite divisibility of the line means that such a definitive end would be endlessly elusive, like Achilles's pursuit of the tortoise. The single line is not singular (*única*) in the sense of being unified or unifying, like the unifying, monotheistic order of "Rome." It is fundamentally divisible, involving a difference that recalls the personification of division in Janus, which does not unify difference in human form, but acknowledges that individual living beings, like the space and time they inhabit, are divided and divisible. The single line will not allow Scharlach to kill Lönnrot (again), but it does not erase their difference or antagonism, like Heraclitus's understanding that conflict is inevitable (*polemos*). Divisibility does, however, undermine the race for sovereignty, the pursuit of victory of one over the other, like the divided scepter described at the end of "The Perpetual Race of Achilles and the Tortoise" (OC 1.261; SNF 47).

The labyrinthine nature of the line that allows for infinity, rather than unity, has to do with undecidability, undermining the rule of symmetry and equivalence on which the figure of sovereignty is based. In distinction to the maze-like metaphor of all roads leading to Rome, which represents a mode of thinking that presumes a determinate end, the labyrinthine line requires an exposure to the unknown, without a predetermined solution. Although Lönnrot transposes Scharlach's scheme onto the line, including his own capture and death, the symmetrical battle between law and outlaw is "corrupt[ed] and upset" by the introduction of infinity ("Avatars" OC 1.268; L 202).

Scharlach agrees to meet Lönnrot again in this labyrinthine line, suggesting that he too wishes there were an escape from the "quadrangular prison" of law and vengeance, although it seems that he is inclined to first settle his account with Lönnrot, who started the carceral logic when he imprisoned Scharlach's brother (OC 1.542; CF 154). On an interesting etymological note, *cárcel* derives from the Latin *carcere*, which means prison but also the starting area of a race. Is it a stretch to see the incarceration that sets off the elaborate act of revenge in this story like the starting gun of a race between two adversaries straining to win on the same track? I even wonder if there is room to imagine the final sentences of the story, "He stepped back [*Retrocedió*] a few steps. Then, very carefully, he fired," as suggesting the possibility not of a conclusion to the race, but a different beginning (OC 1.544; CF 156). The detail of backing up to shoot — after making a promise, furthermore — suggests that Scharlach's actions are already taking place within a line (pro-mise, *retro-cedió*). The adverb *carefully* (*cuidadosamente*) that modifies the shot implies calculation, a final punctuation to the carefully mapped revenge, but by Scharlach's own admission, the end is not definitive. The story ends before the shot finds its mark, hence it is still going, as can also be said of the shot that Lönnrot landed in Scharlach's abdomen, although that shot appears to be carrying out the *sentencia* of the law of symmetry and exchange, a rebound of the imposition of an imperial police logic that tries to subjugate all directions of the city to a single order. Scharlach's promise that there will be another encounter in the infinite labyrinth of a line leaves open the possibility of a different relationship to difference, a mode of shaping meaning and relation that does not end in a battle for sovereignty, that is, a different kind of *sentence*.[16]

Behind this possibility is the force of affect, which underlies both the race for sovereignty and its apparent victory. The name of the *quinta*, Triste-le-Roy, invokes the sadness of the sovereign, a quality that is accentuated by Scharlach's tone when he announces Lönnrot's entrapment: "Lönnrot heard in his voice a tired triumphance [*victoria fatigada*], a hatred as large as the universe, a sadness no smaller than that hatred" (OC 1.542; CF 154). Scharlach's victory comes out not as a sovereign achievement, but as a weary and mournful animosity, as vast as the universe. The fatigue that seems to dissolve intention and undermine completion recalls Maurice Blanchot's description of fatigue: "As if weariness [*la fatigue*] were to hold up to us the preeminent form of truth, the one we have pursued without pause all our lives, but that we necessarily miss on the day it offers itself, precisely because we are too weary" (*The Infinite Conversation* xiii).

Fatigue combined with sorrow or regret also recalls Yu Tsun's "endless contrition and . . . weariness" at the end of "The Garden of Forking Paths," which exceeds the structure of sovereignty for which he is a reluctant instrument. Although there is much that distinguishes "Death and the Compass" from "The Garden of Forking Paths," and the latter story does not overtly invoke Zeno's paradox, there are some similarities worth noting. Like "Death and the Compass," "The Garden of Forking Paths" is structured as a kind of footrace between antagonists, in which once again the racetrack is structured as the pursuit for sovereignty, in this case for global, rather than civic dominance. In both stories the racetrack of sovereignty — the contest between two parties for a single shot at victory — is contrasted with the figure of the labyrinth, or the distinction between a maze-like path to domination, akin to the trenches of the First World War, and the labyrinthine nature of spatio-temporal difference.[17] Whereas the latter is promised (or sent forth, *pro-mettere*) at the moment in which sovereignty appears to be imposed in "Death and the Compass," in "The Garden of Forking Paths" it is sent from a dead ancestor in the form of a fragmentary letter. Both missives evoke the labyrinthine nature of temporal existence as an abyssal pullulation of possibility that threatens to undermine the race for sovereignty in all its guises (OC 1.511, 1.261; *Inquisiciones* 100; CF 125; SNF 47, 6).

# In-conclusion

By way of closure, I want to emphasize the fact that there can be no closure. Borges's work, like any work, is not a totality that can be mastered once and for all. Its resistance to sovereignty is both thematic and structural, as I have endeavored to show throughout this book. Its themes range from the nature of the present and the structure of the subject to the imposition of order. My emphasis on political sovereignty, especially in relation to nationalism, anonymous authoritarianism, and empire does not aim to reduce his rich work to a single register. To do so would impose its own version of sovereignty, reducing the act of reading to a voyage of conquest, as Willy Thayer says in the passage with which I began. However, ignoring the significance of the political elements that recur throughout his work risks reducing an understanding of the political to sovereign positionality, into which readers have either tried to situate him or despaired or disparaged him for the difficulty in so doing. Borges's work suggests that there are always elements — although they are sometimes barely detectable and all too easy to disavow — that evade and have the potential to unsettle any position of sovereignty. This includes the individual sovereign subject (Yu Tsun, Juan Dahlmann, Funes, "Borges" in "The Aleph") as well as individuals who work to impose sovereignty over others (Otto zur Linde, Shih Huang Ti, the secret bodies that endeavor to establish order in "Tlön," the library of Babel, and the lottery system of Babylon). It also involves, more broadly, thinkers who argue that order is intrinsic to the structure of the universe and its components, including most of the Western philosophical tradition, with special attention given to the tradition of political theology that, from Parmenides and Irenaeus to more recent figures from different extremes of the global system, affirms that "one order and only one is possible" (OC 2.112; SNF 211).

What Borges calls the "aesthetic fact" lends the name of aesthetics to the possibility of responding to the infinitely finite singularity that lies beneath or beyond any sovereign claim. This includes constructs such as the Tower of Babel, the Great Wall of China, and the ideal of law that imposes an order to which all roads lead, as well as forms of representation such as the imperial map that endeavors to represent its territory, Carlos Argentino Daneri's poetic effort to encompass the earth, and all the endlessly varied efforts to usurp, immobilize, or definitively understand the inconceivable universe. Not corresponding to a sovereign act of will, intention, or choice, the aesthetic fact names a kind of doing or making (*hacer*) that responds to the infinite and ineradicable fact (*hecho*) of possibility that lies within every structure. It marks the condition of possibility to respond to what calls to us from the temporality of existence, as Borges describes in the passage in "The Wall and the Books" in which the aesthetic fact is named as such, opening paths and relations not determined by the architectures of sovereignty built into walls or books.

The paths that are opened within Borges's work bifurcate or divide claims to sovereignty, whose principal characteristic, as Derrida tells us, is indivisibility, which "excludes it in principle from being shared," including "from time and from language" (Rogues 101). Time and language are of course central concerns in Borges's writing, and are repeatedly shown to challenge metaphysical versions of history and identity based on the ideals of an immutable origin, a (patri-) linear form of succession, and the overcoming of time and difference more generally. In Borges's hands, the intrinsically temporal practices of reading and writing — understood as inextricably linked, and not limited to linguistic practice — stress the uncertain and destinerrant nature of the sovereign mandate, whether from faceless rulers or political-theological structures of inheritance, law, or logos, tracing paths that lead beyond internally or externally imposed life sentences toward different possibilities for life.

# Notes

## *Introduction*

1. Graff Zivin quotes a brief portion of this passage from Jacques Lezra's *Wild Materialism* (Graff Zivin, *Anarchaeologies* 149; Lezra, *Wild Materialism* 70). See Lezra's note explaining his modification of the English translation of the passage. Note that in earlier essays, Derrida used the term *sovereignty* in a different register. See for instance "Force of Law" (292).
2. I am drawing from Weber's 2005 essay "Once and for All" and also the opening of *Singularity: Politics and Poetics*.
3. This corresponds to David Johnson's account of singularity as an untranslatable element that lurks within language, marking the limit of the translatable, which is the condition of possibility of translation, of which both philosophy and literature are forms (7–13).
4. Along these lines, David Johnson suggests that Borges's work — like deconstruction — can be seen as performing the inextricable relationship between literature and philosophy, understood as two modes of translation that trace, in different but related ways, the improper relation between singularity and difference, the particular and the universal, accident and necessity (Johnson 3–21). In a similar vein, Pablo Oyarzún describes Borges's work as staging a radical encounter between narrative fiction and the essay in such a way that marks the differential tension that characterizes "the singularity of the singular, the facticity of the factual, and the contingency of the contingent" (Oyarzún, *Literature and Skepticism* 174).
5. My discussion of the fable of Babel runs throughout this book, but in brief, I see it evoked especially in the fictions in which man-made structures or systems purport to rival or replace God, and repressive mechanisms defend their sovereignty from any hint of the contingency that inevitably underlies and undermines them. See Alberto Moreiras's discussion of the relationship between Borges and Babel in *Tercer espacio* (69–71) and David Johnson's in *Kant's Dog* (187–90).
6. I discuss the relationship between Borges and Kafka at length in chapter 2 of this book.
7. Note the odd dating of the title "A Comment on August 23, 1944." August 23 does not mark the liberation of Paris, but the somewhat desperate day before Allied troops arrived. Perhaps Borges signals this day as a transitional moment between the damaged promise of autonomous resistance and a new (or renewed) global order.
8. See my discussion of this in chapters 5 and 7.

9. Borges addresses this issue in many of his texts, but it is foregrounded in "From Allegories to Novels" (OC 2.131; SNF 339). See Weber's discussion of the salvational dimension of the figure of the individual and its influence throughout modern history (*Singularity* 183).
10. Borges, "Franz Kafka: *La metamorfosis*" (106).
11. There is arguably a political-theological dimension to the structure of the missive in the Western tradition. The Biblical apostles and their Epistles (both deriving from the Greek *stellein*, to send) are considered to be reliable receivers and transmitters of the divine Word, already transmitted immaterially from God to Jesus.
12. All translations from Moreiras's *Tercer espacio* are my own. The essay "El villano en el centro" ("The Villain in the Center") appears in the revised and expanded version of the book, published in 2021. It is the first essay in the added material, and effectively addresses, through a discussion of Borges, the reception of the first edition of the book (1999), which was partly about Borges. Incidentally, I address the relationship between "infamy" (possibly the origin of de Man's comment about villainy) and Borges's work in a chapter titled "Allegory, Ideology, Infamy" in *Reading Borges After Benjamin.*
13. As Daniel Balderston notes, Borges criticism favored a ludic and self-referential interpretation until around 1990, with several intriguing exceptions (see Balderston, *Out of Context* 2–3). With the advent of cultural studies in the 1990s, his work started to be considered in relation to political and historical concerns, although through different lenses, including New Historicism (Beatriz Sarlo, Edna Aizenberg, and Daniel Balderston, with important variations among them), a continued interest in literary craft (Ricardo Piglia, Hernán Díaz, Balderston), and a more philosophically or political-philosophical bent (Alberto Moreiras, Patrick Dove, David Johnson, Pablo Oyarzún, Brett Levinson, and Erin Graff Zivin).

## *Chapter 1*

1. See Oyarzún's excellent description of the figure of heroism in Borges in "The Writing of Courage": "But if in a certain sense . . . nobody dies in time, for we all are, in view of this extremity, straggled and immature, then the characteristic notion of the hero speaks of the lucky one who has been able to go back over the track of delay, turning to contract in the vertiginous instant of intrepidity the totality of life's time. On the contrary, for the writer, for the man of letters and syllables, the weight of all time is heavily felt in the middle of inescapable idleness, without hope of either abbreviation or epitome: however hard he may try to find out its number — and to write is to count and to tell, he knows in advance it is incalculable" (28).

2. "Percibir." As the *Diccionario de la lengua española* has it, "Recibir algo y encargarse de ello. *Percibir el dinero, la renta.*" Also used in English as "perceive." See OED II, definition 8: "The collection or receiving of rents, profits, dues, etc."

   The story makes the connection to Babel explicit with the figure of Buckley: "Buckley did not believe in God, yet he wanted to prove to the nonexistent God that mortals could conceive and shape a world" (OC 1.472; CF 79). Moreiras considers him to be a melancholic figure who acknowledges the lack of God but feels "the inevitable necessity of a new alliance in the symbolic order" (*Tercer espacio* 70).

   Regarding the relationship between Buckley and Berkeley, there is a similar play on the relationship between Britain and America in the opening section of the story. The first mention of the land of Uqbar appears in a volume of *The Anglo-American Cyclopaedia*, published in 1917, the year the US entered the First World War. The story mentions that this volume is a "literal (though also laggardly) reprint of the 1902 *Encyclopaedia Britannica*" (OC 1.461; CF 68). Among other things, this description can be read as a dig against the attitude of the US during major world conflicts: as a poor copy of its mother country, and arriving late (*morosa,* which Andrew Hurley translates as "laggardly") to the war. *Moroso* is also an economic term, as in late on a payment (Donald Yates translates it as "delinquent"). This qualification of *The Anglo-American Cyclopaedia* as a "literal reimpression" that also incurs a debt and/or delay is contradictory. The spurious entry on Uqbar inserted into its pages, a kind of surplus that introduces something new into the "circle of learning" or *cyclo-paedia* (itself a spurious inheritance from the Greek), is associated with an effort to cancel all debts and take over the world more effectively than the European Empires. But the story also suggests that the relationship between original and copy, including memory, inheritance, translation, and even the form of perception itself, always involves some distortion or excess, in which impressions, even reimpressions, are never "literal," but rather, like Bioy Casares's impression of this reimpression, something akin to "literary" ("formulated in words almost identical to those Bioy had quoted, though from a literary point of view perhaps inferior," OC 1.462; CF 69).

3. The *hrönir* are compared to offspring, which recalls the heresiarch mentioned at the beginning of the story who rejected paternity and reflection because they multiply and divulge aspects of the visible world.

   This heretical doctrine is presented as a contrast between its evident Platonism (and/or Gnosticism, which shared a belief in the pleroma and derivations) and the Berkeleian nature of Tlön, in which being is constituted by perception, not an eternal essence underlying what is perceived. Although Tlönian idealism clearly welcomes perceptual and representational progeny, in some cases in a promiscuous and proliferating way, the passage from the discovery of *hrönir* to their methodical production is described as a reigning in of such indiscriminate propagation to a more normative model of breeding. See for instance "Until recently, *hrönir* were the coincidental offspring of distraction and forgetfulness" and "The first attempts [at methodical production of *hrönir*] were unsuccessful" (OC 1.470; CF 77).

4. The fact that the schoolmaster of this school died during the first excavations, as well as the use of the word *exhumar*, often associated with the digging up of bodies, suggests also that the objects the students unearthed may be ciphers of the schoolmaster himself, or how he was viewed by the students. Hence this scene suggests a Freudian band of brothers analogy, in which freedom is ostensibly obtained by the father figure's death, but the patriarchal structure exceeds the father figure, lying rather in the autonomous conception fantasy of the male society that produced Tlön, and which directs the association between revelation, production, and freedom — affiliated with the plays on extraction and coinage — in the first place.

5. Moreiras interprets these *hrönir* that infiltrate our world as the return of the nouns repressed in Tlön, that is to say, the materiality that is denied in the extreme idealist system that produces Tlön (*Tercer espacio* 73).

   The figure of the cone is a witty reference to the relationship between idealist philosophy and geometry, likely prodding at a point of tension between Berkeley and Kant regarding a priori forms. See for instance Meer's description of the centrality of the cone for Kant's theory of the a priori shape of understanding (108), a theory that contrasts with Berkeley's relationship to geometry, see his *New Theory of Vision* (paragraph 125). Also, conical hats (invoked in "The Zahir") are associated with classical Saturnalia, which Derrida links to the longing for a cannibalistic and filicidal golden age of absolute knowledge, together with the forced drinking of a pharmakon that made Saturn throw up his children and thereby lose his fantasy of possession (*Glas* 231–32; 1986 trans, qtd. in Taylor 5).

6. Note the striking similarity between this passage and the description of Funes: "In the teeming world of Ireneo Funes there was nothing but particulars — and they were virtually *immediate* particulars [*En el abarrotado mundo de Funes, no había sino detalles, casi inmediatos*]" (OC 1.524; CF 137). I discuss this reference to near immediacy in chapter 5.

   My reading of "Tlön, Uqbar, Orbis Tertius" shares some elements with Pablo Oyarzún's illuminating and provocative interpretation of the story in *Literature and Skepticism*. He proposes that it performs the tension between representation and reality that lies at the heart of Borges's work more generally, staging on the one hand the fantasy of subjective control over reality, and, on the other, the ways that time and language underlie and unsettle such a fantasy. With a generous reference to my first book on Borges, Oyarzún suggests that Borges approaches writing as a response to the force of history, understood as that which "resists entering the space of universality" in such a way that it can be said to gesture toward the "possibility of doing justice to ... (rebellious) singularity" (Oyarzún 165).

7. As opposed to the Tlönian world-making substantivization, which parallels capitalism, Moreiras considers that Borges puts into practice "another writing: a Babelic writing, a singular writing that never becomes self-identical, an acknowledgement of the local in resistance to any identitarian hypostasis, a writing of the sign as opposed to the symbol and, more than a wager, an affirmation of an aprincipial form of community" (*Tercer espacio* 73). Nonetheless, he ultimately argues that Borges is a melancholic figure — less warlike than Buckley, whom he also considers to be melancholic — who admits the condition of loss and difference associated with Babel but, Moreiras avers, in his texts "it is still possible to hear the immemorial hum of the effort to conjure affliction from affliction," a description that aligns Borges with Heidegger's assessment of Nietzsche as the last of the metaphysicians (*Tercer espacio* 75; see also chapters 3 and 5). I address this in my previous book (*Reading Borges After Benjamin* 137), and hope that my readings in the present book further indicate my respectful disagreement with this interpretation. If there are moments in Borges of longing for knowledge and presence — and indeed, who does not sometimes long for them? — they are far outweighed by his insistence on their limits and contingency, and his critical evaluation of the costs throughout history of the efforts to impose "a single order" on the infinite finitude of the world. Oyarzún also sees Borges as a melancholic figure, but he interprets this not as a desire for presence or remediation, but as part of his conviction of the temporality of the subject. Describing the end of "Tlön, Uqbar, Orbis Tertius," he writes, "With its evocations of Quevedo and Browne, the last sentence marks the instance of death, which determines and makes possible (and impossible) the subject" (*Literature and Skepticism* 172). Finally, consider Jacques Lezra's interpretation of the end of the story as presenting a tension between "classes of *decisions* that lead to what the story calls 'symmetries with the appearance of order'" and an "indecisive . . . , asymmetrical, anti-ideological means for understanding the relation between aesthetic and ethical judgments," which forms the basis of a "fundamentally political form of resistance" (*Untranslating Machines* 36).
8. The references to animals in the story also suggest an alternate form of perception to that of appropriation. The plains of the American West are described as tread (*holladas*) by bulls and bisons (OC 1.472; CF 79). *Hollar* means to tread, and shares a root with the more common *huella*, trace: hence the bulls and bison leave impressions on the land that are fundamentally different from Buckley's perceptual acquisition or Tlön's molding of the world. Likewise at the end of section II we read how the perceptions of a "beggar [,] . . . a few birds, a horse" bear witness to the evanescence of thresholds and ruins, in a way that recalls the beggars and animals that inhabit the tattered strips of the imperial map in "On Exactitude in Science." Animals and beggars in both instances represent creatures whose perceptions fall outside the bounds of the unitary and appropriative nature of the

human "subject of knowledge" (OC 1.469; CF 76). For more on this, see Bosteels's essay on beggars and animals.

9. Antonio Gómez López-Quiñones points out that of the five footnotes included in this story, four of them are purportedly added by the editor, and only the second one is attributed to Dietrich himself (151). López-Quiñones astutely interprets this as introducing not only a literary tension that undermines the self-certainty of the Nazi narrator, but also — especially since the second footnote mentions (world) *consciousness* — the limits of the narrator's consciousness (152).

   Note the resemblance between the opening discussion of ancestry in "*Deutsches Requiem*" and that of "The South," in which the protagonist is said to favor his properly Argentine ancestors who were also men of action, as opposed to the immigrant man of letters. There are in fact several similarities between this story and "The South," including the justification of violence as a proving (in both senses of the word) of individual and collective mettle, the tension between representation and action, and even the appearance of cats, who appear at the threshold between the two as ciphers for an undecidable limit of the human and its *domos*.

10. My reading here is influenced by Giorgio Agamben's discussion of Spinoza's account of the reflexive form of the verb *pasearse*, which divides the ostensible unity of the subject (Agamben 234).

11. López-Quiñones interprets the laconic second footnote of the story as implying that Dietrich was likely castrated by the war (146). One can imagine this description of Jerusalem's torture as a reversal of the sublimation of his own castration, whereby he tries to bury the loss of a single object in an ideology of totality. Fixation, which focuses on a part object that both represents the fantasy of wholeness and reminds the subject of its inaccessibility, is of course a common trope in Borges's fictions (for instance, "The Aleph," "The Zahir," "The South," "The Book of Sand").

12. The figure of the historian is in some way similar to that of military strategists (of which Hart was one, as well). Both can be said to fix being in what Levinas calls "the concept of totality . . . The meaning of individuals . . . is derived from this totality. The unicity of each present is incessantly sacrificed to a future appealed to bring forth its objective meaning" (Levinas 21–22; see also Cassell's *Liddell Hart: A Study of His Military Thought*). In his essay on Borges between the world wars, Kristal posits that the pretext of a secret communication regarding the Battle of the Somme was absurd, since military operations in the area were "no secret," "unconcealed" ("Jorge Luis Borges's Fictions and the Two World Wars," 40). I would argue that Borges's story speaks to how an unconcealed military operation, as well as the accompanying "historical record" that it inspires, does in fact conceal a great deal.

    David Johnson offers an excellent reading of "El jardín de senderos que se bifurcan" in *Kant's Dog*. My reading here offers intersects in numerous ways with his. On the topic of enmity, which Johnson also discusses, see Eva Horn's excellent essay "Borges's Duels."

13. My understanding of telecommunication (both temporal and spatial) in this story has been influenced by Jacques Derrida's work, including "Ulysses Gramophone" and "Faith and Knowledge."
14. The odd construction of "innumerable contrition and sadness" contrasts instructively with the play with number and experience in relation to the "sophism of the nine coins" in "Tlön, Uqbar, Orbis Tertius." A footnote in that story addresses the confusion over multiplicity (different experiences) and grammar (the same verb, *ser*), noting that one of the churches in Tlön sustains that all pain (as well as all orgasms and all acts of reading) are one and the same (OC 1.468; CF 76).
15. The misrecognition and wrong name here mark an important contrast with Yu Tsun's appropriation of Albert's life and name as a tool of wartime communication. If indeed one reads the story as an illustration of the ominous nature of successful communication, understood as arrival at a totalizing commonality, the scene of Yu Tsun's arrival at Albert's pavilion performs a significantly different possibility, in which arrival and communication always involve misunderstanding and alterity.
16. This passage bears a certain resemblance with "The South," namely in the relationship between national identity and iconicity, in tension with transnational passage and encounter. Albert's collection of Chinese artifacts recalls Dahlmann's collection of early Argentine memorabilia through which he constructs his sense of national belonging. Nonetheless, the description of Albert's library is one in which East and West coincide ("libros orientales y occidentales," OC 1.510; CF 123). There are also two porcelain vases that can be seen as representing China, although their description again suggests cultural encounters rather that regional autonomy. The first is from the "rose family," which refers to a style of enamelware introduced in the eighteenth century and adopted widely in Europe, so widely that the name in Mandarin means "foreign colors" (Wikipedia, "Chinese Ceramics," last revised 30 June 2019, viewed 2 July 2019). The second vase mentioned is described as "from many centuries earlier, in that shade of blue that our artisans (*artífices*) copied from the potters of Persia . . . ," referring to the classic blue patterns that are said to have originated in the cosmopolitan (or imperial expansionist) Tang dynasty, which extended all the way to Persia. Both vases represent China but can hardly be seen as icons of an autonomous Chinese identity.
17. This second form of labyrinth corresponds to Yu Tsun's account of Ts'ui Pên's process of construction, which he describes as "disparate labours [*heterogéneas fatigas*]" (OC 1.509; CF 122). The word *fatiga* — which resonates in interesting ways with the description of "endless contrition, and . . . weariness" at the end of the story — suggests both a challenging task and a state in which determination and intentionality are loosened if not

completely let go. Furthermore, after letting go of the effort to imagine his ancestor's labyrinth, the text mentions that the downhill slope "forestalled all possibility of weariness." Here, rather than the typical experience in which work produces fatigue, the receptivity to the crepuscular fragments of the landscape does the work ("obraron en mí"). Note that the repetition of "Lo imaginé" echoes other instances of repetition in Borges's stories, including most notably that of *vi* in "El aleph" and *Lo recuerdo* in "Funes the Memorious," which refer to modes of perception that are interrogated in their respective stories.

18. See Johnson's discussion of this passage (168).

# Chapter 2

1. See Balderston's *Out of Context* (2–3), although I would argue that the more recent turn to historicism merely changes the terms of the entrapment pole of such a "Borges reaction." An amusing illustration that can be read as illustrating both sides of this "reaction" is the Jorge Luis Borges Google Doodle, which is insightfully discussed in *Google and the Culture of Search* (Hillis et al. 117–18). On Borges's relationship to Kafka, see Sarah Roger's chapter "Borges and Kafka," Efraín Kristal, *Invisible Work* (124-30), as well as the essays in *The Yearbook of Comparative Literature*, volume 63 (2017), edited by Patrick Dove and myself.
2. The English translation of the latter is included in *Selected Non-Fictions;* the Spanish is not extant. I do not think the former has been translated into English.
3. Borges adds under his breath that such a search for a home or "a place . . . in some Order" is at once "so German" and "so Jewish" (Borges, "Franz Kafka, The Vulture" 503). This aside resonates with a number of Borges's works that address the figure of "Order" in European fascism, including "Tlön, Uqbar, Orbis Tertius," "*Deutsches Requiem*," and "A Comment on August 23, 1944." Borges also dedicated numerous works to Israel and Judaism, many of which address these topics with deep admiration while also acknowledging the mutable and evanescent nature of lineage and tradition. There are also a few works that appeal to a militarized Zionism. The poem "A Israel" from *Elogio de la sombra* (1969) demonstrates the full spectrum of this erratic approach, beginning with a lost labyrinth of blood and ending in a troubling salute to Israel's divinely ordained and militarily defended frontiers.
4. Wills describes *dorsality* thus: "The dorsal turn is also a turning back in the sense of a return, which also signals an original turning of the back, the senses of departure and abandonment. It is deployed along the axis that links home to exile, which . . . defines home as originary exile" (*Dorsality*

13). Werner Hamacher, following Walter Benjamin, describes the structure of deferral in Kafka's work as performing a non-arrival at law and judgment, including the law of (literary) representation (299). I regret that due to my focus on Borges I do not engage more with Hamacher's essay or with any other of the many rich and provocative reflections on Kafka's works, including North's, especially the question of how his notion of the yield relates to the structure of deferral. I am grateful to Patrick Dove for linking my observation about dorsality to the emperor's imperative that the wall "dé la vuelta del imperio."

5. Here, I am referring specifically to the beginning of the second paragraph, in which Borges introduces his topic and then says: "That, at least, is the opinion of certain Sinologists," which is followed by an unresolved string of conjectures (OC 2.15; SNF 346). Weinberger's translation does not quite do justice to the ideas I am trying to stress in the final paragraph, so in what follows I am relying more on my own translations. Regarding the temptation, and indeed, the tendency, to take Borges's "I" statements at face value, see Oyarzún's observation that we should keep in mind the fact that Borges "spent most of his life disavowing the [idea] that there could be something like Borges himself, immune to the other" (*Literature and Skepticism* 160).
6. See "From Allegories to Novels" and "Nathaniel Hawthorne"; see also Jenckes (*Reading Borges* 61–62, and 152, note 20). It should be mentioned that Pater and Croce subscribed to different notions of aesthetic form, which it is beyond the scope of this chapter to develop.
7. Pater is somewhat ambivalent about transcendence in the conclusion to *The Renaissance Studies*. He insists that art enables a certain centralizing economy (allowing us, for instance, to "be present always at the focus where the greatest number of vital forces unite in their purest energy") but says that the profit in this economy is ultimately ephemeral (n.p.). The metaphor of the "gemlike flame" incorporates this ambivalence.
8. *Hecho* is the past participle of *hacer* ("to make or do") and translates most commonly as "fact." Patrick Dove aptly translates it as aesthetic event or act in his provocative analyses of the passage (*The Catastrophe of Modernity* 177, 185–86; "Two Sides of the Same Coin?" 93–96). Moreiras also presents an incisive analysis, with an emphasis on the element of improductivity (*Tercer espacio* 125). See also Jenckes (*Reading Borges* 132–35).
9. As a footnote at the end of the essay indicates, an important point of reference for Borges's engagement with the concept of tradition is T. S. Eliot's "Tradition and the Individual Talent." In this essay, Eliot famously argues that aesthetic work is produced in relation to the past ("not only the pastness of the past" but also its bearing on the present) and modifies that past ("what happens when a new work of art is created is something that happens simultaneously to all the works of art that preceded it," [25–26]). Although Borges's idea initially seems quite similar to Eliot's, as the laconic footnote seems to indicate, there are important differences between the two. Eliot affirms that tradition consists of "monuments (that) form an ideal

order among themselves" and encompasses "the timeless and the temporal together," and he suggests that each new work alters "the *whole* . . . order" (26). In this sense, literary tradition for Eliot resembles Shih Huang Ti's imperial territory, with permeable walls and a *deleznable* or changeable interior. Indeed, his description seems to abstract the idea of European empire, which in 1919 was in ruins, to the phantasmatic figure of the mind, specifically "the mind of Europe" (27). For Borges, however, there is no ideal or total order, individual works do not constitute monuments, and there is no such thing as a unified mind of Europe or any other region. His example, after all, is Kafka, a peripheral and minor figure in the strongest sense.

10. This furthermore recalls Jansen's observation that Borges's invocations of Tacitus tend to exemplify lost literature, which, nonetheless, could still be found in some form or another (Jansen 13).
11. My reading here resonates with Erin Graff Zivin's analysis of "Kafka and His Precursors" in "Deconstruction and Its Precursors" (147–48).
12. The other examples of Kafka's precursors illustrate how perception is not necessarily secured by knowledge (for instance, we do not recognize the unicorn because we do not know what it looks like; analogously, Achilles looks like he is running but is not since Zeno knows that change does not happen — nevertheless it does) and how the small and familiar contains the great and unfamiliar and vice versa, or rather how the *domus* is never what we think it is.
13. Derrida's "Before the Law" and "Des Tours de Babel" clearly inform my reading of Borges here. Such a condition of possibility contrasts instructively with the nature of potentiality as Giorgio Agamben describes it — in tension with Derrida's reading — in relation to Kafka's parable *Before the Law*. Agamben interprets the man who stands before the law in Kafka's parable as "an image of law in the time of its messianic nullification," which he links to Benjamin's understanding of a state of exception (*Potentialities* 172). Agamben arrives at this interpretation via Benjamin's correspondence with Gershom Scholem, in which the latter describes the structure of the law in Kafka's works as a "stage in which revelation . . . does not signify, yet still affirms itself by the fact that it is in force" (169). Agamben connects this idea of a state of law "being in force without significance" ("*Geltung ohne Bedeutung*") to the Kabbalistic understanding of origins of the Torah as "a heap of unarranged letters" "without meaning," which "consisted only of the totality of possible combinations of the Hebrew alphabet" (165, 164). The putative emptying out of the law by Kafka's meek protagonist in *Before the Law* constitutes in this reading a desemanticization of earthly law and a return to law and language as pure linguistic potentiality and cipher of "all possible meanings" (165). The "perfect nihilism" that returns law to its linguistic and thereby medial and potential state constitutes in this way an inversion of the Tower of Babel, whereby the path from human meaning to linguistic jumble is understood as Messianic fulfillment. I consider this

reading to be an extreme version of the "Kafka reaction," which interprets Kafka as simultaneously restrictive and emancipatory — a total garden, into which Agamben confoundingly places Derrida in a later essay in the same volume. Agamben effectively shapes Babel into a new structure, a new *domus*, whereas Kafka and Borges (like their successors, Benjamin and Derrida) persistently *postergan*, stress the deferral and the dorsality of the structuration of the proper, opening it up to a different relationship to difference, including the difference of time, which constitutively does not "produce itself" (*una revelación que no se produce [OC 2.15;* SNF 346*]).* For a compelling reading of Agamben's interpretation of Kafka, see Ferris.

## Chapter 3

1. See Pascal, section V (n.p.), and Derrida's "Force of Law: The 'Mystical Foundation of Authority.'"
2. Although Borges seems to have admired Bloy for his ability to express tension between faith and knowledge, it is a tension that is ultimately resolved, and resolved, furthermore, in defense of an anthropo-theological sovereignty: as, for example, in the text from which this citation comes, *L'Ame de Napoléon*, in which Bloy affirms that "son nom seul demeure, son prodigieux Nom, et quand il est prononcé par le plus pauvre de tous les enfants, c'est a rougir pour n'importe qui d'être un grand homme. Napoleón, c'est la Face de Dieu dans les ténèbres" (Bloy 8).
3. See McNamara, Paul, and Frederik Van De Putte, "Deontic Logic."
4. *Ars dictaminis* is also a branch classical rhetoric concerning the art of letter writing, which is relevant to the fact that this narrative is later described as an epistle. Regarding Borges's allusion to Pascal's sphere, see my discussion of this figure in *Reading Borges After Benjamin*, chapter 4.
5. Hurley translates this line as "became congruent with the unlimited width and breadth of humankind's hope," a translation that obscures the sense of sovereign overreach in the original (CF 115).
6. The question of naming totality recalls once again the metonym of Rome, mentioned in "A Comment on August 23, 1944" as a recurrent name for Order, and whose "secret name" is mentioned obliquely in "The Total Library" as one of the things included in the library's holdings (SNF 216). See also "Historia de los ecos de un nombre" regarding the secret, "true" name of Rome, which according to De Quincey, Quintus Valerius Sorano "committed the sacrilege of revealing . . . , and was executed" (OC 2.136; SNF 405). See my discussion of this essay (*Reading Borges After Benjamin* 125–29) as well as Johnson's (184–85).
7. The word *cifra* is a recurrent one throughout Borges's work. It comes from the Arabic word for zero, an integer or whole (intact, integral) number that

is the opposite of wholeness. The search amidst texts for a master signifier, even one that may be the null category of signification, recalls Johnson's discussion of the letter *alif* in the Quran (xx).

8. This line finds correspondence in "Historia de la eternidad" when Borges observes that the thought of there being no eternal record or justification of events in the universe "rather uncomfortably makes ghosts of us" (SNF 136). Here he talks about the "invention" of eternity, which he compares to other inventions intended to preserve things from time, such as devices of mechanical reproduction like phonographs and cinema, which, he observes, are poor substitutes for eternity (OC 1.388; SNF 137).
9. I am influenced here by Derrida's multifaceted invocation of kind, genre, or *Geschlecht*, which includes the category of the human, gender, and also national identity (see Krell, *Phantoms of the Other*, for an illuminating overview of Derrida's use of this term). Borges's engagement with the limits of a privative conception of *Geschlecht* can be seen as focusing on the first and last of these categories, but rarely the second, although the gendered homogeneity of the library may be understood as significant in this regard.
10. On "indemnificatory autoimmunity," see my discussion of this term in *Witnessing Beyond the Human* (xxviii). I'll add here that the name of Trinity for the first atomic bomb can be seen as anachronistically corresponding to Borges's description of "horrible imaginings" associated with the figure of the Christian Trinity mentioned in "The Total Library" (SNF 216), and also his discussion of the Trinity in *A History of Eternity*, where he describes it in terms that are strikingly similar to the figures of the total library and the world-as-text: "We perceive real events and imagine those that are possible (or future); in the Lord this distinction has no place, for it belongs to time and ignorance. His eternity registers once and for all (*uno inteligendi actu*) not only every moment of this replete world but also all that would take place if the most evanescent instant were to change — as well as all that are impossible. His precise and combinatory eternity is much more copious than the universe" (OC 1.385–86; SNF 134).
11. See Dove's intriguing discussion of the period or point in the story's concluding affirmation that the library is "unlimited and periodic" ("Architectures of Totality" 38–40). Oyarzún's description of the structure of subjectivity in Borges's writings as a punctum pierced by the point of inscription is also suggestive in relation to this section of "Biblioteca" (*Literature and Skepticism* 162).
12. See my mention of the figure of distraction in relation to "The South," "Funes the Memorious," and "The Garden of Forking Paths," all influenced by North's book *The Problem of Distraction*.

    Incidentally, Roberto Bolaño reworks the description of writing as distraction from "the present condition of humanity" in interesting ways in a number of his works, for instance in *Amuleto*, when Auxilio Lacouture reads poetry in a bathroom stall during the siege of the university; the poetry readings during the Chilean dictatorship in *Estrella distante* and Sebastián

Urrutia's reading of the classics after the Pinochet coup in *Nocturno de Chile*. The description of "young people [who] prostrate themselves before books and like savages kiss their pages, though they cannot read a letter" (OC 1.505; CF 118) would seem to be the inspiration for the numerous appearances of the *poetas bárbaros*, for instance in *Estrella distante* (138–39). Bolaño pushes at the sense of ritualized respect for the authority represented by literature, which tips into a "barbaric" hypostatization of the materiality of the text. The materiality of the texts can be linked to the body, and specifically the female body (or the feminization of all bodies), which seems implicit in the final footnote of "The Library of Babel," where the word *cuerpo* — which usually means body, although in this context it refers to font size — is associated with the only woman in this exclusively male world. Characters such as Carlos Wieder, associated briefly with the *poetas bárbaros,* can be seen as using aesthetic form to subjugate the feminized bodies of texts, which, as described in the "The Library of Babel" footnote, is uncomfortably silky and slippery (Borges, OC 1.505; CF 118).

13. This anecdote explains the image that is featured front and center on the book's cover. Burton describes melancholy thus: "*Melancholy*, the subject of our present discourse, is either in disposition or in habit. In disposition, is that transitory *Melancholy* which goes and comes upon every small occasion of sorrow, need, sickness, trouble, fear, grief, passion, or perturbation of the mind, any manner of care, discontent, or thought, which causes anguish, dullness, heaviness and vexation of spirit, any ways opposite to pleasure, mirth, joy, delight, causing forwardness in us, or a dislike. In which equivocal and improper sense, we call him melancholy, that is dull, sad, sour, lumpish, ill-disposed, solitary, any way moved, or displeased. And from these melancholy dispositions no man living is free, no Stoic, none so wise, none so happy, none so patient, so generous, so godly, so divine, that can vindicate himself; so well-composed, but more or less, some time or other, he feels the smart of it. Melancholy in this sense is the character of Mortality . . . This *Melancholy* of which we are to treat, is a habit, a serious ailment, a settled humour, as Aurelianus and others call it, not errant, but fixed: and as it was long increasing, so, now being (pleasant or painful) grown to a habit, it will hardly be removed" (Burton 1.164).

14. See Sanjinés's theory of these *pozos* as "extrasemiotic" (70).

    On another note, Burton recounts a tale about Mercury and Charon that can be seen as a possible inspiration for "Biblioteca." With a certain resemblance to the fable of Babel, Charon, ferryman of the underworld, goes with Mercury to a high point. What this Godlike perspective provides him is not a vision of human unity, but swarm-like strife: "a vast multitude and a promiscuous, their habitations like molehills, the men as emmets, *he could discern cities like so many hives of bees, wherein every bee had a sting, and they did nought else but sting one another, some domineering like hornets bigger than the rest, some like filching wasps, others as drones.* Over their heads were hovering a confused company of perturbations, hope, fear, anger, avarice, ignorance, &c., and a multitude of diseases hanging . . ." (Burton 1.48). As Jonathan Basile indicates, the hexagonal shape of the library's galleries resembles the hexagon of a beehive (*The Library of Babel* n.p.).

15. Vehement protests erupted in which the "people" (*el pueblo*) fight to have equal access to the lottery, along with the rich — in other words, this structure of equivalence, now a neat composite of state and market, extends to all sectors of society "equally" (OC 1.490; CF 103). All *subjects*, that is. The leaders behind the sovereign structure of the Company operate in mystical secrecy, an inequivalence or difference that conditions the structure of subjugation. Moreiras reads the depiction of popular power and its embrace of free-market totalitarianism as a critique of the emergence of the national popular under Juan Perón in Argentina, as one manifestation of a global trend toward the strengthening of the state form after the financial crash of 1929, as a mode of paving the way to a condition in which national states "become subsidiaries of a . . . spectral transnational state" of global capitalism, "a new social regime 'of perpetual metastability' based on the market as final mechanism of control" (*Exhaustion* 176).
16. Laraway describes the narrator's tattoo and mutilation as a kind of numismatic branding of citizens as coin-like tokens of equivalence and exchange, the material objects of circulation in the peculiar economy of the lottery.
17. "Interpolación." Note that "interpolation" is also mentioned in "The Library of Babel," first in the description of totality ("the interpolation of every book into all books" [CF 115]), and second in relation to infinity ("I have just written the word 'infinite.' I have not included [*interpolado*] that adjective out of mere rhetorical habit" [OC 1.505; CF 118]).
18. "That is, it is a law (of reason) for us and part of our vocation to estimate everything great that nature contains as an object of the senses for us as small in comparison with ideas of reason; and whatever arouses the feeling of this supersensible vocation in us is in agreement with that law" (Kant, *Critique of the Power of Judgment* I, ii, section 27).
19. Moreiras reads the idea that truth — including both the Company's and the narrator's — can never be ascertained as implying that nothing lies outside of the ideologization of chance (*Exhaustion* 178–79). He stresses in particular the use of the word *indifferent*, which he attributes to the narrator's attitude vis-à-vis the state of Babylon. Although the narrator does not outwardly proclaim an opposition to the Company's totalizing tactics, his "hurried statement" can be seen as marking a difference and a distance, which is always already intrinsic to temporal existence, despite institutional efforts to interpolate it. Furthermore, I do not see that the term *indifferent* applies to the narrator — on the contrary, he describes a sense of *asombro* or astonishment (Hurley translates it as "bewilderment") at the structure of his society and the subversive murmurs that lurk at its limits (OC 1.488; CF 101). That said, I concur that the story stages the relationship between direct power and ideology, and with it, the relationship between difference and

indifference — as Moreiras puts it, quoting Althusser, "how to escape the circle while remaining in it" (*Exhaustion* 179) — in interesting ways.

By the end of the story, operations attributed to the Company cannot be determined definitively as distinct from falsification or mere impersonal event. The narrator asks how we could know for certain that someone is falsely impersonating an agent of the Company, since it is possible that the impostor is executing a secret directive from the Company, which may be unknown even to himself. He describes this "silent functioning" as "comparable" to God, but he also acknowledges that, itself based on conjecture, it provokes "all manner [*suerte*] of conjectures," a phrasing that can be seen as playing on the double sense of the word *suerte*, luck or kind, suggesting that the mystical foundation of authority that supposedly determines one's luck is itself open to a multitude of interpretations, like a throwing of the conjectural dice (OC 1.492; CF 106). The word *comparable* (this falls out of the translation, which uses "like") rhymes with the word used to describe the first of the conjectures, *abominablemente*, which bears within it a departure from the prediction (and thereby control) of fortune (from *ab,* away from, and *omen*). These abominable conjectures are associated with heresy, a word that, indicating a distinction from orthodoxy, entails choice (Gr. *hairen*, to choose). In other words, the silent workings of the Company allow space for heretical murmurs (OC 1.488; CF 102) that question the assertion of a mystical ground of sovereignty over chance and choice, and indicate the internal and "heretical" fold intrinsic to the structure of religious doctrine. For an intriguing reading of the figure of heresy, see David Wills (*Matchbook* 115–21).

The abominable conjectures that conclude the story include the ideas that the Company ceased to exist centuries ago; that it is omnipotent, but only affects miniscule things like the call of a bird, the shades of rust and dust, waking dreams at dawn; that it never existed at all, and never will exist; and that it is impossible to determine whether or not the Company is real, since everything is an infinite play of chance. Rather than indifference, such a conjecture would seem to imply that reality is intrinsically heterogeneous or in-different.

## *Chapter 4*

1. I am drawing somewhat freely here from his remarks on an Order in "A Comment on August 23, 1944" and "Franz Kafka, The Vulture," as I have already elaborated in the introduction and chapter 2. Specifically relevant for my purposes here is the following line in "Franz Kafka, The Vulture": "There is only a single man in his work: the *homo domesticus*, so German

and so Jewish, desirous of a place, no matter how humble, in some Order — in the universe, in a ministry, in an insane asylum, in jail" (SNF 503).

2. The term *Creole* (*criollo*) in Argentina refers to the descendants of white European settlers. See especially Beatriz Sarlo's interpretation of Borges as anti-immigrant in *Jorge Luis Borges: A Writer on the Edge* and Ricardo Piglia's influential essay "Ideología y ficción en Borges," both of which I discuss in *Reading Borges After Benjamin*.

3. Dove's analysis of "El sur" in *Catastrophes of Modernity* is the finest one I know. I intend my analysis as a complement to it, with some slightly different points of emphasis.

   On another note, the names Dahlmann and Glencairn etymologically evoke valleys (Glen, Dahl), a space between mountains, hence a kind of interstitial space. The combination of Mann and Cairn suggests the Roman demigod Terminus, guardian of boundaries.

4. The portrayal of a German Argentine nationalist who, in 1939, seeks to disavow his German ancestry, is suggestive in a number of ways. On the one hand, it is a pointed gesture to Argentine nationalists who may or may not subscribe to fascist ideals (Argentina was notoriously "neutral" throughout the war), although the echoes between Dahlmann's nationalism and Nazism are likely leveled at Argentine fascists, whom Borges repeatedly criticized. The fact that Dahlmann is also an alter ego for Borges adds a peculiar twist to this association, however. It may be that Borges is criticizing his own previous nationalist or regionalist tendencies, noticeable in some of his early work, although, as I try to show in my first book, his collecting of *criollo* images is done with the brooding eye of the allegorist, which perceives the discontinuities of history rather than iconic presence.

   Note that Argentina was not as far away from the Second World War as it might seem. The war arrived at the mouth of the Río de la Plata in the Battle of the River Plate in 1939, the year mentioned in the first sentence of the story.

5. The qualification of this death as Romantic stresses the process of the internalization of exposure as symbol, a motif that in American literatures was especially linked to the figure of the frontier (Sarmiento's invocation of the Romantic aspect of the pampa is iconic in this regard). As numerous critics have noted (from Paul de Man to the editors of the book series Lit Z), however, Romanticism also exposes the structure of such internalization, opening thinking and representation to an externality that cannot be contained. Life and death are prominent figures in both versions of Romanticism, appearing as either sublated into an ideal of immortality or stubbornly resisting such sublation in a discontinuous form of survival, performing what Sara Guyer and Brian McGrath call, in their description of the Lit Z book series, "another relation to the present." Although the mention of Romanticism in "The South" is brief, it can be read as indicating a tension that is central to the story, and indeed to all of Borges's writing.

6. *Aforar* is also a theatrical term that means to frame the scene, hiding parts of the stage that shouldn't be seen. It also means a stripping of legal protections, from the Latin *forum*, as I also address in my reading of "The Aleph." See the *Diccionario de la lengua española*'s entries for "Desaforar" and "Aforar."
7. Prior to 1939, Borges had written poetry, essays, and a volume of short stories based on rewritings of other texts (*Historia universal de la infamia*). One wonders if the name Pierre doesn't connect Menard to the stone-like liminal men that we see in "The South" and "The Man on the Threshold." Oyarzún's description of Walter Benjamin's interest in stories of criminals and rascals as concerning "the opening of a space in which the outlaw appears before or on the margins of any sentence" comes to mind in relation to Borges's worrying of the thresholds of law and language (*Doing Justice* 106).
8. Recall Otto Dietrich zur Linde's matronymic last name in "*Deutsches Requiem*," which means essentially "to the limit." Note that Dahlmann disavows his German inheritance, but appears to know German, since the copy of *A Thousand and One Nights* that precipitated his initial injury is a translation into German.
9. Hurley translates the word *acometiendo* as modifying Dahlmann's imagined ferocity, rather than the sky: "morir en una pelea a cuchillo, a cielo abierto y acometiendo," "dying in a knife fight under the open sky, grappling with his adversary" (OC 1.567; CF 179). Admittedly the construction is somewhat ambiguous. Note that the *Diccionario de la lengua española*'s second definition of *acometer* concerns the sudden onset of a "sickness, dream, or desire."
10. Dove describes the end of the story (with some different points of emphasis from my reading) as offering a "summons to language which, in placing a limit upon what is possible, gives shape to possibility — that is, the possibility of engaging the other" (*The Catastrophe of Modernity* 97).
11. Hurley translates "hondo conventillo" as "long, narrow rooming house" (OC 1.671; CF 288). *Conventillo* generally translates as tenement. The modifier *hondo* (*hondo conventillo*) is a little ambiguous in Spanish, and I am choosing to keep the strangeness in the English translation. Finally, I think it is important to keep the conjugation "and" (momentary and repeated) rather than replacing it, as Hurley does, with "yet."
12. The fact that the narrator is a member of the British council who used to work in India can be seen as a pointed allusion to the way that the British version of colonial power was manifest in a soft fashion in nineteenth- and twentieth-century Argentina, at the same time that it intervened more forcefully in other parts of the world. This soft colonial power contributed to political turmoil in Argentina dating from the 1930s, which can be seen as a deep house with a succession of sovereigns, like a series of patios.
13. This recalls Borges's description of literary classics in "On the Classics": "A classic is not a book . . . that necessarily possesses these or those merits;

it is a book that generations of men, impelled by different reasons, read with pre-established fervor and mysterious loyalty" (OC 2.161, translation mine). Although such books "promise a long immortality, . . . we don't know anything about the future, except that it will differ from the present" (OC 2.160).

14. Djelal Kadir astutely observes the relationship between law and writing as central to Borges's oeuvre, which he describes in relation to the parable "El espejo de tinta," in which an executioner, named Abu Kir (father reader or father of reading), "carries on writing's generic sentence, even as his offices require that he carry out (that he 'throw the book' of) the Court's sententious law" (Kadir 54). Reading, as a mode of spilling writing's differential fluidity, disrupts — sentences — any pretension to self-presence through representation.
15. See Fishburne and Hughes. Although I do not want to reduce the complex history of Peron and Peronist support, which upended oligarchic and neocolonial forces, it is not a stretch to see both the depiction of the colonized masses taking over the house of judgment, while leaving it intact, and the invocation of Juvenal, best known for his satirical description of popular power in ancient Rome, as subtle critiques of Peronism. Writing in the United States during the era of Donald Trump, there are distinct resonances between Trump's unflagging popularity and Juvenal's description of a crowd swayed by "bread and circuses." Dewey's misquotation of Juvenal, *Ultra aurorem et Gangen*, seems to confuse the original (*Usque auroram et Gangen*) with a combination of two imperial mottos "The sun never sets on the British Empire" and "Non Plus Ultra," the latter of which, perhaps not unsurprisingly, is inscribed in Trump's pleasure palace, Mar-a-Lago.
16. The question of the relationship between faith and fiction seems quite pointed in relation to Kipling's poem "Evarra and His Gods," which, as Daniel Balderston points out, appears to be invoked in "The Man on the Threshold." The poem describes a maker of idols who hears the acclaim of crowds where there is really only the lowing of cows, in another distant (and undoubtedly dubious) allusion to the dangers of populism ("Liminares: Sobre el manuscrito de 'El hombre en el umbral'" 34).

## Chapter 5

1. Hurley translates the title "Funes el memorioso" as "Funes, his Memory." I have chosen to refer to the story in English as "Funes the Memorious."
2. In *Kant's Dog*, Johnson affirms that Kant is a primary philosophical interlocutor of "Funes the Memorious." He notes the resonance between the description of Funes's perception of dogs ("Not only was it difficult for him to see that the generic symbol 'dog' took in all the dissimilar individuals of

all shapes and sizes, it irritated him that the 'dog' of three-fourteen in the afternoon, seen in profile, should be indicated by the same noun as the dog of three-fifteen, seen frontally") (OC 1.524; CF 136) and Kant's example of a dog to indicate the relationship between sense perception and conceptualization: "The concept of a dog signifies a rule in accordance with which my imagination can specify the shape of a four-footed animal in general, without being restricted to any simple particular shape that experience offers me or any possible image that I can exhibit *in concreto*" (Kant, qtd. in Johnson 105). Johnson explains that Kant's description of the function of the imagination involves an element of mediation that, as potentially unruly, autonomous, and automatic, threatens the conceptualization of the process of conceptualization, which he endeavors to control by claiming that a unity of consciousness (transcendental apperception) precedes all such mediation (Johnson 107–15). Johnson suggests that in "Funes the Memorious," Borges demonstrates the necessity for a synthesis of time (without which the subject is nothing more than a "heap" of representations), but also the impossibility of an unmediated and atemporal unity of consciousness. Such a lack of (temporal) mediation would allow for neither life nor the recognition or recounting of life, which involve *time*, understood as the "impossible limit of interiority and exteriority," a limit that troubles the distinctions between sensibility and the understanding, the singular and the universal, literature and philosophy, and the accidental and the necessary (118, 92).

3. *Mate* in this context refers to a dried gourd used as a cup for containing and consuming yerba mate, a traditional beverage common in the Río de la Plata region. Colloquially, it refers to the head. I may be stretching it a bit to suggest that the word *armas* can be seen as evoking the English homophone for part of the body, in addition to the sense of insignia (a coat of arms, related to the sense of arm as weapon). But given Borges's relationship to English, I don't think it's too much of a stretch; furthermore, in Uruguay in particular, mates figure as prosthetic extensions of the arm, much like weapons. And, at risk of stretching this association beyond repair, the image of arms that hold a container, which, like the head, internalizes and contains, and does so under the sign of belonging backed up by force, constitutes a convoluted hieroglyph of the story, especially if we think of the arms that hold the *mate* as arms that write, externalizing that which cannot be fully held, the prosthesis of holding undermining the logic of containment.

   The description of Funes's hands as "slender leather-braider's fingers [*manos afiladas de trenzador*]," refers on one level to the task of rope braiding, an important component of nineteenth-century Uruguayan ranching culture. It can also be seen as evoking Irenaeus's theory of the Christian Trinity (three twisted together as One, just as past, present, and future are condensed into a timeless present).

4. It seems like a Borgesean conceit that the ideal of linguistic immediacy was only conceived as such through repetition, in which God's capacity for

naming (Let there be light) was not named as such until the Gospel of John, which is, furthermore, not penned by its supposed author (Attridge 128).

5. I am indebted to Michael Naas for "re-animating" these ideas in his compelling book *Plato and the Invention of Life* (116–35). Kadir also refers to the pharmacological dimension of writing in Borges as manifest in "El Espejo de tinta" (50–51).
6. Marder notes that Benjamin turned to Freud in order to understand why modern experience was not as fragmented or divergent as Nietzsche's description of the man who did not possess the power of forgetting would suggest (Marder, *Dead Time* 28). Clearly the defensive structure of consciousness produces a directedness that contributes to the building of civilization and the like. Nietzsche's example is "extreme," an exaggeration of consciousness that doesn't acknowledge its own limits, including its temporal structure.
7. In keeping with Río de la Plata culture, the two examples of "tripartite" names that appear in the story do not follow this format (the narrator's cousin's name appears as both Bernardo Haedo and Bernardo Juan Francisco, and Funes's mother's name appears as María Clementina Funes). Nevertheless, I think the implication is there.
8. Ragaller proposes that Nietzsche's eternal return is akin to childbirth, which she contrasts to the Hegelian dialectic, although she rejects the idea that the dialectic is, as Derrida suggests, a return to the father (Ragaller 15).
9. See Boretto Ovalle, n.p. In "A Fragment on Joyce," Borges observes that he was undecided about whether to set this story in Fray Bentos or Junín, Argentina. My analysis clearly addresses the final decision to set it in Fray Bentos, although there are some interesting holdovers from the Junín option, including the mention of a "lake scene" (OC 1.519; CF 131), which remains like a (Nietzschean) snapshot from this moment of indecision.
10. See Derrida's discussion of the anxiety of conception in "The Night Watch."
11. Gonzalo Díaz Letelier points out that in the prologue from 1953, Borges revises his characterization of Plato, which he (implicitly) distinguishes from its treatment in Plotinus (Díaz Letelier 141). I agree with Díaz Letelier's assertion that Borges's work invites us to think the errancy and disagreement of relations, which echoes Erin Graff Zivin's reading in *Anarchaeologies: Reading as Misreading*.

    At the end of "A History of Eternity," Borges outlines a third version of eternity, which he claims is the only one to which he can subscribe. He bases this on an excerpt from an earlier work, in which he describes an experience of déjà vu, which he poetically characterizes as an encounter with an unchanged past (OC 1.388; SNF 138). Although his sense of irony is less evident in this section than it is in the rest of this acerbic and very funny essay, I submit that it should not be taken at face value, just as we should never take his use of the first person at face value. First of all, there is the very structure of (self) quotation, which, in the hands of someone like Borges — one need think only of Pierre Menard, or, chronologically closer, the pieces in *Universal History of Infamy* — is never an exact or reliable repetition. In "The Doctrine of Cycles," Borges mentions that repetition introduces difference, unsettling any apparent sameness or reliability in déjà vu, quotation, or perception itself, which is acknowledged as a form of memory, through a filtered Freudian lens (OC 1.415–18; SNF 119–21).

12. The putative opposition between realism and nominalism appears throughout Borges's work, sometimes explicitly, sometimes not. He repeatedly notes the modern predilection for nominalism and corresponding distaste for realism, while undoing any real opposition between the two, since language and thought — even when directed at particulars — inevitably employ abstraction, and yet for finite beings living in a finite world no abstraction is absolute. In "A History of Eternity" he ironically claims that both concepts resist interpretation and commentary: "realism, a doctrine so distant from our essential nature that I disbelieve all interpretations of it"; "Now . . . we all do nominalism *sans le savoir*, as if it were a general premise of our thought, an acquired axiom. Useless, therefore, to comment on it" (OC 1.386; SNF 135). It is as if critical commentary — a form of repetition — would disrupt the sense of the absolute on which both categories rely. See also the discussions of realism and nominalism in "From Allegories to Novels," "Preliminary Note," "A New Refutation of Time," and "Nathaniel Hawthorne." Although he associates the structure of the novel with nominalism and suggests that Joyce's *Ulysses* exemplifies it, I would venture that Borges acknowledged that Joyce was also interrogating this opposition, as does, perhaps, most fiction ("A History of Eternity" OC 1.386; SNF 134–35).
13. Borges mentions Irenaeus in several essays, including "A Defense of Basilides the False," "A Defense of the Kabbalah," and "A History of Eternity."
14. In addition to "Funes el memorioso," it is possible to detect resonance of these quotations in "The Aleph" and "The Zahir," "*Deutsches Requiem*," and "The Garden of Forking Paths." The emphasis on the infinite richness of the everyday could be said to run through nearly all of Borges's writing. In "A History of Eternity" he stresses the sexual undertones of the desire to possess such (ephemeral) pleasures, quipping that "eternity is the style of desire," and quoting Lucretius on the "fallacy of coitus," suggesting that the striving for eternity can be understood as a striving for "more solid possessions," or what he says of Irenaeus in particular, "un belicoso placer" (OC 1.387, 383; SNF 135–36, 131).
15. Moreiras suggests as much, especially in relation to the quotation of Nietzsche in "The Doctrine of Cycles" regarding the idea of the eternal recurrence: "The instant that this idea presents itself, all colors are different — and there is another history!" ("Doctrine" OC 1.416; SNF 120; Moreiras, *Tercer espacio* 110). He focuses his reading of "Funes el memorioso" around the question of Borges's relation to Nietzsche's affirmative embrace of the eternal recurrence as an end to metaphysics. However,

he considers, cum Heidegger, that Nietzsche fails in this endeavor, and argues that Borges, by association, does as well (*Tercer espacio* 101–26). Although I ultimately disagree with Moreiras's approach to Borges as a nostalgic thinker of metaphysics, I am deeply indebted to his provocative and nuanced readings. One idea that stands out in his brilliant analysis of "Funes" is his comparison of Funes's mnemonic ability to the "elegant hope" of the narrator at the end of "The Library of Babel," in which he affirms his desire for an ordered repetition — repetition as producing Order — that would "resist the arbitrary or random constitution of the real" and provide meaning to existence (*Tercer espacio* 109).

16. See Samuel Weber's analysis of Nietzsche's eternal recurrence as an experience of reading, including the reading of the self (through consciousness and memory). Weber describes the pyramidal block where Nietzsche recounts his encounter with the "most abyssal thought" of the eternal recurrence as an obstructive figure of sedimented meaning, including a sedimented sense of time. Nietzsche's fable-like narration turns this obstruction into a gateway that marks a space of the conflictual but convergent forces of the past and the future: "They contradict one another, these ways; they repel each other head-on — and here, at this gateway, is where they come together. The name of the gateway stands inscribed above: moment [*Augenblick*]" (quoted and translated by Weber, *Singularity* 302). Weber writes, "Reading always entails both the recognition of conventional meaning (the 'moment' as the object of an eye-glance, as a kind of block) and the desedimentation of this momentarily blocked meaning into something that marks a transition and a passage: a gateway . . . [It] is not just the reader's sense of self-presence that risks being pulverized, but . . . the self-presence of the here and now singularized in and as the moment" (303–04). Reading — an action that externalizes the encounter of consciousness with its limits, both temporal and "material" (that is, through different kinds of sedimentation, different spaces of return) — approaches the moment, or the here and now, not as ground nor as block, but as a radical engagement with the differential dynamic of time, or being in and as time (*Singularity* 305–06). Weber suggests that ultimately, the blinking of the moment in Nietzsche is closer to Heidegger's *Dasein* than he acknowledges.
17. In *Twilight of the Idols*, Nietzsche condemns philosophers for their "hatred of the very idea of becoming, their Egypticity. They think that they are showing respect for something when they dehistoricize it, *sub specie aeterni*, — when they turn it into a mummy. For thousands of years, philosophers have been using only mummified concepts" (166–67).
18. "Language began at a time when psychology was in its most rudimentary form: we enter into a crudely fetishistic mindset when we call into consciousness the basic presuppositions of the metaphysics of language — in the vernacular: the presuppositions of *reason*. It sees doers and deeds all over: it believes that will has causal efficacy: it believes in the 'I,' in the I as being, in the I as substance, and it *projects* this belief in the I-substance onto

all things — this is how it *creates* the concept of 'thing' in the first place . . . Being is imagined into everything — *pushed under everything* — as a cause; the concept of 'being' is only derived from the concept of 'I' . . . I am afraid that we have not got rid of God because we still have faith in grammar" (Nietzsche, *Twilight of the Idols* 169–70).

Nietzsche's name for the ungrounded subject, the subject exposed to the conflictual gateway of time, is *Übermensch*, a term that Weber helpfully translates as "transhuman" (Weber, *Singularity* 2).

19. Borges, citing Nietzsche: "'Inmortal el instante,' dejará escrito, 'en que yo engendré el eterno regreso. Por ese instante yo soporto el Regreso'" (*Unschuld des Werdens*, II 1308)" (OC 1.415; SNF 119). The citation is from a posthumously published fragment on Zarathustra, which reads "Unsterblich ist der Augenblick, wo ich die Wiederkunft zeugte. Um dieses Augenblickes willen ertrage ich die Wiederkunft" (Nietzsche, *Unschuld des Werdens*, II 1308; see also *Nachgelassene Fragmente* November 1882–February 1883). The allusion to conception and pregnancy (*zeugen, ertragen*) is echoed in other parts of Nietzsche's writings on the eternal recurrence, including most notably his description of the conception of this idea in "Ecce Homo" as a peculiar rebirth, as of a phoenix, that had an eighteen-month gestation period, like an elephant (124). Both animal references can be seen as unsettling Borges's description of Nietzsche's "grammatical (first) person" as prophetic parent: the phoenix because the rebirth is marked by the ash to which it will return; the elephant, whose size would burst and kill any human-sized casing, and whose gestation period is double that of a human's. The repetition, excess, and doubling implied by these analogies divide and disrupt any presumed parental unity. See Regaller on the metaphor of engendering in relation to the eternal recurrence.

20. This passage resonates with the opening of "A History of Eternity," where Borges introduces the notion of eternity as "a daughter of mankind" (OC 1.373; SNF 123) and contrasts this progeny with *time*. Shifting metaphors slightly, he describes time in a Heraclitan vein as a river, but then mentions two (not Heraclitan) interpretations of this figure relating to which direction the river flows, including the common conception of time as flowing from past to future, and its opposite, which Borges says is no less illogical, which is Unamuno's suggestion that time flows backward from its source (*manantial*) in "the eternal tomorrow" (qtd. in OC 1.373; SNF 123). The forward flow of the river can be linked to a model of patrimony (think gene pool) that may or may not recognize its inheritance but is rooted in an atemporal space of the subjective present and projects its prophetic style toward the future (which relates to Borges's account of Nietzsche in "The Doctrine of Cycles"). Unamuno's river is no less atemporal or prophetic but, in Borges's hands, sounds like a macabre fairytale in which the parent ingests its adoptees.

As I describe in my chapter on Zeno, Borges's description of infinity, in which he again appeals to a metaphor of birth, contrasts in important ways to these two models of time, which are in fact models of eternity (*hija de los hombres*). In "The Perpetual Race of Achilles and the Tortoise," Borges posits that infinity, or the infinitely finite nature of time, disrupts any stable sense of subjective grounding in the present, which is to say any solid parental footing or recognizable offspring. He describes the very word *infinity* as a "troubling word (and then concept) that we have recklessly engendered and that once accepted into a thought, explodes and kills it" ("The Perpetual Race" OC 1.261, translation mine; see also SNF 47). Here we're in the realm of a different, more monstrous birth, which explodes its conceptual eggshell, which was already troubled to begin with (*palabra de zozobra*). This description of an explosive engendering that overtakes the parent is of course much closer to Nietzsche's thought than Borges's dig about a prophetic "I" that digests the past and endows the future with its greatness.

Borges's characterization of Nietzsche's lack of quotation marks notwithstanding, Werner Hamacher stresses the prominence and significance of quotation marks in Nietzsche's work, including around the word *individuum* (162), which he interprets as unsettling any apparent solidity of autonomous perspective and of communication. He refers specifically to aphorism 125 of *The Gay Science*, "where Nietzsche lets a madman proclaim, 'God is dead,' he writes: 'This monstrous event is still on the way and wanders . . . '" Hamacher suggests that this description of the wandering, arriving citation is intrinsic to Nietzsche's thought, performing an indeterminacy of meaning and a suspension of address, hence of communication (171): "The monologue of singularity never arrives, never comes home, never enters any 'house of Being.' It is enormous, uncanny, and monstrous — it is *ungeheuer* because it, without arriving, keeps coming" (171). Although in "The Doctrine of Cycles" Borges merely points out the grammatical techne underlying Nietzsche's prophetic pronouncements, the "enormous dialogue" in "Funes" can be seen as an extended play on the incommensurability between the wandering event of singularity and the prophetic voice that claims to house it.

21. See Johnson's discussion of philosophy and language (96–97).
22. Note that the other flower mentioned in the story, *santonina* (OC 1.520; CF 133), also has an "allegorical" name. Interestingly, *santonina* is a variety of artemisia, which derives from the Roman goddess Artemis, virgin protector of fertility and childbirth. Also known as wormwood, it is a medicinal herb traditionally used as an antiparasitic purgative. If in the opening scene Funes's fixation on the passionflower can be interpreted as a symbol of Irenaean unification of time and difference, perhaps his subsequent contemplation of "a fragrant switch" of artemisia/wormwood can be seen as a different stage in the "sacralization" of his memory, namely the purgation of his unknown paternity.
23. Borges mentions ethnic physical traits in several of his stories. Although generally without elaboration, they are not simply bits of local color or

allegorical attributes. See for instance my discussion of the man with the "cara achinada" in "The South" in chapter 4, Jewishness in "Death and the Compass," "yellow" skin color in "The Garden of Forking Paths." See also my discussion of the "infamy" of race in *Universal History of Infamy* in *Reading Borges After Benjamin*, chapter 3.

24. This sentence is repeated almost verbatim in "The Aleph," just as the anaphoric repetition of "I recall" at the beginning of Funes is repeated by the repetition of "I saw" in "The Aleph," both of which perform the impossibility of re-lating self-presence, as contrasted with phantasmagoric ideals of totality.

    The reference to the time that has passed since he spoke with Funes as "half a century [*medio siglo*]" (from L. *saeculum*, referring to the average length of human life) can be seen as emphasizing the difference between the narrator, for whom everything is distanced and in parts, and Funes, for whom every instant is an entire life ("seeing it as it had never been seen, even had it been stared at from the first light of dawn till the last light of evening for an entire lifetime," [OC 1.519; CF 131]).

25. The town is now a UNESCO world heritage site, interestingly enough — a different kind of commemorative project (see Graham-Harrison). Recall that one speculation is that Funes's father may have been a doctor at the meat-packing plant, "an Englishman named O'Connor" (OC 1.520; CF 132), hence associated with the expropriating factory, although, as the name suggests, possibly not really English, but Irish, hence a colonized subject working for the colonizer.

26. Moreiras describes Funes's transcendence of writing as a "perfect mimesis" that thematizes the disappearance of writing, understood as a scene of difference (*Tercer espacio* 124, 119). He acknowledges that the narrator is not exempt from such difference, and in fact is obliged to inhabit it. He stresses the importance of the word *casi* for both the ideal of unmediated presence represented by Funes, which both disrupts it and allows him to live, and for the wishful witness of almost-immediacy in the figure of the narrator, who, he affirms, uses it to mediate between the incompatible totalities of memory and presence, thereby enabling his narration — as a writing against writing, so to speak (*Tercer espacio* 112). Johnson also stresses the importance of the qualification "almost" (*casi*), describing it as a gap in the ideal of infallible memory that enables the telling of this story (Johnson 95).

27. Funes insists that his infallible mental abilities leave Christianity in the dust, stating that before his accident, "he had been what all Christians are: blind, deaf, befuddled, devoid of memory" (OC 1.522; CF 134, translation modified). In this sense he can be understood to be a Nietzschean (post-theological) version of Irenaeus. Sergio Villalobos-Ruminott has an intriguing analysis of Funes's fall in *Heterografías de la violencia* (53).

28. Irenaeus: "He has declared the cup, a part of creation, to be his own blood, from which he causes our blood to flow; and the bread, a part of creation, he has established as his own body, from which he gives increase unto our

bodies. When, therefore, the mixed cup [wine and water] and the baked bread receives the Word of God and becomes the Eucharist, the body of Christ, and from these the substance of our flesh is increased and supported, how can they say that the flesh is not capable of receiving the gift of God, which is eternal life — flesh which is nourished by the body and blood of the Lord, and is in fact a member of him?" (*Against Heresies* 5:2). Nietzsche: "It is with works of art as with wine — it is better if one has need of neither, keeps to water, and through one's own inner fire and sweetness of soul, again and again transforms the water into wine on one's own account" (*Human, All Too Human* 237).

29. In "A Fragment on Joyce," Borges affirms that only one as monstrous as Funes would be capable of a consecutive reading of *Ulysses* (SNF 220).
30. The word *cipher* (*cifra*) recurs throughout Borges's work in varying ways, as I discuss in relation to "The South" (the gaucho as cipher), "The Garden of Forking Paths" (the objective of deciphering a message and thereby reducing the division of enmity to a One), as well as the figure of the One in "Death and the Compass" and the Zeno essays. On numbers and names in "Funes the Memorious," see Johnson (99–104).
31. *Manta de carne* refers to a cut of meat, although it likely plays on the polysemy of *manta*, which also means blanket or poncho. Likewise, *caldera* refers both to a kettle and a crater, which resonates with the mention of sulfur, perhaps relating to the volcanic area in the Northwest of Argentina. Luis Melián Lafinur was the Uruguayan uncle of the Argentine poet Alvaro Melián Lafinur, mentioned in "The Aleph." The May Revolution that set off the Argentine war of independence from Spain was triggered by Napoleon's invasion of Spain.
32. The Battle of Quebracho was fought by Federalist forces affiliated with Rosas's government of Argentina, against the French and British, who were — at least in theory — supporting Uruguayan sovereignty, as well as the Unitarians, with whom Sarmiento was aligned.
33. See "Vago" and "Solar." In "A Fragment on Joyce" Borges mentions that this story was set in either Junín or Fray Bentos. Junín is surrounded by lakes, while Fray Bentos is bordered by the Uruguayan River (SNF 220).
34. The fact that Saturn was the Roman name for the Greek Titan Cronus is also very suggestive, given. The relationship between sons and fathers. Boretto Ovalle mentions that *El saturno* did, in fact, exist.
35. The narrator describes himself as distracted at least twice, in his first encounter with Funes and later in his reaction to the telegram informing him of his father's fragility (OC 1.520–21; CF 132–33). Distraction is another example of the narrator's difference from the putatively near immediacy of Funes's perception.
36. This detail in Funes resonates with other stories in interesting ways. First the description of Funes's ability to perceive the multiple faces of death in a long wake reappears in a central scene in "The Zahir" and also evokes the photographs of Beatriz Viterbo in "The Aleph." In fact, these three

stories have much in common, all departing from a loss (Funes's accident and/or his absent father, and the death of the women in "The Zahir" and "The Aleph"), which provokes a fantasy or vision of total containment. In a different register, Funes's surprise at seeing his face and hands resonates with the end of "*Deutsches Requiem*" when Dietrich, looking in the mirror "in order to know who I am," notes a distinction between his mind, which sustains a sovereign idea of a total and enduring order, and his body, which does not (OC 1.622; CF 234).

37. Moreiras says of this passage, "Ireneo's face is at the same time atemporalized and profoundly marked by time. He will die two years later, in 1889. In January of that year Nietzsche was interned in the Jena asylum" (*Tercer espacio* 113).
38. See Weber's discussion of Nietzsche's description of the encounter with the pyramidal block (Weber, *Singularity* 284–88).
39. The story is set during the 1880s, a decade of cinematographic innovation. "Half a century" later places the story's (fictional) writing in the late 1930s. Hurley softens the peculiarity of this description: "I saw the face *that belonged to* the voice that had been talking all night long" (CF 137).

    Regarding the mention earlier in the story of recording technology as a means of verifying Funes's abilities ("Those are the things he told me; neither then nor later have I ever doubted them. At that time there were no cinematographers, no phonographs; it nevertheless strikes me as implausible, even incredible, that no one ever performed an experiment with Funes. But then, all our lives we postpone everything that can be postponed," [OC 1.523; CF 135]), Moreiras observes that this statement contrasts the temporality of human experience, marked by delay and deferral, with the ideal of instant self-coincidence represented by both Funes and technological reproduction (*Tercer espacio* 123).

## *Chapter 6*

1. In "Pascal's Sphere," Borges describes a shift in the idea of cosmic unity as a topography of sovereign stability in the Baroque: "In that dejected century, the absolute space that inspired the hexameters of Lucretius, the absolute space that had been a liberation for Bruno was a labyrinth and an abyss for Pascal" (OC 2.18; SNF 353). He sees this shift exemplified by a manuscript in which Blaise Pascal evokes the figure of absolute space as an infinite sphere, but subsequently changes the word *infinite* to *terrifying* (*effroyable*): "Nature is a terrifying sphere, whose center is in all parts and whose circumference is in none." Although the epigraphs to "The Aleph" do not properly align with the historical parameters that Borges describes in "Pascal's Sphere," they exhibit more in common with the Baroque than with

the Renaissance. In both, the ideal of unity is neither reassuring nor liberating, and sovereignty must adapt to the lack of absolute ground.

The unworking of figurative nutshells of sovereignty in "The Aleph" is echoed in the pair of vignettes dedicated to Dante's *Divine Comedy* in *El hacedor*, in which Borges interrogates the ideal of prosopopoeic figuration and the hierarchy of humans over animals in a way that can be seen as unworking any absolute structure of *re-ligio*, whether secular or religious (what Dante calls "La forma universal di questo nodo," [*Paradiso* Canto 33, line 91; Borges, OC 2.189, 196; CF 316, 323]).

2. In "Nine Dantesque Essays," Borges describes *Divine Comedy* as a Ulysses-like voyage to a celestial Ithaca, which, of course, surpasses Ulysses, who was swallowed up off the austral shores of Mount Purgatory before being sent back to (Eurasian) hell ("Nine Dantesque Essays" SNF 280–83).
3. Note that the word *abarrotado* [teeming] is also used to describe Funes's mind (OC 1.524; CF 137) and the barrage of media that accompanies Tlön's invasion of the world in "Tlön, Uqbar, Orbis Tertius" ("Handbooks, anthologies, surveys, 'literal translations,' authorized and pirated reprints of Mankind's Greatest Masterpiece filled the world, and still do," [OC 1.473; CF 81]).
4. It does not take much imagination to connect the idea that there is a world in the basement of the family house, forbidden to the young child, to the phallus, understood as a symbolic key to unbounded (world-possessing) patriarchal sovereignty. The name "Aleph," furthermore, is a near anagram of phallus. See Michael Naas's discussion of Derrida's understanding of the "phallic effect" as a simulacrum of sovereignty that brings together the spontaneity of life — that is, that which is untouched by technology — and machine-like autonomy and capacity to produce or ensure presence (Naas, *Miracle and Machine* 210–11).
5. Note that in the prologue to "Nine Dantesque Essays," Borges describes the "dogma" of unity that extends at least from Parmenides to Dante as subscribing to the idea that "rotation [is] the most perfect form of movement, and the sphere its most perfect body" (SNF 269).
6. Balderston considers this tendency in "The Universe in a Nutshell" (55). See also Moreiras's emphasis on seriality in "El villano en el centro" (*Tercer espacio* 296–97) and Jaime Alazraki's discussion in *Borges and the Kabbalah* (116–24).
7. The description of Argentino's poem included in the story begins with allusions to Odysseus's voyage and Xavier de Maistre's parodic encomium to domestic confinement, *Voyage autour de ma chambre* (OC 1.660; CF 276–77). The hidden implication is that, by virtue of the Aleph, Argentino can travel the world like Odysseus, while never leaving home, like de Maistre, although the latter reference appears to miss the point that de Maistre's text is a pointed criticism of his experience of house arrest, suggesting that Argentino has not, in fact, learned to distinguish between literal and figurative (including parodic) uses of language. The conceit of traveling

the world from the comfort of home was likely another element of Borges's self-parody, since he was known for fictionalizing the idea that one's understanding of the world is always modified by one's own experience (see, for instance, his poem "Fundación mítica de Buenos Aires," where he claims that his "patria" was founded in the neighborhood where he grew up [OC 1.87]). This is not Schopenhauerian, as some have claimed, since he is not claiming that his perspective creates the world, only that his understanding cannot be disentangled from it. Incidentally, Xavier de Maistre was the younger brother of the arch conservative Joseph de Maistre.

8. The fact that the Aleph is described as a "world" that he "discovered" as a child evokes the conquest of the New World, an association that is reinforced by Argentino's patronymic, which closely resembles the name of the nation, named so after the silver that was brutally extracted from the far end of the imperial territories, and transported through the land that later would bear the name of that precious metal.
9. It may be a stretch to point out that the Latin root of *veneros*, *vena*, connotes penis, as does the Hebrew letter Z, or Zayin. I would relate this to my proposal in footnote 4, above, that Argentino's Aleph may be related to a phallic phantasm. There are numerous subtexts to this story, including a sexual one, as Estela Canto reveals in her memoir, *Borges a contraluz*, so it may not be surprising to find a few *disjecta membra* beneath the surface. On the sexual subplot of the story, see Alberto Moreiras's "Lugares privados en 'El Aleph,' de Borges" ("Private Places in Borges's 'The Aleph'") in *Tercer espacio y otros relatos*.
10. The prefix *Zun-*, which is shared by the two proprietors and the lawyer that Argentino proposes to hire to fight them, Zunni, can be seen as evoking the mechanical sound of the construction of modernization (*zun, zun, zun*), as well as the heliotropic force of secular sovereignty, in distinction to Hobbes's "kingdom of darkness." It is tempting to associate the prefix with the character Yu Tsun from "The Garden of Forking Paths," and so with another homophonic resonance, the English "soon," that is, an ominous insinuation that "soon, soon, soon" the apparatuses of modern sovereignty (law, capital, and national or imperial identification) will usher us into a *hic* and *nunc stans* in which time is undifferentiated (such as that willed by Yu Tsun: "He who is to perform a horrendous act should imagine to himself that it is already done, should impose upon himself a future as irrevocable as the past. That is what I did . . . " [OC 1.508; CF 121]).
11. The *Diccionario de la lengua española* indicates that *regatear* derives from *recatear*, which derives from *recatar*. The first definition of *recatar* (from L. *re-captare* or recapturing) is "Encubrir u ocultar lo que no se quiere que se vea o se sepa." Etymonline notes that the etymology of "bargain" is disputed, but suggests this derivation: perhaps from Frankish *borganjan* "to lend," ultimately from Proto-Germanic *borgan* "to pledge, lend, borrow," from PIE root *bhergh-* (1) "to hide, protect."

12. See Balderston, "The Universe in a Nutshell: The Long Sentence in Borges's 'El Aleph.'"
13. Philemon Holland produced the first English translation of Pliny at the beginning of the seventeenth century, which can be understood as linking the imperial pretensions of ancient Rome to those of the emergent British Empire. Furthermore, in a coincidence that Borges would have likely appreciated, he tutored George Berkeley, although it was the one who became the eighth Baron Berkeley, not the philosopher.
14. Interestingly, the letters are seen in a drawer in *the* desk ("un cajón del escritorio" [OC 1.667; CF 283]), the direct article referring to a particular desk in the house above, perhaps the one where Argentino stores his poem, also described as *the* desk, suggesting that there is only one desk in the house ("abrió un cajón del escritorio . . . " [OC 1.660; CF 276]). That Beatriz's letters appear to be stored in the same desk as Argentino's ponderous poem suggests that his poem, in addition to constituting the conversion of riches extracted from the recesses of his house and consciousness, can be seen as a conversion of the letters he received from his cousin, a translation of a hidden writing into something like a global blazon, an enumeration of parts that presume a whole.
15. See Dove's excellent reading of this story in "Metaphor and Image in 'El Zahir,'" in which he discusses the distinction between an onto-theological understanding of image and appearance, based on revelation, and Borges's approach to the literary image, which he connects to the description of the "aesthetic event [*hecho estético*]" in "The Wall and the Books," as the "imminence of a revelation that does not take place" (Dove 177; Borges OC 2.15; SNF 346).

    In addition to the Norse myth of Fafnir, the association between memory and coins — which is a recurrent one in Borges's writings — evokes the Roman goddess Juno, who combined aspects of the Greek goddesses Hera (marriage and family) and Mnemosyne (memory). One of Juno's epithets was Moneta, which resulted from the fact that coins were minted near her temple.

## *Chapter 7*

1. Susan Petrilli acknowledges this subtext of the Parmenidean One in "Text Metempsychosis and the Racing Tortoise," where she compares the figure of translation to Achilles, in an impossible race with the tortoise-like original (156). As she notes, Borges's story "Pierre Menard, Author of the Quixote" includes a reference to Zeno's paradox of Achilles and the tortoise in which Menard published a work dedicated to presenting a chronological summary of "solutions" to the paradox. The second edition of this fictional

work includes as an epigraph a line attributed to Leibniz, "Ne craignez point, monsieur, la tortue," which Petrilli interprets as advice not to fear the original, as Menard exemplarily did not (Petrilli 157). Fishburn and Hughes locate the reference to Leibniz's discussion of Zeno in a letter to Simon Foucher in 1692, which they explain as concluding that infinite divisibility can be summed up as a finite quantity (Fishburn and Hughes 51). In a letter to Foucher dated 1693, Leibniz renounced his earlier approach to the mathematics of movement and embraced infinite divisibility: "I believe that there is no part of matter that is not, I do not say divisible, but actually divided, and consequently, the least particle must be considered as a world full of an infinity of different creatures" (Leibniz n.p.).

2. Borges includes a list of thinkers in relation to this distinction, including thinkers as diverse as Parmenides, Plato, Leibniz, and Kant, on the one hand, and Heraclitus, Aristotle, Locke, Hume, and William James, on the other. He proposes that the former thinkers believe in their ability to understand and represent the universe as cosmos or order; while the latter ones acknowledge the limited nature of their understanding. Such broad brushstrokes are clearly satirical. As I describe earlier, in "From Allegories to Novels" he acknowledges the collapse of this distinction in modernity, when everyone associates themselves with the latter yet in such a way that they reproduce the former.
3. The wording of this description invites reflection: First, the term *rasgo* suggests a physiognomic feature, thereby playing on the *"adventure"* of thinking "that a coordination of words . . . can resemble (*parecerse*) the universe" (OC 1.272–73; L 207–08). However, as I mentioned in relation to the appearance of the word *rasgo* in "El Aleph," it also relates to writing, which in turn derives from the verb *rasgar*, which signifies rupture or tearing ("Rasgo"). Perhaps more than seeing in Schopenhauer's illustrious coordinations of words a resemblance to the universe that might help us understand it, he sees a scratch or tear that resembles the precipice of infinity that rends Zeno's racetrack to truth.
4. See Beiser, *Weltschmertz: Pessimism in German Philosophy*, for a cogent account of this aspect of Schopenhauer's thought.
5. The second definition for "halucinación" in the *Diccionario de la lengua española* reads, "Sensación subjetiva que no va precedida de impresión en los sentidos" ("Halucinación"). As we have seen, Borges plays with the extremes of philosophical certainty in his fictions, stressing that perception does not take place in a vacuum, but is modified by the unconscious, or what he calls "los túneles del sueño, ese proteo" ("Yo," OC 3.89).
6. I have been unable to identify the source of this reference. Even Warnes, who quotes it, does not name its source. My reading shares certain similarities to that of Hernán Díaz's discussion of Borges's critique of "dogmatic idealism" (68–69).
7. Warnes stresses that Novalis's notion of magical idealism was not absolute, but involved a synthesis of realism and idealism, and an acknowledgment of

the "limits imposed by the physical world," including, exemplarily, sickness (Warnes 490–91). This is elaborated by his understanding of Romanticism: "Indem ich dem Gemeinen einen hohen Sinn, dem Gewöhnlichen ein geheimnißvolles Ansehn, dem Bekannten die Würde des Unbekannten, dem Endlichen einen unendlichen Schein gebe so Romantisire ich es" (quoted 489). See also Terry Pinkard's understanding of Novalis's refusal of the subject/ object binary as a "relational" notion of consciousness that led to a "conception of self-consciousness that was forever out of reach" (quoted in Warnes 490). Cahen-Maurel makes the association between magic, art, and the classical figure of the pharmakon, in which art as mere illusion threatens the ground of philosophy (162).

8. See definition 9 of "saludar": "Proclamar a alguien por rey, emperador, etc." ("Saludar").
9. The relationship between Zeno's paradox and life is also mentioned earlier in "Perpetual Race," in Borges's account of John Stuart Mill's refutation (which, Borges adds, does not refute, but merely explains, the paradox), in which the "linked precipices corrupt space and, even more vertiginously, living time [*el tiempo vivo*], in their desperate persecution of both immobility and ecstasy" (OC 1.258; SNF 44).
10. Weinberger's translation of this passage differs in important ways from mine: "Such a deconstruction, by means of only one word, *infinite*, a worrisome word (and then a concept), we have engendered fearlessly, once it besets our thinking, explodes and annihilates it" (SNF 47). The original is this: "Esa descomposición, es mediante la sola palabra infinito, palabra (y después concepto) de zozobra que hemos engendrado con temeridad y que una vez consentida en un pensamiento, estalla y lo mata" (OC 1.261).
11. The allusion to Zeno's paradox in "Tlön, Uqbar, Orbis Tertius," in which the "sophism of the nine coins" is compared to the scandalous reputation of the "Eleatic aporias," can be seen as a parody of "the concrete growth of the perceived" ("Perpetual Race" OC 1.261; SNF 47). In this context, furthermore, the growth of what is perceived is measurable economically, since the privilege given to perception is so extreme that each time a coin is seen its value replicates. In this example, what is won or gained (*ganar*) is economic value, rather than a footrace. Such growth is systematized in the "methodical production" of the *hrönir*.
12. There is a kind of performative irony in the fact that this essay was rejected as juvenilia by Borges, and consequently left out of the *Obras completas*. One might respond, misquoting the essay, "no hay tal obra completa."
13. Petrilli notes that Levinas quotes Valéry's reference to Zeno's paradoxes ("Zénon, cruel Zénon . . . Cette flèche") in the context of suggesting that "Achilles who does not succeed in catching up with the slow tortoise is the identity of self which does not succeed in standing up to its own alterity, in leaving its own shadow" (Petrilli 163).
14. Dyson points out Borges's acknowledgment that Lönnrot is a Swedish name, and notes that *röd* in Swedish means "root" or "source," and *lönn*

means concealed or hidden (Dyson 143). He also observes that Lönnrot's name may be connected to Elias Lönnrot, a Finnish physician, "a major proponent of nineteenth-century Finnish cultural and linguistic independence from Sweden," once again pointing to an instance of coloniality and resistance beyond the usual examples (144).

15. The length of time has religious resonance in both Christianity and Judaism, initially related to a period of mourning.
16. The mention of metempsychotic repetition should be understood in a philosophical and historical register, not a mystical, transmigratory one. This scene of a life and death encounter — amidst the ruins of an old order, on the limits of sovereignty, between a Jew and a Christian — has elements that have repeated countless times throughout history, on large and small scales, and indeed were playing out in a very different way on the world stage at the time of the story's publication. Such repetition is not deterministic. It is not that antagonisms such as these *have* to repeat, but they tend to, probably related to the structural continuity of different efforts to impose a single order.
17. I again take the distinction between a maze, as a prosthesis of sovereignty, and a labyrinth, as a mode of relation to otherness, including the other within, from North (*Distraction* 102). This distinction constitutes the focus of "The House of Asterion," a short story in which the Minotaur narrates his reflections on life. His "house" was constructed as a prison to keep the Minotaur's monstrosity separate from human existence. The doors of the house are open because the distinction between human and inhuman is presumed shut, which is confirmed when the Minotaur ventures outside and the townspeople run away screaming. For him, however, the doors are infinite in number and always open to all species of living and animate beings: "its doors (whose numbers are infinite) stand open night and day to men and also to animals" (OC 1.608; CF 220). Although he is always alone, he keeps himself entertained with his own difference from himself, playing solo hide and seek, playacting paying himself a visit, and laughing at his own mistakes. Perhaps a lifetime of imprisonment instills a sense of the inevitability of sovereignty, or a longing for a sovereign, as he indeed begins to long for a redeemer who will turn the labyrinthine nature of his existence into a meaningful structure.

# Works Cited


"Acometer." *Diccionario de la lengua española*. Real Academia Española. 23rd edition, 2014, updated in 2022. dle.rae.es.

"Aforar." *Diccionario de la lengua española*. Real Academia Española. 23rd edition, 2014, updated in 2022. dle.rae.es.

Agamben. *Potentialities: Collected Essays in Philosophy*. Translated by Daniel Heller-Roazen, Stanford UP, 1999.

Alazraki, Jaime. *Borges and the Kabbalah*. Cambridge UP, 1988.

Alighieri, Dante. *Paradiso*. Translated by Allen Mandelbaum, Bantam, 1984.

Attridge, Harold. "Johannine Christianity." *The Cambridge History of Christianity*, edited by Margaret M. Mitchell and Frances M. Young, vol. 1, Cambridge UP, 2006, pp. 125–43. Cambridge History of Christianity. 9 vols. Accessed 21 Aug. 2023.

Balderston, Daniel. "Liminares: Sobre el manuscrito de 'El hombre en el umbral.'" *Hispamérica*, vol. 41, no. 122, 2012, pp. 27–36.

Balderston, Daniel. *Out of Context: Historical Reference and the Representation of Reality in Borges*. Duke UP, 1993.

Balderston, Daniel. "The Universe in a Nutshell: The Long Sentence in Borges's 'El Aleph.'" *Variaciones Borges*, vol. 33, 2012, pp. 53–72.

Barthes, Roland. *Essais critiques*. Seuil, 1991.

Basile, Jonathan. *Library of Babel*. https://libraryofbabel.info/. Accessed 21 Aug. 2023.

Beiser, Frederick. *Weltschmertz: Pessimism in German Philosophy 1860–1900*. Oxford UP, 2016.

Berkeley, George. *An Essay Toward a New Theory of Vision*. HTML version by Al Haines. Project Gutenberg, 2003. Accessed 21 Aug. 2023.

Berryman, Sylvia, "Democritus." *The Stanford Encyclopedia of Philosophy*, Spring 2023 ed., edited by Edward N. Zalta and Uri Nodelman. Accessed 21 Aug. 2023.

Blanchot, Maurice. *The Infinite Conversation*. Translated by Susan Hanson, U of Minnesota P, 1993.

Bloy, Léon. *L'âme de Napoléon*. Mercure de France, 1912. Gallica, Bibliothèque National de France. https://gallica.bnf.fr/ark:/12148/bpt6k6305341f/f9.item.r=face#. Accessed 21 Aug. 2023.

Bolaño, Roberto. *Amuleto*. Vintage, 2017.

Bolaño, Roberto. *Estrella distante*. Anagrama, 1996.

Bolaño, Roberto. *Nocturno de Chile*. Vintage, 2017.

Bond, Brian. *Liddell Hart: A Study of His Military Thought*. Rutgers UP, 1977.

Boretto Ovalle, René. "Tras las huellas de Borges," *Spdrionegro*. 26 Nov. 2016, Uruguay, https://sites.google.com/site/spdrionegro/biblioteca/centro-de-manejo-documental/personas-y-personajes/jorge-luis-borges. Accessed 4 Mar. 2021.

Borges, Jorge Luis. *The Book of Imaginary Beings*. Translated and edited by Norman Thomas di Giovanni, Penguin Books, 1969.

Borges, Jorge Luis. *Inquisiciones.* Seix Barral, 1993.

Borges, Jorge Luis. *Jorge Luis Borges: Selected Fictions*. Translated Andrew Hurley, Viking, 1998.

Borges, Jorge Luis. *Jorge Luis Borges: Selected Non-Fictions*. Translated by Esther Allen, Suzanne Jill Levine, and Eliot Weinberger, Penguin Books, 1999.

Borges, Jorge Luis. *Labyrinths: Selected Stories and Other Writings*. Translated and edited by James Irby and Donald Yates, New Directions, 1964.

Borges, Jorge Luis. "Nota preliminar." *Pragmatismo. Un nuevo nombre para algunos viejos modos de pensar*. Translated by Vicente Quintero, Emecé, 1945, pp. 9–13.

Borges, Jorge Luis. *Obras completas*. Emecé, 2006. 4 vols.

Bosteels, Bruno. "Beggars Banquet: For a Critique of the Political Economy of the Sign in Borges." *Variaciones Borges*, vol. 29, 2010, pp. 3–52.

Browne, Thomas. *Hydriotaphia, urn-burial, or, A discours of the sepulchral urns lately found in Norfolk together with the Garden of Cyrus, or, The quincuncial lozenge, or network of plantations of the ancients, artificially, naturally, mystically considered : with sundry observations*. In the digital collection *Early English Books Online.* https://name.umdl.umich.edu/A29860.0001.001. University of Michigan Library Digital Collections. Accessed July 18, 2025

Burton, Robert. *The Anatomy of Melancholy*. George Bell and Sons, 1896. 2 vols. Hathi Trust. Accessed 21 Aug. 2023.

Cahen-Maurel, Laure. "Novalis's Magical Idealism." *Symphilosophie*, 1, 2019, pp. 129–65.

Cantor, Estela. *Borges a contraluz*. Espasa-Calpe, 1989.

Celan, Paul. "Speech on the Occasion of Receiving the Literature Prize of the Free Hanseatic City of Bremen." *Selected Poems and Prose of Paul Celan*, translated by John Felstiner, Norton, 2001, pp. 395–96.

Deleuze, Gilles. *The Fold: Leibniz and the Baroque*. Translated by Tom Conley, U of Minnesota P, 1988.

Deleuze, Gilles, and Félix Guattari. *Kafka: Toward a Minor Literature*. Translated by Dana Polan, U of Minnesota P, 1986.

de Man, Paul. *Aesthetic Ideology*. U of Minnesota P, 1996.

de Man, Paul. "A Modern Master." *The New York Review of Books*. 19 Nov. 1964. https://www.nybooks.com/articles/1964/11/19/a-modern-master/. Accessed 21 Aug. 2023.

de Man, Paul. *The Resistance to Theory*. U of Minnesota P, 1986.

Derrida, Jacques. "Before the Law," translated by Avital Ronell and Christine Roulston. *Acts of Literature*, edited by Derek Attridge Routledge, 1992, pp. 183–220.

Derrida, Jacques. *The Death Penalty*, vol. 1. Translated by Peggy Kamuf, U of Chicago P, 2013. 2 vols.

Derrida, Jacques. *The Death Penalty*, vol. 2. Translated by Elizabeth Rottenberg, U of Chicago P, 2017. 2 vols.

Derrida, Jacques. "Des Tours de Babel," translated by Joseph Graham. *Difference in Translation*, edited by Joseph Graham, Cornell UP, 1985, pp. 165–205.

Derrida, Jacques. "Faith and Knowledge," translated by Samuel Weber. *Acts of Religion*, edited by Gil Anidjar, Routledge, 2002, pp. 40–101.

Derrida, Jacques. "Force of Law: The 'Mystical Foundation of Authority,'" translated by Mary Quaintance. *Acts of Religion*, edited by Gil Anidjar, Routledge, 2002, pp. 230–98.

Derrida, Jacques. *Glas*. Translated by J. P. Leavy Jr. and R. Rand, U of Nebraska P, 1986.

Derrida, Jacques. "The Night Watch," translated by Pascale-Anne Brault and Michael Naas. *Derrida and Joyce: Texts and Contexts*, edited by Andrew Mitchell and Sam Slote, State U of New York P, 2013, pp. 87–108.

Derrida, Jacques. "Plato's Pharmacy," translated by Barbara Johnson. *Dissemination*. U of Chicago P, 1981, pp. 61–171.

Derrida, Jacques. *The Post Card: From Socrates to Freud and Beyond*. Translated by Alan Bass. U of Chicago P, 1987.

Derrida, Jacques. "Ulysses Gramophone: Hear Say Yes in Joyce," translated by François Raffoul. *Derrida and Joyce: Texts and Contexts*, edited by Andrew Mitchell and Sam Slote, State U of New York P, 2013, pp. 41–86.

"Desaforar." *Diccionario de la lengua española*. Real Academia Española. 23rd edition, 2014, updated in 2022. dle.rae.es.

Díaz, Hernán. *Borges, Between History and Eternity*. Continuum, 2012.

Díaz Letelier, Gonzalo. "Anarqueologías errantes, Borges disjunto y el perro yagán." *European Journal for the Philosophy of Communication (Empedocles)*, vol. 11, no. 2, Dec. 2020, pp. 137–45.

Díaz Pozueta, María. "From Philosophical Idealism to Political Ideology in 'Tlön, Uqbar, Orbis Tertius' and 'Deutsches Requiem." *CR: The New Centennial Review*, vol. 9, no. 3, 2010, pp. 205–28.

Dove, Patrick. "Architectures of Totality: Structure, History, and Polemos in Kafka and Borges." *The Yearbook of Comparative Literature*, vol. 63, 2017, pp. 22–43.

Dove, Patrick. *The Catastrophe of Modernity: Tragedy and the Nation in Latin American Literature*. Bucknell UP, 2004.

Dove, Patrick. "Metaphor and Difference in 'El Zahir.'" *Romanic Review*, vol. 98, no. 2/3, 2007, pp. 169–87.

Dove, Patrick. "Two Sides of the Same Coin?: Form, Matter, and Secrecy in Derrida, De Man, and Borges." *The Marrano Specter: Derrida and Hispanism*, edited by Erin Graff Zivin, Fordham UP, 2018, pp. 81–102.

Dyson, John. "On Naming in Borges's 'La muerte y la brújula.'" *Comparative Literature*, vol. 37, no. 2, 1985, pp. 140–68.

Eliot, T. S. "Tradition and the Individual Talent." 1919. *Points of View*, Faber and Faber, 1941, pp. 23–24.

*The English Bible, King James Version: The Old Testament*. Edited by Herbert Marks. Norton Critical Edition, 2012.

Ferris, David. “Agamben and the Messianic: The Slightest of Differences?” *Messianic Thought Outside Theology*, edited by Anna Glazova and Paul North, Fordham UP, 2014, pp. 73–92.

Fishburn, Evelyn, and Psiche Hughes, editors. *A Dictionary of Borges*. Revised ed. Duckworth, 1990.

García, Carlos. “Borges and Kafka.” *Fragmentos*, Florianópolis, no. 28/29, 2005, pp. 49–59.

Graff Zivin, Erin. *Anarchaeologies: Reading as Misreading*. Fordham UP, 2020.

Graff Zivin, Erin. “Deconstruction and Its Precursors: Levinas and Borges After Derrida.” *The Marrano Specter: Derrida and Hispanism*, edited by Erin Graff Zivin, Fordham UP, 2018, pp. 138–52.

Graff Zivin, Erin. *The Wandering Signifier: Rhetoric of Jewishness in the Latin American Imaginary.* Duke UP, 2008.

Graham-Harrison, Emma. “Fray Bentos — A Town in Uruguay, Not Just a Meat Pie.” *The Guardian*. 8 July 2018. Accessed 21 Aug. 2023.

Guyer, Sara, and Brian McGrath. Lit-Z series description. https://fordhampress.com/series/lit-z/.

“Halucinación.” *Diccionario de la lengua española*. Real Academia Española. 23rd edition, 2014, updated in 2022. dle.rae.es.

Hamacher, Werner. “The Gesture in the Name: On Benjamin and Kafka.” *Premises: Essays on Philosophy and Literature from Kant to Celan*, translated by Peter Fenves, Harvard UP, 1996. pp. 294–336.

Heraclitus of Ephesus. *Fragments*. Translated by Brooks Haxton, Penguin, 2001.

Hillis, Ken, Michael Petit, and Kylie Jarrett. *Google and the Culture of Search*. Routledge, 2013.

Hobbes, Thomas. *Leviathan: A Norton Critical Edition*. Edited by David Johnston, Norton, 2019.

Horn, Eva. “Borges’s Duels: Friends, Enemies, and the Fictions of History.” *Thinking with Borges*, edited by William Eggington and David E. Johnson, The Davies Group Publishers, 2009, pp. 161–82.

Huret, Jules. *Enquête sur l’évolution littéraire*. Bibliothèque Carpentier, 1891. in Wikisource https://fr.wikisource.org/wiki/Enqu%C3%AAte_sur_l%E2%80%99%C3%A9volution_litt%C3%A9raire. Accessed 21 Aug. 2023.

“Interpolación.” *Diccionario de la lengua española*. Real Academia Española. 23rd edition, 2014, updated in 2022. dle.rae.es.

Irenaeus. *St. Irenaeus of Lyons Against the Heresies.* Translated and annotated by Dominic J. Unger, with further revisions by John J. Dillon, Paulist P, 1992.

Jansen, Laura. *Borges’s Classics: Global Encounters with the Graeco-Roman Past*. Cambridge University P, 2018.

Jenckes, Kate. *Reading Borges After Benjamin: Allegory, Afterlife, and the Writing of History*. State U of New York P, 2007.

Jenckes, Kate. *Witnessing Beyond the Human: Addressing the Alterity of the Other in Post-Coup Chile and Argentina*. State U of New York P, 2017.

Jenckes, Kate, and Patrick Dove, editors. *The Yearbook of Comparative Literature* (Special issue on Borges and Kafka). Volume 63, 2017.

Johnson, David E. *Kant's Dog: On Borges, Philosophy, and the Time of Translation.* State U of New York P, 2012.

Jorge Luis Borges Google Doodle, published 23 Aug. 2011, YouTube, https://www.youtube.com/watch?v=RFcFWkeEEbE. Accessed 21 Aug. 2023.

Kadir, Djelal. *The Other Writing: Postcolonial Essays in Latin America's Writing Culture*. Purdue UP, 1993.

Kafka, Franz. "Building the Great Wall of China." *Kafka's Selected Stories*. Translated and edited by Stanley Corngold. Norton, 2007, pp. 113-24.

Kant, Immanuel. *Critique of the Power of Judgment*. Translated by Paul Guyer and Eric Matthews, Cambridge UP, 2000.

Krell, David. *Phantoms of the Other: Four Generations of Derrida's Geschlecht*. State U of New York P, 2015.

Kristal, Efraín. *Invisible Work: Borges and Translation*. Vanderbilt UP, 2002.

Kristal, Efraín. "Jorge Luis Borges's Fictions and the Two World Wars." *Borges in Context*, edited by Robin Fiddian, Cambridge UP, 2020, pp. 35–42. https://www.cambridge.org/core. Accessed 21 Nov. 2021.

Laraway, David "Borges and Company: The Corporate Body in 'La lotería en Babilonia.'" *Bulletin of Spanish Studies*, vol. 88, no. 4, 2011, pp. 563–85.

Leibniz, Gottfried. "Letter to Simon Foucher." June 1693. Translated by Lloyd Strickland. *Leibniz Translations*, 2013, www.leibniz-translations.com/index2.php. Accessed 21 Aug. 2023.

Levinas, Emmanuel. *Totality and Infinity: An Essay on Exteriority*. Translated by Alphonso Lingis, Duquesne UP, 1969.

Levinson, Brett. "The Possibility of the Unicorn in Borges and Kafka." *The Yearbook of Comparative Literature*, no. 16, 2017, pp. 44–61.

Lezra, Jacques. *Untranslating Machines: A Genealogy for the Ends of Global Thought.* Rowman and Littlefield, 2017.

Lezra, Jacques. *Wild Materialism: The Ethic of Terror and the Modern Republic*. Fordham UP, 2010.

López-Quiñones, Antonio Gómez. "En los márgenes de Borges: Los pies de página en 'Deutsches Requiem' y 'Pierre Menard.'" *Variaciones Borges*, no. 12, 2001, pp. 139–65.

Marder, Elissa. *Dead Time: Temporal Disorders in the Wake of Modernity (Baudelaire and Flaubert)*. Stanford UP, 2001.

Marder, Elissa. "Figures of Interest: The Widow, the Telephone, and the Time of Death." *Deconstructing the Death Penalty: Derrida's Seminars and the New Abolitionism*. Edited by K. Oliver and S. Straub, Fordham UP, 2018, pp. 175–85.

Marder, Elissa. *The Mother in the Age of Mechanical Reproduction: Psychoanalysis, Photography, Deconstruction*. Fordham UP, 2012.

Meer, Rudolf. "Immanuel Kant's Theory of Objects and Its Inherent Link to Natural Science." *Open Philosophy*, vol. 1, 2018, pp. 342–59, De Gruyter Open Access, https://doi.org/10.1515/opphil-2018-0025. Accessed 21 Aug. 2023.

McNamara, Paul, and Frederik Van De Putte, "Deontic Logic." *The Stanford Encyclopedia of Philosophy,* Fall 2022 edition, edited by Edward N. Zalta and Uri Nodelman, https://plato.stanford.edu/archives/fall2022/entries/logic-deontic/. Accessed 21 Aug. 2023.

Moreiras, Alberto. *The Exhaustion of Difference*. Duke UP, 2001.

Moreiras, Alberto. *Tercer espacio y otros relatos*. Splash Books, 2021.

Naas, Michael. *Miracle and Machine: Jacques Derrida and the Two Sources of Religion, Science, and the Media*. Fordham UP, 2012.

Naas, Michael. *Plato and the Invention of Life.* Fordham UP, 2018.

Nietzsche, Friedrich. "Ecce Homo: How to Become What You Are." *The Anti-Christ, Ecce Homo, Twilight of the Idols, and Other Writings*. Translated by Judith Norman, Cambridge UP, 2020, pp. 69–152.

Nietzsche, Friedrich. *Human, All Too Human: A Book for Free Spirits*. Translated by R. J. Hollingdale, Cambridge UP, 1996.

Nietzsche, Friedrich. "Nachgelassene Fragmente November 1882 — February 1883," *Nietzsche Source Digital Archive*, www.nietzschesource.org/#eKGWB/NF-1882,5[1]. Accessed 21 Aug. 2023.

Nietzsche, Friedrich. "On the Uses and Disadvantages of History for Life." *Untimely Meditations*, edited by Daniel Breazeale, Cambridge UP, 2020.

Nietzsche, Friedrich. "Twilight of the Idols, or How to Philosophize with a Hammer." *The Anti-Christ, Ecce Homo, Twilight of the Idols, and Other Writings*, translated by Judith Norman, Cambridge UP, 2020, pp. 153–229.

Nietzsche, Friedrich. *Thus Spoke Zarathustra*. Translated by Adrian del Caro, Cambridge UP, 2006.

Nietzsche, Friedrich. *Unschuld des Werdens*, II Leipzig: Alfred Kroner Verlag, 1931.

North, Paul. *The Problem of Distraction*. Stanford UP, 2012.

North, Paul. *The Yield: Kafka's Atheological Reformation.* Stanford UP, 2015.

Oyarzún, Pablo. *Doing Justice: Three Essays on Walter Benjamin.* Polity, 2020.

Oyarzún, Pablo. *Literature and Skepticism*. State U of New York P, 2022.

Oyarzún, Pablo. "The Writing of Courage." *CR: The New Centennial Review*, vol. 11, no. 1, 2011, pp. 25–37.

*Oxford English Dictionary*, Oxford UP, 2010.

Pascal, Blaise. *Pascal's Pensées*. E. P. Dutton, 1958, Project Gutenberg, 2006.

Pater, Walter. *The Renaissance Studies in Art and Poetry*. Sixth ed., Project Gutenberg, posting date 2009, https://www.gutenberg.org/files/2398/2398-h/2398-h.htm.

"Perceive." *Oxford English Dictionary*. Second edition. Oxford UP, 1933.

"Percibir." *Diccionario de la lengua española*. Real Academia Española. 23rd edition, 2014, dle.rae.es.

Petrilli, Susan. "Text Metempsychosis and the Racing Tortoise: Borges and Translation." *Semiotica*, vol. 140, no. 1, 2002, pp. 153–67.

Piglia, Ricardo. "Ideología y ficción en Borges." *Punto de Vista*, vol. 2, no. 5, 1979, pp. 3–6.

Ragaller, Irene. *A Telling Silence: Nietzsche on the Downfall of the Dialectic.* 2006. Cardiff U, PhD thesis.

"Rasgo." *Diccionario de la lengua española.* Real Academia Española. 23rd edition, 2014, updated in 2022. dle.rae.es.

"Recatar." *Diccionario de la lengua española.* Real Academia Española. 23rd edition, 2014, updated in 2022. dle.rae.es.

"Regatear." *Diccionario de la lengua española.* Real Academia Española. 23rd edition, 2014, updated in 2022. dle.rae.es.

Rodríguez, Fermín. "Sueños de la llanura. Ficción y política en Borges." *Variaciones Borges*, vol. 53, 2022, pp. 87–109.

Roger, Sarah. "Borges and Kafka." *Borges in Context*, edited by Robin Fiddian, Cambridge UP, 2020, pp. 188–94. https://www.cambridge.org/core. Accessed 21 Nov. 2021.

Rojas, Carlos. *The Great Wall: A Cultural History*. Harvard UP, 2010.

Rottenberg, Elizabeth. *For the Love of Psychoanalysis: The Play of Chance in Freud and Derrida*. Fordham UP, 2019.

"Saludar." *Diccionario de la lengua española.* Real Academia Española. 23rd edition, 2014, updated in 2022. dle.rae.es.

Sanjinés, José. "The Extrasemiotic in Borges' 'The Library of Babel.'" *The Latin Americanist*, vol. 57, no. 1, 2013, pp. 65–78.

Sarlo, Beatriz. *Jorge Luis Borges: A Writer on the Edge*. Verso, 1993.

Sarmiento, D. F. *Facundo*. Edited by Roberto Yahni. Cátedra, 1997.

Shakespeare, William. *Hamlet*. Norton, 2019.

Schulte-Albert, Hans. "Classificatory Thinking from Kinner to Wilkins: Classification and Thesaurus Construction, 1645-1668." *Literary Quarterly* 49, no. 1, 1979, pp. 42–64.

"Solar." *Diccionario de la lengua española.* Real Academia Española. 23rd edition, 2014, updated in 2022. dle.rae.es.

Spagnuolo, Marta. "Eduardo Acevedo Díaz-Carlos Argentino Daneri, persona bicéfala en 'El Aleph.'" *Variaciones Borges* 48, 2019, pp. 53–77.

Taylor, Mark C. "Archetexture of Pyramids." *Assemblage*, vol. 5, 1988, pp. 16–27.

Thayer, Willy. *Technologies of Critique*. Translated by John Kraniauskas. Fordham University P, 2020.

"Vago." *Diccionario de la lengua española.* Real Academia Española. 23rd edition, 2014, updated in 2022. dle.rae.es.

Villalobos-Ruminott, Sergio. *Heterografías de la violencia: Historia, Nihilismo, Destrucción*. Editorial La Cebra, 2016.

Waisman, Sergio. *Borges and Translation: The Irreverence of the Periphery*. Bucknell UP, 2005.

Warnes, Christopher. "Magical Realism and the Legacy of German Idealism." *The Modern Language Review*, vol. 101, no. 2, 2006, pp. 488–98.

Weber, Samuel. "Once and for All." *Gray Room*, vol 20, Summer 2005, pp. 105–16.

Weber, Samuel. *Singularity: Politics and Poetics*. U of Minnesota P, 2021.

Wills, David. *Dorsality: Thinking Back Through Technology and Politics*. U of Minnesota P, 2008.

Wills, David. *Matchbook: Essays in Deconstruction*. Stanford UP, 2005.

# Index